FROM MOUNTIE TO BUSH PILOT

SASKATCHEWAN BOY JOINS THE ROYAL CANADIAN MOUNTED POLICE AND THEN GOES BUSH FLYING

JACK CLARKSON

Contents

FROM MOUNTIE TO BUSH PILOT   JACK CLARKSON

Chapter 1 ---------------------------------- 09
Chapter 2 ---------------------------------- 12
Chapter 3 ---------------------------------- 15
Chapter 4 ---------------------------------- 19
Chapter 5 ---------------------------------- 21
Chapter 6 ---------------------------------- 29
Chapter 7 ---------------------------------- 30
Chapter 8 ---------------------------------- 38
Chapter 9 ---------------------------------- 45
Chapter 10 --------------------------------- 62
Chapter 11 --------------------------------- 69
Chapter 12 --------------------------------- 78
Chapter 13 --------------------------------- 83
Chapter 14 --------------------------------- 99
Chapter 15 --------------------------------- 102
Chapter 16 --------------------------------- 109
Chapter 17 --------------------------------- 113
Chapter 18 --------------------------------- 123
Chapter 19 --------------------------------- 141
Chapter 20 --------------------------------- 153
Chapter 21 --------------------------------- 163
Chapter 22 --------------------------------- 176
Chapter 23 --------------------------------- 191
Chapter 24 --------------------------------- 165

THE CALLING SKY   GORDON PETER CHENKIE

Chapter 1 ---------------------------------- 207
Chapter 2 ---------------------------------- 209
Chapter 3 ---------------------------------- 221
Chapter 4 ---------------------------------- 231
Chapter 5 ---------------------------------- 245

Preface

This is a story about a young fellow growing up in small town Saskatchewan and wanting to have an interesting career with a reasonable amount of compensation for his efforts. The period of time was the 1930's and that taught him a bit about money --- and 25 cents was enough to spend on a Saturday night for a picture show or some ice cream.

His first thoughts were to join the Royal Canadian Mounted Police upon finishing school. I joined the R.C.M.P. in 1950 and took training in Regina and Ottawa and then had a posting to Manitoba. Numerous incidents are related of dealing with people who had too much alcohol and in some cases, breaking the law. One notable case was while on Highway Patrol out of Winnipeg, dealing with bank robbers who had shot one of our members.

There was something missing and that was not having a lot of money at the end of the month. I took my discharge and went to work at Imperial Oil for a couple of years. BORING. Next came aeroplanes and a commercial flying license and getting a job flying in the bush. Subsequently, starting an air service and building it up and then losing it on the idea of over expansion.

Mr. Maude, Vicar of the church, having shepherd's pie with Jack and Michael

Chapter 1

From the way things turned out I believe that I was born twenty years too soon. However, that is something that is impossible to change. It was not until some seventy years later, that I began to understand the beginnings of why I am here in the first place. It took a couple of trips to England and a trip to the Highlands of Scotland to check on the family tree of the Clarksons, Johnsons and Mathesons. The Clarksons was a surprise although it did not sink in right away and only came from snippets of information gathered on visiting different relations, and checking a few grave yards. I always heard about the old man, Robert Clarkson, and what a strict old man he was. He, I thought was my grandfather, no; it turned out he was my great –grandfather. Sidney, my father's uncle, who I thought was his brother, showed me a picture of my grandmother, who of course, was Sidney's sister, Polly. I had to complete the cycle so we contacted the Vicar of the church in the area and it was Mr. Maude. I had his name from records at home, and he was also a farmer and had rented 12 acres of prime land that my Father owned and agreed to meet us at the local Church and graveyard.

The Church of England cemetery and buildings looked like something out of an Alfred Hitchcock movie, lonely, sinister, and the grave markers all turned black at the top from the air of the North Sea. We were only a few miles from the sea. The boys and I each took an area of the cemetery to inspect for the names, and it was getting late in the evening, and foggy, inclement weather. Eerie!! Not actually a place you would want to be. John was on one side of the cemetery, I was in the center and Michael was on the side of the hedge row. We were getting more than half way through our inspection and advising each other of any Clarkson gravestones, and what the names were. All of a sudden there was a holler out of Michael and he passed everyone running, in high gear to the church. A pheasant flew up from hedge row just he was passing and that was enough to put the fright in him. That ended our searching but we did find that Robert Clarkson was buried in plot number 286, and Arthur and Polly, (My Father's Mother) in another area. This was confirmed in the church records with an inspection of dusty old books from back in the 1930's. Mr. Maude was very accommodating and we went out for supper at a pub down the road, but not until he had pointed out a place for us to stay for the night. We met his son, now the farmer of the land, and I had to have a plate of shepherd's pie, one of my Fathers favourite dishes and the other was chips rolled up in newspaper, an English custom. It was an enjoyable evening at the English Pub with a few local people.

The Bed and Breakfast included a pub as well and not very well attended. We paid for our room and I had one or two drinks with the boys and decided to go to bed. They do not turn the heat on in the room until it is paid for. I went to bed but could not sleep as it was too cold. I got up and put all my clothes on and then went to bed. That seemed to work until the boys came to the room about 3:00 am, apparently the bartender, a Lancashire man, kept them entertained with stories until the wee hours of the morning. Closing time was when you finished drinking. The boys said they tried all the different types of beer and had an enjoyable evening. The next day we went to Robin Hoods Cove and learned that it had been a hide-away for a large sailing vessel, just in case the Sheriff of Nottingham got to close to Robin Hood and his men and they had to put out to sea.

There was a terrible smell coming from the front end of our little rental car and I believe the boys had switched to methane gas or something similar. I then realized that last night's beer was making a comeback.

The trip to the cemetery only made me more interested and I found that Robert Clarkson had been the Superintendent of Police in Yorkshire County in Northern England. I also found out from viewing some records in the Dominion Archives in Ottawa, that he had been to Canada in 1856 to fight in the Fenian Raids which was prompted by the Irish wanting to take over Canada, (Upper Canada) and trade it back to the English so England would give them back Ireland. Robert was in the Niagara Peninsula region for two years and was mentioned in dispatches but had no major role to play. This may be why he got a police job when he went back to England. Being a strict old fellow, and getting up in age, and having had his wife die, he looked upon Polly to look after him. She apparently had a boyfriend, Botterill, being his last name, and he may have wanted to go to Canada, and she claimed she had obligations to fill looking after the old man. A boy child was born, but that did not solve the situation. Wilfred, my father, was brought up, by Polly, and he learned farm work at a very early age. Mind you, he got his schooling but there was a war, in 1914, and he would be nine years old. When he was eleven or twelve, he had the chore of driving prisoners (German Soldiers) back to the prison compound which was nearby, with a horse and cart, after they had worked in the fields for the day. Other than learning farm work and being a hard worker, he had no other trade.

Chapter 2

Somewhere in around 1925, Wilfred decided to go to Canada, presumably to meet his father for the first time. He came over on the CEDRIC, probably worked his fare off on the boat, and he was in the Ottawa area (Britannia Bay) for a spell, and then moved west. Charlie Clarkson, a relation, and I believe an uncle, was managing a farm for the Speers Family, who had several farms and one of them being near Whitewood, Saskatchewan- four miles south. The others are in Lake Francis, Manitoba, a horse farm or ranch, and a mixed farm at Griswold, also in Manitoba. Wilfred was a farm hand on all of them. I believe that he made contact with his father, Frank Botterill, who lived in the Fleming, Saskatchewan area, having immigrated to Canada much earlier. They were both on their own but I am told that he went to Botterill's funeral when he died in 19? Many years later, my sister Janet and I located his grave in a cemetery on the north side of Number One highway, near Fleming. Wilfred, worked on the Whitewood farm the most, and perhaps it was because of the neighbors across the road, four and one-half miles south of Whitewood. They were the Matheson Family and there seems to be a young girl by the name of Jemima (Born 1910) that was an acquaintance.

The Matheson Family, Angus and Isabella, along with several children came from the Highlands of Scotland in 1843 and settled in West Zorro, an area near Woodstock, Ontario. It was a heavily wooded area and clearing the land was a real chore but with organized clearing bees they would clear an acre at a time. This was really a hard time for everyone, before they could end up with productive land for farming. Angus died and was buried in the local Presbyterian Cemetery and Isabella and her son moved to a different area, Bruce County, I believe, but contact with them was hard to find. Another son, Robert, and two of his boys, Angus (my Grandfather) and Forbes, decided to go west as the railroad was being pushed through. They settled on a homestead near Whitewood, Assiniboine Territory, which is what the area was called before Saskatchewan became a province in 1905. It was hard work, clearing bush, breaking land, and planting and harvesting crops, all with horses. Angus must have found a little spare time because he met and married Henrietta Johnson, a graduate nurse, fifteen years younger than him, and they settled in Whitewood, Sask. Henrietta's family (Johnson's) immigrated from the Isle of Muck, Scotland, to Cape Breton Island, and then homesteaded in the McKay District north of Whitewood. Angus had a team of horses from the farm (Pat and Nellie, where their names) and he did chores around town, plowing gardens, hauling dry wood for heating the houses, and Henrietta ran a nursing home that stood for almost one hundred years. Henrietta also went on house calls to the sick in the country and she travelled on horseback using a side saddle and sometimes by buggy or cutter. Jemima, my mother, was born in 1910 and as I said before, met Wilfred and they were married in 1929 and after working out at farms for a year or two settled in Whitewood.

Grandpa Angus Matheson and me

Toad on a Post

Grandma Henrietta

Always a Pet in my life

Teasing my dog, Rover

Chapter 3

Somewhere in these busy times, I was born and had a taste of the dirty thirties.

I was talking to my cousin, Blanche, around Christmas time this past year and I asked her what her most memorable Christmas was. She told me that when she was around five years old, her older sister, Tuni, was working as a house maid or cook, at my uncle Forbes place, the Matheson Homestead, as Forbes never married and I guess wanted the place cleaned up for Christmas. Tuni asked Blanche, who lived nearby, to come with her to Forbes place to spend Christmas Eve, and then sleep over, as a lot of people may be coming the next day. She agreed and after she put up her stocking for Santa and left some lunch out for him, they went to bed. Sometime around three in the morning she heard quite a racket with sleigh bells ringing and she knew it must be Santa. It turned out that Forbes, not having any children, was going to make sure, that Blanche knew that Santa was in the neighborhood. When she woke in the morning, everything was as it should be, stockings full, presents under the tree, and the lunch gone. That really made her Christmas.

Then I remembered a Christmas, when my Mom and Dad were working for an older farmer, considered pretty stingy, or like a scrooge. He had a lovely team of black drivers, with nice harness to match, bells, and buffalo robes and a light cutter. They got permission to take the team for an overnight stay at our friends place some seven or eight miles away. The roads were never ploughed in winter but there were trails on top of the snow made by horse teams and sleighs. We were not cold snuggled up in the robes, but Father had to drive and the horses were anxious to run. He had to watch that we did not upset or take the wrong turn. I can remember peeking out and seeing a clear night, with the moon and stars out, and the steam coming off the horses. Boy! was it cold. Father would have to slow them down once and awhile but they sure were having fun running. After what seemed like a couple of hours, we could see the coal oil lamps in the windows of the house we were going to and then lanterns came out with men carrying them to direct us to an open stall in the barn.

Another Pet I had growing up

There were other animals in the barn and our team was unharnessed and rubbed down, and horse blankets put on them and fed. They had done a good job and now it was time to visit with our friends, and have a lunch, and find a bed with the other kids for the night. I can't even remember what I got for Christmas but we did not need too much in those days. That was surely a fun Christmas; just to get away was good, because that old man was pretty strict. Father hauled wood for the stoves and grain to town, and pretty soon the winter was over. Everyone a had pretty good respect for my old man, as he was a tough old bird, Oliver Hoggarth, told me that, and Oliver was a well respected farmer in the area, and pretty soon it was time to start school.

I also did a lot of going back and forth to the farm, either the Speers farm that Uncle Charlie ran, or Forbes farm, the old Matheson place, and sometimes to Fred Jordan's place, as he had a small Shetland pony that I was mighty interested in riding. Fred Jordan lived next to the Matheson Place so it was quite convenient, to hop over the fence. That little horse Sandy, took me on a wild ride out of the fields where the men were working after I had delivered them lunch. He put his head down to drink at the water trough and I fell in .It took me quite awhile to live that one down, but then that horse was 21 years old and he had to train a lot of kids.

Over at the Speers farm, just across the road, they were harvesting and changed the four horse teams pulling the binder after about a half a day. Fresh horses were brought out to the field and the tired, thirsty ones were taken to the barn to take the harness off and fed. Everyone else must have been working so this job fell to me, even though I was only about 12 years old at the time. The ones going to the field were no problem but the ones going to the barn wanted to walk faster and faster. I was probably 90 lbs soaking wet and in barefeet and that alone is hard on the feet walking on stubble. Well anyway, they ran away from me, ran through the trees and messed up all the harness. It took awhile to catch them and salvage the harness and get them fed, by then I had some help.

Threshing outfit in operation

During another harvest I was a field pitcher out in the McKay district, on Uncle Dick's farm. Anybody tall, gets the field pitcher job as you walk from wagon to wagon to top off their loads, and the driver stays on top and spreads the sheaves around to make a nice full load. We were working close to the house so we went in for lunch, horses got fed but the water trough was up on the hill the way we were going to work in the field. So they got watered on the way out. I was catching a ride in the rack, and at the water trough, the driver took the bridles off the horses to let them drink. The lines were tied around the post on the rack, but with no bridles and bits in the horse's mouth, the lines would be no good to me. The horses bolted at the water trough. They wheeled around and headed for the barn yard. I could do nothing but bail off the rack and I kind of rolled up in a ball and threw myself over the side. I did not get hurt too bad but it could have been worse. The harness and rack were wrecked pretty badly. I think that fellow always brought a wild team to work in the fields; they were certainly a one man team and not fully broke-in yet.

Team hauling sheaves

Uncle Forbes' car

Jack and two sisters: Janet and Joyce

Chapter 4

I also worked at the Round Lake Indian Residential School, which had a farm, a big garden, cattle, chickens and pigs. This would be in the busy fall harvest period, and we usually got some time off from school to help out, or at least we took it. Recently, I was reminded of this when I picked up my old principal, Gordon Mack, (93 now) and brought him out to my son John's place in Cochrane, Alberta for lunch. We were reminiscing about the old school days and he said that three of you boys came back to school about a month late, and were not ready to settle down yet. Most of the other students had gone through this period and we were disturbing the class. He decided the only way was to give us all the strap and he did. Funny I can't seem to remember that but I am sure it probably happened. When do you contradict your seniors? Anyway, we enjoyed our lunch.

I worked with the native kids, and the three boys, whose father ran the school, were also on hand. It was a United Church Indian Residential school at Round Lake in the Qu'Appelle Valley about 20 miles north of Whitewood, Sask.

I brought a big load of oat sheaves out of the field one day that they were going to use as feed, and did I ever pile it high as I was cleaning up the last of the field. Then I found that with the fields in the valley they always sloped towards the river. And after a couple of bumps in the road it looked as though I was going to lose the top of my load or upset. I had to stop and re-pile the top of my load placing it on a slight angle to the high side. I made it into the farmyard, but I remember having to raise the telephone lines to get the load under where the road went. Sure was a big load and I was probably about 15 or 16 at the time. I seemed to get along pretty good with horses and maybe it was because I did not really abuse them.

A number of years later, I was at my cousins funeral in Whitewood, and at our luncheon after the funeral, I saw a native guy and his wife sitting down the table from me. I remembered him as Elmer George, one of the boys who went to the Residential School at Round Lake. His sister, Salina, married my cousin, Myles, who had just passed away. Elmer was dressed nicely in a Western Style suit and I sent him a note, as the hall was really crowded. I said "Elmer, did you ever get the strap when you went to school." He wrote back, "Yes, one time the teacher, Miss Currie, gave me the strap for not filling her wood box." (Her quarters were separate and was heated by wood stove) I believe that there was never any abuse at this school and some fine people spent time there.

Chapter 5

By this time I am getting pretty tall, but not much meat on me. A bean pole, in other words. My father bought a couple of lots in Whitewood, probably paid $25.00 each for them. They were covered with poplar trees mostly and he cleared the land by hand, with enough room for a good sized garden and a house site. Then he got some rough lumber and started to build a house. Never built a house before but there was not much that he would not do. I believe that he had back trouble the rest of his life from this job. He planted trees and made a home for us at 401 Balfour Street and in the meantime he started working at the local Ford Dealership as a parts man, and he could remember parts numbers in his head like no one else could. This job lasted for 25 years, but war intervened and he was one of the first in town to sign up. He was going to go and save the old country single handed, I believe. But his bad back from moving trees and working hard, did not give him a good medical report and he ended up staying in Canada in stores his entire army career.

Wilfred Clarkson – R.C.A.S.C.

Of course, he was 34 years old and that is like grand-paw status in the army. Most of the guys and girls were in the 19 to 25 age group. My mother was President of the Royal Canadian Legion and I guess we all did our part. I can remember knitting socks at school for the men overseas. After the war, father got a job with the Post Office sorting mail and caretaker

My father, Wilfred Clarkson, and his mother, Polly

work, and spent another 20 years doing that job. He took my mother to England once, but she did not care for it, said the only time she got warm was when she went to the bathroom. To save heat and expense, they keep their houses on the cool side. She also said, that at news time they brought out a radio and listened to the news and then put the radio away again. I do not know whether they liked the solitude or just did not want to use the power and thereby save on the light bill. I am sure things have changed a lot. They never mentioned his mother, at least not to me, and then again I do not remember what year it was. I said to Father more than once, why don't you bring your mother over to Canada. Little did I know that she had made herself a recluse and wore old fashioned clothes and lived with only memories of a much finer life that she could have had. .

In the mean time, I had not got into too much trouble and was doing pretty good at school, at least until about Grade 9 and then I seemed to get too busy. I did a lot of hunting, especially for deer and between my father and I, we seemed to have deer meat on the table all the time. My father had 270 Bolt action rifle and he had one bullet up the spout and one bullet behind his ear and he very seldom had to use the second bullet and he shot his last deer when he was 82. The job of delivering groceries from the local store came open and I was recommended for the job. At that time, especially in the winter time, people used to phone in their grocery order and the store had it delivered for them. It was six days a week and Thursday I used to have to get off at recess in the morning to do my job, much to the displeasure of the teacher. The rest of the time the delivering was done after school and on Saturdays, I worked in the store until delivery time. Oh yes, and the delivering was done with horse and small sleigh in the winter and a democrat in the summer. I had to look after the horse as well, but the barn was only a block away from my place. Come to think of it, I don't think I got paid for looking after it on Sundays. I started out at 25 cents per hour and went to 55 cents per hour after four years. Well, at least I was able to buy my own clothes and have some spending money. This horse, Baldy was something else again. It never kicked but it sure liked to bite. Baldy was part Percheron and part Blood and did this horse ever like to run, always in a pacing mode, never broke into a gallop and had a few tricks. I used to tether him to a weight with a rope on it outside the store while I was getting the orders ready. He would pick up the rope with the weight on it with his teeth and walk across the sidewalk to the store window and would not leave until he got an apple. He upset me a few times with the sleigh but never with the buggy. He ran away on me once and tried to get in the barn with the sleigh behind. He had a nice pasture for the summer and after I left I hope that they gave him a good retirement. He was that kind of horse that deserved it.

Baldy, the delivery horse

Besides all the work at the store the boss had two nice daughters. And they both worked in the store from time to time. A friend of mine, Monty, and I decided to go on a harvest excursion to Ontario for the summer holidays from school. We got on the train in Whitewood and eventually ended up in Orillia, Ontario at the county municipal office. The farmers that needed men came to the office to take their pick. They quizzed us about what we knew and what we had been doing and then either hired us or went to the next one. There was a lady there and the word spread fast that she was looking for hoers for her large potato acreage. Needless to say we were busy talking to someone else or just turned our back on her. No one wanted to hoe potatoes for the summer. I got hired by Don McKay who had some haying to do and then some custom combine work to do as he had just bought a new Massey Ferguson self propelled combine. Don and his wife, Noreen lived near Ripley, Ontario in a large stone house. Seemed like a good set up to me. They were good Presbyterians and so was I. The haying was hard because it was all put up in the loft by slings and then had to be spread out in the loft. It was hot, but I survived and had the odd weekend off to see my friend Monty. He sort of lucked out, in that he was hired by this family, three boys and a big spread, close to Lake Huron, and the boys had a musical band and where always going to dances on the weekend. So we would meet once and awhile in ORILLIA or some other town and enjoy the evening. I remember one thing that happened and that was I finished harvesting a field and was going to take the combine to another one. As I came through the gate I hooked the breather pipe of the combine on the telephone wires and bent it back. I straightened it by hand and just then the boss came along in the car. He said that he would take the combine to the next field as he knew where it was. He seemed in a hurry and I did not get a chance to tell him about the pipe. I drove the car down following him and as he pulled off the road into the field, he hooked the breather pipe on the telephone wires and bent it. I kind of figured that I did not have to tell him about my problem. We stayed the summer, got our pay and headed for Niagara Falls by bus. After we paid our train fare home I think we had a little over $100.00 each. But it was a good experience and we saw a different part of the country. I got my job back at home and started another year of school. This job made it tough to play hockey and I needed the job, but I did play spare goalie.

Things went pretty well at school. We had a teacher that was an Albino person, and he sure was a nice guy and a very good athlete who taught us lots. Same old thing during the winter, only I think this was the winter that there was lots of snow. The roads were blocked and even the train could not get through. We were called from school to go out and help get the snow off the tracks or at least break the drifts down so the train snowplow could push its way through. I can remember getting kind of warm and taking off my parka and hanging it on the cross arms of the telegraph poles. Another chore we had was to dig a hole at the cemetery for an old fellow that died. The ground was frozen and we had to thaw it out by burning straw in the hole and then go down and chip away again. No backhoes for doing that job and I think we were a little shy of the six feet down on that particular hole, but I won't mention who went in it. I think two of us got paid $12.00 for this job. There was a fellow named Zimmer who had a team of skinny horses and pulled around a saw mandrel and sawed up wood for the different households. The wood came from the bush in tree lengths and had to be sawed up to use in the stoves. It took at least four men or husky boys to operate this sawing machine and we got 25 cents each for a cord. Sometimes we would buy a small package of Turret cigarettes and maybe on Saturday nights we would get someone to buy us a bottle of Emu 999 wine. I do not think we really abused either, only just to make us big shots for a little while. There were always dances at Round Lake on Saturday nights in the summer months and most people wanted to go.

Life is not without its sad moments and they usually come as a surprise. I was doing my delivery run with groceries and I had to go across the railroad tracks. Whitewood is on the main CPR line and there are double tracks running through the town. I came around the corner and up towards the crossing in town and a long train was blocking the road. Little did I know that the train had stopped because they had hit a man that was walking across the tracks at the crossing? The man turned out to be my grandfather. It was the day before his birthday and I suppose he was going over to see an old friend for some reason. His wife, Henrietta had died in 1942, and he still had a brother, Forbes, on the farm that would soon move into town.

School, job, Church activities, yes, I was in the young people's group, and also in the church choir, and my mother even had me taking piano lessons. When summer holidays came along, a new adventure appeared and it would be out on the west coast. A relation of mine, who I had never seen before was working as head bell hop on the Princess line, a ferry boat service owned by the CPR. These steam ships travelled between Vancouver and the island carrying passengers, cars and campers, etc. I thought I was going to be working as a junior bell hop, catering to passengers, etc. I bummed a ride out west with a family from Whitewood and eventually ended up away out on Douglas Street in Victoria. I guess I took too long getting there because that particular job was filled, so my relation knew that the Hudson Bay Store needed waiters in a restaurant they had opened. So I put on some kind of a uniform and worked there for about 10 days and another job came open on the Princess Joan. Only this time it was in the engine room and I was called 'wiper, third class' the job entailed cleaning brass in the engine room, plus the floors and generally doing what I was told. Wipers go from third class, to second and then first, all had different jobs to do, getting progressively better. The next step up would be fireman, third class and lo and behold, within two weeks I was fireman third class, due to a turnover of personnel. Firemen, worked three shifts, and lived on the boat, sleeping in the fo'c'sle, which is the front of the ship, below the water line, two bunks per room. Meals were taken in the staff kitchen. The engine room was down of couple of flights of stairs from the deck that the cars where carried on, and passengers staterooms, as they were called, were above that. This particular ship had three scotch boilers and Yarrow and each boiler had three burner chambers fired by a tube that sprayed out bunker oil. They of course, had to be lit and a rod with a coil of cloth soaked in fuel in a holder was close at hand but you needed a match or lighter to start it, unless there was one burner left running more or less at a low flow or idle. One particular night, we left at Midnight from Vancouver and it was about a six or eight hour run, depending on whether or not we went to Nanaimo first then Victoria, coming under the Lions Gate bridge and just beyond, the wheel house spotted a small boat in their path and called down to the engine room to reduce power. I had already got the steam up to 248 lbs. pressure because I thought we were under way at full power and at 250 lbs. it blows. Well, it trips a relief valve, like on your water heater, and the pressure goes out the smoke stack, along with a bunch of black ash and makes a real noisy sound, like a whistle or fog horn. Most of the passengers were in bed and they came out on the open deck to see what had happened and this black soot settled on their night attire. The Captain, was on deck too, looking for the unlighted small boat that was probably out there with a net for some illegal fishing. My way of reducing power, in the engine room, seeing as it was at the max, was to throw the main valves off on each boiler, it only took seconds, and all the flames went out. Then they called all clear and wanted power again. And what do you think; I never had a match to get my initial torch lighted so I could start the boilers. I had to climb up two flights of iron stairs and run to my room, through parked cars and campers, parked side by side, to get a match, and then back again. I cut my arm on something sharp on a vehicle and was bleeding, I still have the scar, but I got back and lit the torch, and then the boilers. Someone came down to see if there was a problem, and I said "not anymore" They saw my arm and bandaged it, and we were under way again. I think I got the nickname "Prairie Schooner "after that.

Being a fireman eventually leads to being a Stationary Engineer after a number of years but I thought I had better things to do back home. However, it was a very interesting summer, and I paid for my way back home on the bus. The year was 1948, and as I was leaving home, I dropped into the local Hospital, as my mother was having a baby. Another girl, three now, and I named her Beverly June Alyson, as I liked that movie star. It was a good job we had a big garden and lots of wild deer meat.

This is the Princess Joan and it was the night boat luxury liner of the day that ferried passengers and about 70 cars to and from Vancouver and Victoria, with a side trip to Nanaimo as traffic demanded. It left each port at midnight and arrived about 07:30. Most of the approximately 430 night passengers had staterooms, but those of more modest means could rent a bunk in the dorm forward, (she was licensed to carry 1000 day passengers). This ship went into service in 1930 and had sister ships Elizabeth, Alice, and Adelaide. During the Second World War – many of the Royal Canadian Navy, Engine Room Trainee's, received valuable training aboard these vessels. The last sailing of these night boats was on Tuesday, Feb. 24th, 1959 and they were put up for sale. A Greek Shipping Co. bought the Princess Joan and it became the "Hermes". The boat went to the North Sea for accommodation of the oil crews and in 1974 it was scrapped. This was a good experience for a "Prairie Schooner" and I enjoyed it very much.

Chapter 6

Whitewood is a unique town, as probably are many more in the area with a diverse population. French people, with as many as fifteen counts, came from south of the Loire Valley in France in 1885 and settled at or near Whitewood, in the St. Hubert's district. They set up large homes and started ambitious enterprises and then scattered around the globe when their businesses failed. The counts brought entourages that included servants and experts in agriculture. Many of those people remained behind. One Count tried to set up a sugar beet plantation and distillery. The beets grew well, however the government did not allow the Count to distill into alcohol the product of his farm. Another watched his sheep farm fail after his chief sheep herder was run over and killed by a cart. Another count tried to start a cheese factory before he discovered the feed available to cows in Saskatchewan produced milk that was not suitable for fine cheese. The Counts left, the workers were left behind, and they became today's farmers and business people. One house in town is being restored and that was owned by the Duquette family and I knew those people. To the north there was a Finland Colony, west a lot of Swedish people, and Scotch, Ukrainians, Germans, Hungarians, and others mixed throughout the area. It was a good town to grow up in. One thing that should be noted and that is at least 260 men and women from a town of approximately 800 people and the surrounding district joined up to fight in the second world war, and good number never came back or were permanently disabled.

Chapter 7

Sometime, during the spring (1948) my friend (Pat King) and I decided to get our application ready and apply to join the R.C.M. Police. This involved getting several letters of recommendation, school marks and presenting ourselves at the training headquarters in Regina, Sask. After an interview with the Personnel Officer, we were sent for medicals. Everything seemed okay, until we had to expand our chest four inches. What chest, I was skinny as a rail. They measured you with a cloth tape when you exhaled and then wanted a big breath, and there was to be four inches difference in the measurement. I failed my medical on this and so did my friend. Since then, I often wondered how they measured the girls they were hiring. Anyway, they told us to go home and beef up with lots of work, and come and try again. Maybe, they had a full complement of trainees at that time and just wanted to put us off. However, Pat went working for his Dad for the summer, an Imperial Oil agent and I went harvesting. Pat went to work for Sears in Regina in the fall, and then joined the following year.

I had been talking to some friends that worked for the CPR as telegraph operators and they seemed to be doing pretty good, only I would have to go to school and learn the Morse code. I was told that Old Joe Skinner gave a course on telegraphy and it started in the fall. A bunch of us kids going to Winnipeg shared on the local taxi and we left home. We arrived in Winnipeg, the big city, and not having any place to stay I was dropped off at a cheap hotel, the Woodbine. I found board and room and then went to meet Joe Skinner. He had 12 students starting on Monday and I could be one of them. Joe Skinner had a gimpy leg and was an old telegraph operator and wanted something to do in retirement. The class was held daily in the basement of the old CPR station on Higgins Avenue and we had a noon break playing pool in Jack's place, near the corner of Higgins and Main. I guess I learnt it okay but I was not a whiz and then we progressed to bugs, a faster way to send messages. I also took a typing course at Success Business College. Just before Christmas, I got a "Dear John" letter from my girlfriend in Whitewood and that made me realize that something's are not forever. So I went home for Christmas, which I tried to do for many years and then went back and finished my course by spring. In the meantime, I had been making contact with the hiring officials of the CPR regarding a job as a telegraph operator. I had an interview in Brandon, and they did not care about my chest size, and was given a station agent relieving job for the summer. I went to numerous small towns and ran the station for two or three weeks at each place while the agent was on holidays. It was a good learning experience. When I wanted to move from one place to the other, I had a pass that would allow me to catch a ride in the caboose of a freight train. One particular nice place I worked at was Stockholm, Sask. and they were having a Hungarian wedding at the place where I was to board. The wedding party lasted for days and I still consider those people my friends. I got shifted around quite a bit and finally ended up on Midnight shift in Moosomin, Sask., not far from home. There was a CST. E.J. Webdale, R.C.M.P. stationed in that town that used to come and visit me on the night shift. He convinced me that I should try again as they were looking for recruits. I always remember that he had two fingers partly off on one hand and he had to convince them that he could type and was not handicapped with these two stubby fingers. He must have got through to me, as sometime that spring I was renewing my application. This time I was accepted and went into recruit training in Regina, Saskatchewan.

This was not to be a tea party. There were 30 of us from all parts of Canada organized into a squad (D) and the first thing they did was give us a short haircut. Then we got fatigue pants and jackets, boots, and gym shorts and running shoes. We slept in alphabetical order in one large room and we were expected to keep it clean. Six o'clock was wake up time and then it was a mad rush to the bathroom, and get outside at 6:30 a.m.. I thought maybe we were going to eat, NO; the horses were going to eat. Then I thought we were going to jump on a bus or truck and go to the stables, NO, we were going to run over there. Anyway, at the stables we started a routine, clean the horse's stalls out, and groom them, even a wet sponge to clean their nose and under their tails (guess which one we did first) and some fellows were detailed to feed them. There were a few horses in box stalls and they were the unpredictable ones. They were all nice looking horses, all black, some with white socks and then the fellows that were on the ride came over after they were fed, and got them out for the days riding. Then back to the barracks, walk, NO, run, I don't know what all the hurry is about. Clean up, breakfast, and on the parade square for 8:30 a.m. and inspection, see if our boots

Dormitory – Stetson Hat on my bed   A wrestling Demonstration by the Instructor

are polished. Hell no, I just came from the barn. Then we went to classes until noon, lunch, and more classes in the afternoon, and gym. At gym, we took calisthenics, running, boxing, wrestling, and maybe played a few games. At the pool, we learned to swim, even if you thought you knew how, and learned to save someone. One sad thing happened at the pool. We were told to flat dive into the shallow end of the pool and go to the deep end a save another recruit, and bring him back to shallow water. One of our members, J.R., slipped on his dive and lay motionless on the bottom. We put him on a board and took him out of the pool but to my knowledge he never recovered. He had broken his neck, and ended up in a wheel chair for life. I could see that it was going to be a long three months. Friday night came along and we thought we might go out, NO, only every other weekend, and then no leaving town, only if you have a pass and a good reason. After awhile we got into the routine and made a few new friends. Cleaning our rooms, washing and polishing the floor and having inspection on Saturday morning seemed to be a chore but every once and awhile the evening was livened up with a few pranks, on another squad. Soon we were fitted with uniforms, and this gave us more clothes to wash and care for. More boots to polish and Sam Browne belts to polish, and brass buttons to polish, did I say polish, and then there were revolvers to clean. We were carrying a 45 Colt, and this was pretty interesting learning to shoot them. Lining up properly and marching became a big deal with lots of hollering by a gruff Sergeant/Major. One Sgt./Major was tall and he stood ramrod straight and he had a handle bar mustache and I am sure you could hear his voice in downtown Regina, turned out to be a nice guy at the end of our training. If one particular recruit caused trouble and all of the squad suffered for it, he was given the horse trough treatment out behind the barn. Thrown in the horse trough, boots on, and he usually shaped up, especially because he had to spend a lot more time polishing his boots and getting his fatigues dried out. One particular English fellow got it really bad when he was thrown into run off from the stables one Saturday morning. Our classes involved everything from the Criminal Code, to Provincial Statutes, mock court cases, deportment, and typing. Then, of course, there were exam papers on what we had learned.

The R.C.M.P. has their own cemetery in Regina and while we were there the Commissioner's son was killed in a traffic accident and he was buried in Regina. We became part of the funeral entourage, with the riderless horse, boots in the stirrups backwards, and the twenty-one gun salute. At least we knew if we did not make it we would get a good send off.

One Sunday, with a day off, we decided to rent a car and go out Ft. San and visit one of the fellow's sisters who was taking some nursing training at the hospital. We thought of this on Saturday, so we could not apply for passes to leave the city. It was a nice drive there and back except for the deer we hit on the way back. In order to not get in trouble we had to pay for the damages which amounted to $400.00, divided four ways. Our salary at that time was $108.00 per month. Good job I got a final payment from the CPR of $300.00 for two weeks work as it came in handy.

No major problems so far, we were even shaping up marching. After about three and a half months we were told that we would be sent to Ottawa, (Rockcliffe) for the second part of our training. This would be more of the same, with new instructors. We found that there was a pub down the road a couple of miles at the Eastview Hotel, and we would run down there in the evenings and have one of those quart bottles of beer that we had never seen before and then take a taxi back. We still had to do the chores with the horses and there was a big man, Van Patten, in charge of the stables and the ride. One morning after we had the horses cleaned and fed he told us to stand at attention at the stalls by the horse we had looked after. They played "Reveille" on the trumpet and then fired a .303 rifle with blanks inside the stable and the horses started jumping around in their stalls, only we were not to move, not even an eyelash. Pretty hard to do when you got a horse jumping around behind you. This was to get them used to gun fire, and to see what kind of chicken Mounties they had. They used to ride the horses through some sand dunes that were close at hand and everyone liked that, at the full gallop mind you.

Notice the troop, on the next page, with full riding gear, and horses at the gallop. Also, not one of the horses has white socks. If a colt is born at their horse ranch in Fort McLeod, Alta. and it has white socks, even one, they will invariable sell it off or keep it for training, if it turns out to be a good horse, but all the horses in the ride that travels around the country performing will be all black. The policemen and women who are in the ride get no extra pay, and after a spell in the ride, they will return to regular police work.

One of the other chores that we did not like was taking an R.C.M.P member that was in jail for a walk in the morning. Apparently, he was on detachment in Dundas Harbour, in the N.W.T. and started living with a local person. The charge was 'co-habiting with a woman other than his wife' and this was his second offense. He was charged under the R.C.M.P.

act and got six months in jail for it. My, how things have changed. Another member "went over the hill" as they say. He left, ran away, to marry his sweetheart. At that time a member could not get married for five years, and before that it was as much as twelve years until you could ask permission to get married, and meet some other criteria that they had in place. We had a nice time in Ottawa and even took part in the Remembrance Day parade on November Eleventh, on Parliament Hill.

We had our usual, "hi-jinks" and one of these involved one of our members and a parade in the morning with revolver drill and inspection. Someone got a hold of a certain member's Sam Browne belt and revolver, after he had cleaned it all and then went to the bathroom, just before parade. They stuffed a "condom" in the barrel with part of it hanging out. When the drill instructor called for "draw pistols", this was done on command and fairly quickly. Our member was in the front row and could not be missed by the instructor. He walked over and said (Name withheld) "when did you clean your pistol last". The incident kind of broke up the rest of the squad, and fortunately the instructor thought it was funny too. We also did driver training in Ottawa, which seemed to be a lot of driving around doing the instructor's errands. We were getting ready for the "pass out" party which meant we were done our training and would be going out on detachment, to really learn police work.

"Got to show off my uniform at home"

Chapter 8

There was a lot of speculation as to what Province we would be going to because at that time they did not send you to your home Province. I happened to draw Manitoba and here I am a number of years later and still in Manitoba, but a lot of water went under the bridge since then. Flin Flon was to be the detachment I was assigned to first, and there were probably ten other members already in place, as we did town policing in this town as well. Flin Flon, a town, now a city, in NW Manitoba, situated on the border with Saskatchewan, about 600 KM's north of Winnipeg, named by a prospector upon his discovery of gold after Professor J. Flintabbatey Flonatin, a character in J.Murddock's novel "The Sunless City," a story about the discovery of a strange world paved with gold beneath the Rocky Mountains. As there was no more room in the barracks for me to stay, they billeted me in the Corona Hotel, just down the street from the barracks. I think I ate wherever I could find a meal, and depending on how much money I had. The owner of the hotel and some of his buddies had a session; it seemed daily, over a bottle of Scotch in the office. They always wanted me to join in, but that was not in my calling to drink and then go to work. The members had three shifts to put in and it was sometimes difficult getting enough sleep.

I believe that we worked six days a week and were to be available at other times, if required. Part of our evening duties were to 'shake door knobs' which meant we checked the doors of businesses on the streets to make sure they were locked, and this was a foot patrol. At least we got to know people in town, which was important. I met Ray Hicken, who first had a shoe repair business and then started a "Chicken Delight", and then Jimmy Bell, who was in the hardware business. This friendship evolved into being asked to go fishing in the spring which I thoroughly enjoyed. I also, met Mr. Freedman, who had a convenience store across from the hotel. Who could forget that when you opened the door of his shop, that you had to step down into the store. Mr. Freedman was also the Mayor of town, and a very nice man. Also, the Justice of the Peace was a man who we had contact with on many occasions. Somehow or other, I met Pat Martin who worked at the mine, which of course gave employment to a great number of the people in town. Pat was a nice guy, who liked to play cards for money, but not with me, and onetime he told me he made enough money to buy a new Pontiac car. I think we did a lot of fishing together. This was a town that had lots of sports, from golf, to baseball, and of course, the Flin Flon bombers, and a junior hockey team. Some notables have passed through there, such as Clark and Leach. The rink was always full on hockey nights and it was a privilege to be on duty on hockey nights, just to make our presence known. Sometimes, things got a little dicey, as we did not stand for open liquor in a public place.

One particular night after I had been there for a couple of weeks, I was paired up with Nick, a more senior member and we got a call from the Flin Flon Hotel, and the Chinese Owner, said "Come quick, a big fight." We jumped in the car and went down to the hotel, and as we walked into the beer parlor we found many guys standing around and it was obvious there had been trouble. Tables knocked over, chairs upside down, beer and beer glasses, all over the floor and some blood here and there. I followed Nick into the scene and followed him right back out, mind you a little bewildered. He went to the phone and called for more members.

The telephone operator in the switchboard office was told to turn on the red light, which lit up several lights on hydro poles in different places in town, and if members saw this, they were to respond. Four members turned up, a couple in civilian clothes, one even in bedroom slippers. We went back into the parlor and sorted things out. Apparently, one fellow had slammed another with a salt shaker on the back of the head, which opened his head up pretty good. A fight started and that is when we got the call. We arrested eighteen miners and marched them two by two down the street to the police station. They went in unwillingly, and then into the crowded cells, and it was a chore taking their boots and belts off them, which is a necessary part of being thrown in jail. After a noisy night, court was convened at 10:00 a.m., and each was fined $55.00 and costs, which they all paid or made arrangements to pay. Now what part of our training told us about this situation, I do not remember. I guess you call it "on the job training". Nick was a marvelously cool guy under pressure and I learnt a lot from him. He spent many years in Northern Towns, where you had to use your own ingenuity. One night in the winter, I was driving around town, and came to a stop sign on Hapnot Hill and I put on the brakes, and did a 360 and ended up at the stop sign, and there was quite a drop off on one side. It was slippery, but he had his eyes closed, getting a little shut eye, and I was thankful for that.

We also did foot patrols up in the warehouse district, on the north side of Main Street, kind of on a hill.

Somewhere around midnight I was coming back from my rounds dressed in my Buffalo Coat and fur hat, for it was very cold and as I came by one warehouse that had the loading platform on posts, about a dozen sleigh dogs came barking out to the end of their chains and scared the heck out of me. I took some awfully big steps clearing out of that area. Apparently, a dog musher from Brochet was travelling through town going to The Pas trappers festival and dog races, and he knew the grocery warehouse owner and got permission to leave his dogs under the platform and he probably stayed at his house. The coldest morning I can remember was minus 54 and the smoke from the mine and houses seemed to be just hanging in mid-air.

Spring was starting to come slowly, and there was word that a trapper and his wife did not come back from the trapline. The name does not matter but the relations had advised us of this and a general search was started. One trapper from Schist Lake used to come to town on Thursday's and after shopping used to visit the Sergeant in charge. He related a story that he had a dream and dreamt that the missing trapper had killed his wife and himself on their trapline. This seemed odd as the old fellow was well trusted and a friend of the Sergeant's. I liked this old fellow and the Sergeant suggested I take the police canoe and motor and go out to his cabin on Schist Lake and have a look around and visit with him. The police canoe was an 18 foot semi-freighter equipped with a 5 H.P. motor stored out at Channing. I caught a ride out there in the police car and got the outfit ready and also put a good sized rock in the bow so it would plane properly. The river led out of Channing and after a trip of about twelve miles I was at his cabin on Schist Lake. He welcomed me and I played with his dogs for awhile. He was raising cocker spaniels and had a new bunch of pups. He told me the same story as he told the Sergeant. I had nothing to think that there was anything different, so in the late afternoon, I left to go back to Channing.

Late in the day a report came into the office a plane from Flin Flon, (the Johnson Brothers, in a Seabee) that they had spotted a red gas can floating in a bay on Lake Athapap, near Bakers Narrows. A search of this bay turned up a gas can thought to be owned by the trapper in the area. Next they found his camp and found a man and woman, dead in a tent camp and partially devoured by animals. Everything was taken back to Flin Flon and an inquest was convened. The Doctor's report showed that the woman had a bullet hole in her skull and the man had also been shot in the head. It was decided that it was murder—suicide. The court released what was left of the bodies to the relations and sent me out to the garbage pit with the tattered clothing, etc. that was not needed, except that it was pitch dark and there were rats running all over the place. ERIE!! End of case.

A couple of weeks went by without too much happening and one day as I was walking down the street in civilian clothes, Archie Peterson, another member, pulled up beside me and said come with me. He said there was a fire in a log cabin out in Channing. The fire department did not go to Channing as it was out of their jurisdiction, but there were people trying to put the fire out. Someone said that there were two kids in the house. Archie put on a smoke mask and we tied a rope around his waist and he went in a window to see if he could find the kids. They were found under a bed and he brought them out, one at a time, and handed them to me at the window. Poor little guys had perished. Archie had done a good job going into the house, after that I think they let it burn.

Well I had a pretty good summer, got lots of fishing in. I even bought a fishing pole with steel line on it so I could fish for trout out on Lake Athapap. Also went fishing out at the Sturgeon Weir river and that was good for pickerel. Three of us portaged into a lake somewhere east of Beaver Lake and had a terrific fishing trip.

There seemed to be an increase of break-ins of several business places in town, garages were particularly hard hit and we could not seem to catch anyone, even with increased surveillance from us. We put a member in a garage overnight with hopes of catching them red-handed but to no avail.

This carried on for months and we switched overnight stays randomly but they seemed to know our movements. And well they did, because one of the culprits was a taxi driver and he would keep track of us and radio our whereabouts to the others. Our Dominion of Canada license number was DG 2002 and he would say 2002 at Hi-way Motors, or at Gail Motors, or they went to Creighton, which is across the border in Saskatchewan. Then they would do their dirty work and we would have another break in. I was not involved with the undercover work that solved these crimes but someone on our staff deserved a lot of credit. Three or four fellows went to court and got time in jail for their efforts. One particular young fellow, though old enough to go to Stoney Mountain Penitentiary ended up hanging himself in there, he could not stand the sex action that prevailed inside the big house. I was told by one of the culprits that one night as we checked Gail Motors, he and a couple of others were at the garage getting ready to break in, when we came along. He went under a car outside and said he could have put his hand or leg out and tripped me as I walked by. Close but no cigar.

Some other residents of town were in a different kind of activity and I spent time with them. I guess the following letter is self-explanatory.

JACK CLARKSON

Sgt. N. J. Calverley,
  R. C. M. P.
    Flin Flon,
      Man.

Dear Sir:

      I hope this letter will express to you my apreciation of your help in making our Scout and Cub camps a success by lending us Constable Clarkson to make a personal appearance.

      Constable Clarkson was very popular with the boys and did a very good job of establishing friendly relations between the boys and the R.C.M.P. Ii imagine he will be greeted on the street by boys he does not even remember.

      I must apologize for keeping Constable Clarkson a bit late last Sunday, and I hope he did not get into trouble over it.

           Thanking you again,
           I remain yours sincerely

           Victor C Hook

           District Commissioner
           Boy Scouts Association.

Chapter 9

I got transferred to Winnipeg and was to go on Highway Patrol. I cannot remember the date exactly, but two of us were assisting the Virden Detachment when there was a foot and mouth disease in cattle and they did not want them going across the border from Saskatchewan in trucks. This was quite a boring job. We were there in March and April (1951) and lived in the Virden Hotel. I remember my partner (Stewart) used to open the window and sleep on top of the covers in the nude. I just about froze but he explained that he spent many years in the Arctic and that's the way he slept. He was also married to an Eskimo woman. The healthy old devil probably lived until one hundred and ten.

Back to Winnipeg and I got paired up with Bill R. and we were on a roving patrol around the outskirts of the city. City Police handled inside the city unless we were in fresh pursuit of someone. Later, I think we were called the "Tip toe Patrol" and maybe for good reason. I drove for the most part unless Bill could visualize a chase and then he took over. He was a past master at catching someone in a car. Flash the headlights on bright when the car ahead would not stop , just at the exact time they were going around a sharp corner, invariably they would miss the corner and we would catch them with a load of booze or stolen property. Or catch the back bumper when the car ahead was going around a corner. Bill was a fairly big man and liked to drive with the seat fully forward and his arms wrapped around the steering wheel, my poor knees in those cramped quarters with breeches and high boots on.

As far as the tip toe patrol was concerned, Bill could spot a car and mile or maybe two miles away, from the reflection of the moon on the chrome. A car parked out on a lonely road by itself was either up to no good or they were drinking. We would go around, maybe five or six miles, if necessary, and get in behind it with our lights out. Then about a quarter mile back, we would walk quietly, no flashlights, until we got to the car, one on each side and open the doors quickly. Some of the sights we saw are not worth talking about. One particular scene was feet pointed in both directions, and a very stunned couple. Bill asked for a driver's license which was retrieved from pants on the floor, and found that this person was a doctor with an address in a very affluent part of town. He said "so you are a doctor, I sure as hell would not want to take my wife to you". We did get lots of liquor infraction busts and I am sure he would give a speeding ticket to his own grandmother. Those were the days when you had to clock a speeder for a mile or so from a half mile back, no radar or camera's. We knew a lot of license plates of supposed bad guys off by heart, and some of them still come to mind. One thing, we never worked midnights, just days and evenings. I used to get my lunch at Ideal Lunch on McPhillips Street and one night he said don't bother with lunch, and about seven o'clock we took our break. We stopped at a house on Mountain Ave. and it was packed with people. They were having a Ukrainian supper, you know the kind, twelve meatless dishes and boy was there lots to eat. The people were his friends or relations and they made me welcome. But we did not have a drink of spirits because we were still on duty. First time that I knew the Ukrainians had two Christmas's to celebrate. We also used to stop at Manitoba motors on Main Street, and talk to Dave, his brother and the old man. There was always some kind of a car deal in the making that was interesting, and it kept us up to date on makes and models. Bill knew were to get a bargain, and well he needed to know, because the paychecks did not go too far.

One morning we heard from dispatches that two men and a girl were travelling west by car through the United States and breaking into service stations and small restaurants, taking what they needed and moving on. The last place they stopped at was a farm yard near Plum Coulee and they stole a fairly new Plymouth Cranbrook, green in color, and then headed north towards Winnipeg. Information from the farmer indicated that they were armed. Bill's intuition must have been working overtime and he was driving. He said "They will probably come into the city on the south west side, staying off Highway No.75." We kind of expected them around eleven am, so we were cruising the south-west quadrant of the city. After awhile we gave up, thinking that they slipped by us. So we went into the city for me to get some lunch and ended up going East on Ellice Ave, just off Ferry Road. Guess what, we met them and the first thing he said is don't turn around to look at them when we go by. They peeled off Ellice and went south on King Edward, which was a gravel road at the time. We followed at a high rate of speed and they turned East on Ness Ave., but did not make the turn and went in the ditch. We were there to see them bail out of the car and run in different directions. I was probably a faster runner than Bill and I caught one guy behind a two story house that had a high fence joining onto the next house. I brought him back to the police car. A crowd was gathering and other people were coming to see what happened, except two people, a boy and girl, walking hand in hand away from the scene. Bill said" that's probably them, go get them". I jumped in the police car and drove down the street about a block and put them both in the back seat, and then I backed up to where the car went in the ditch. We all got out and Bill said "Did you search them" I said "No", but then commenced to search the guy and he pulled out a sawed off .22

out of his belt and gave it to me. It was loaded. Twice he could have shot me. That was the end of their crime spree. We took them to Headquarters and they were questioned and then taken to Vaughan Street Jail until a court date was arranged.

A letter of commendation was received by Cst. Rachel and myself from the Commissioner, L.H. Nicholson stating that "it was drawn to my attention the efficient manner in which these two members effected the arrest of the above noted individuals, following a chase, at high speed through a populated area. The skill and good judgment with which they carried out their assignment are indeed commendable." I might mention policeman instinct in my partners mind, was a factor in being at the right place at the right time.

Shortly after this incident, Bill was advised he could be transferred to Ottawa and after fourteen years on Highway Patrol maybe this was a good move. All the young constables paid special attention to the north main drive-in, picture shows and concession stands owned by Mr. Silverberg. We looked after traffic and we got the last of the hot dogs and drinks in the evening... Also I think there were free passes for the Highway Patrol on our day off. Nice man, Mr. Silverberg and the girls in the concession stands were nice too.

There seemed to be a rash of break-ins outside of Winnipeg and sometimes explosives were used to blow the safes. A new patrol was started with new members and it was from 10:00 p.m. to 6:00 a.m., six days a week, and each night we were to go a different direction. We were nick-named 'Charlie's Angels" and that may have been a misnomer but a Corporal named Charlie was in charge. This did not give a person much of a chance for any night life but we spent a lot of time at Sargent Park swimming pool during the day. Each patrol that went out would put on three to four hundred miles a night randomly checking garages, stores and other business places in the small towns. We caught numerous highway traffic and liquor infractions. One particular liquor infraction was on the river road near St. Andrews, Manitoba. My partner and I pulled in on a car parked along the river bank and as we did a bottle was thrown out the window. I retrieved it and asked the driver to open the trunk of the car, to check for more liquor or whatever. As he did, he struck me across the arm that was holding the bottle and it smashed on the bumper. Thinking we were in for trouble, I brought a pretty good punch up from the ground and knocked the driver into the river. Fortunately it was shallow and he regained his feet and climbed up the muddy bank, about 15 feet. We probably should have arrested him but we took particulars from him and the other three passengers and as there appeared to be other persons capable of driving the car, we just gave him a ticket for illegal liquor and instructed him on a court date. Later on, towards morning we were told to come into the office and make a full report in writing. Apparently, the driver talked to his lawyer and planned on suing me for $5000.00 for the poke in the chin. Special investigators took over and even went out to the scene and retrieved broken pieces of glass and took photos. They also interviewed everyone involved. In about three weeks, his court date came up and all details were put before the magistrate and the gentleman was convicted and paid a small fine. Therefore, he dropped any idea of suing. Whew, anxious times, $20.00 per month until $5000.00 was paid off would take a long time.

One particular night, there was information out that a notorious gang, called the 'Boyd Gang' had escaped from the Don Jail, in Toronto and they were headed west and fully armed. They were supposed to be seen in Thunder Bay; Fort William at the time, and still headed west and a description of the car was supplied. Whitemouth detachment received word that four men had booked into a motel at West Hawk Lake, on old No. One Highway, The police officer at Whitemouth assembled about six men and went to West Hawk and surrounded the cabin they were supposed to be in. My partner and I were covering a junction in the road, called Sieg's corner, further west about 30 miles. Daylight came and the policemen called on loud halers to come out with their hands up, NOW. They did, sort of bleary-eyed, and still in their night attire wondering what was going on. Policemen were behind the woodpile and across the road with guns trained on them. Good job their pajamas stayed up because if they had of dropped their hands they might have been shot. After much talking the atmosphere became more relaxed and then the car was searched. They were telling the truth; they were religious people delivering pamphlets to people out west. The car was full of them. The Boyd Gang was caught on their own turf a week later. Oh well, another night in the life of a constable.

One of my partners on Highway Patrol, Al, had completed many years in the Boy Scouts and it showed. He would sit in the passenger seat of the police car and look up at the stars. He could read them. Pretty soon he would tell me what time it was, exactly, except that he would sometimes forget to add daylight saving time. Sometimes, I would hit the brakes, just to throw him off, or bang his nose on the windshield, but that did not seem to bother him, he was really a nice guy. Another time, my partner and I, not Al, were really tired. Neither one of could stay awake about 4:00 in the morning, too much of the swimming pool, or something. So we pulled into a driveway, off the Hodinott Road, into a farmer's field and behind some bushes to have a little sleep. We thought we were better to be off the road seeing as we were so tired. About 8:00 a.m. we heard a tractor go by and that woke us up, and now we were late to go off shift. Explain that to Charlie!

Seems like we were always on the night shift and so we were, all summer long. Another member was always checking the girls out on the street when he was in downtown Winnipeg and his partner wore really thick glasses, an older fellow, getting ready for pension. This particular day, the driver was checking the sidewalks and they came up to a red light and did not stop in time and hit the car ahead. Guess what, it was really a nice girl and the driver arranged to have lunch with her, fortunately, there was no damage to speak of. Can you imagine trying to explain that to Charlie, our boss?

Saturday nights used to see the patrols roaming the country side, and sometimes finding a dance at a local hall, and of course we were always looking for liquor infractions. I guess we felt we had to prove out worth each night with one kind of ticket or the other. Bob and I were on such a patrol and ended up northwest of Winnipeg. Bob was a pretty husky fellow and played hockey for the Dauphin Kings for a spell. I guess it was lunch time at this particular dance and a lot of people were outside having a barley sandwich. We went in different directions checking cars and people at them. I spotted a guy drinking a beer beside a car with several friends. I told him to give me the beer and he reached over the car door and grabbed me by the shirt and tie, and made me stand on my toes, while he calmly poured the beer out and even shook the bottle. Some of these farm boys are pretty strong. Bob came along about this time, and we decided to take Mr. Farmer to Winnipeg and lock him up. He came to the police car okay and we drove down the road a few miles and stopped to talk to him, see if he would admit drinking the beer and we would give him a ticket for it. As we were sitting there another car pulled up behind and about 5 or 6 guys bailed out and wanted to talk to us, as we were all out of the police car by now. I thought this was going to be a real confrontation. I forced him back in the car with a couple of sharp jabs and away we went to Winnipeg and Vaughan Street jail. He got a lawyer and got out shortly after, with a promise to appear in court. Court day came and he appeared and paid a normal fine.

Some of our other constables went east the next weekend and got shook up at a barn dance (Jimmy's Barn). A bunch of guys started to rock the police car, in an attempt to roll it over but they got out of there. We were down the road a few miles stopping cars and checking them and one car would not stop for our road block. We chased the car and it turned south on a gravel road with us gaining on him. Over a railroad track and then about a half mile down the road there was an abrupt 90 degree turn. The car missed this corner and went through ditch, through a fence and small bushes and hit a farm disc that was parked in the field. He was injured so we took him to the Selkirk Hospital and had him admitted. Turns out he had several warrants out for his arrest, something to do with the 'Bear Skin Club' that was active in the Lockport Area previously. A good night for us.

Somehow, my partner and I ended up on day shift on Sunday, and in the afternoon we were on routine highway patrol in the Lockport, Manitoba area but the events that led up to this began on July 18th, at 2:23 p.m., about two days previous.

"Come on!!! Down on the floor!!!! This is a stick up!!!!"

With those words, two men their faces masked with sunglasses entered the East Kildonan, Greater Winnipeg Branch of the Imperial Bank of Commerce. One man brandished two revolvers, and the other who waited near the door, nursed a sawed-off Shotgun. It was evident they meant business.

There were nine persons in the bank at the time – six being employees. One, a 19 year old ledger clerk, had the presence of mind to trip the alarm before hitting the deck. This brought the East Kildonan police chief to the scene. The Police office is situated only about 100 feet from the bank. The chief met with poor reception, however. He was kicked, hurled to the floor, and stood over by the shotgun wielding bandit. (I learned afterwards that the bank manager and the police chief went for coffee each day and the way the manager had of getting the police chief to come and pick him up, was to give the alarm a short burst – consequently the police chief was just going for coffee - not going to greet bank robbers - and was therefore unprepared.)

Meanwhile, his companion had been over to the vault, but finding it locked, scooped up the cash out of the tellers' cages, stuffing it into a bag he carried. The amount he picked up was $6,920.67.

The whole thing took only about 75 seconds. Then they were away, fleeing in a sleek, black, 1950 model Oldsmobile. This was Greater Winnipeg's first bank hold-up in five years.

Immediately, the East Kildonan Police, Winnipeg City Police and the R.C.M.P., swung into action. Road blocks were placed at strategic points throughout the Greater Winnipeg area.

But the picture was gloomy. Friday went by - nothing. Then Saturday came and went - still nothing. Now Sunday -- but it was different. Sunday brought the first break in the now nearly two day old robbery. But what a day it turned out to be!!! The scene was shifted to Vivian, Manitoba, a small hamlet 30 miles east of Winnipeg. The Canadian National Railway station agent saw two men emerge from the bush, walk to the pump house, fill a jug with water and then return from whence they came. Funny, he thought. And their appearance! Could it be the two bank robbers the police were looking for?

Just then the CNR pump house operator came into the station. It appeared his daughter had spotted the same two men on Friday evening. They packed guns. Yes, it was shaping up now. The agent contacted the dispatcher in Winnipeg. He telephoned the Winnipeg City Police, and they notified the R.C.M.P. Two constables, John and George, who were out on patrol were sent to investigate. They found others in the Vivian area who had noticed the same two men and their descriptions tallied with those furnished by the bank officials. They advised Winnipeg R.C.M.P. that the two men were likely suspects and said they would check the bush area that the men were last seen near. It was suggested that back up patrols should converge in the area. That is where my partner, Al, and I came in.

Our trip from Lockport to Vivian was far from uneventful. It was Sunday afternoon and the traffic was bumper to bumper on the winding Henderson Highway, and of course we were trying to make time. I was driving and many times we found ourselves stuck out in the on-coming traffic lane with cars beside us. A little bit of siren and on one occasion a friendly member, Sgt. Alex Gillespie, who was out for a drive with his wife, slackened off his speed and let us in front of him - not before we told him what we thought was happening out the car window as we sped along.

We made it to the Vivian area, probably in pretty good time. We had been told the two constables were going to check the first gravel road west of Vivian, to the south in the area of some gravel pits. We drove down that road and met another police car proceeding north. We stopped to converse with them and while we were talking, shots were heard to the south of us. As this was a narrow gravel road with deep ditches the other police car had to go to the main road about a mile away to turn around. Al and I sped to the area we thought the shots had come from. We met George who was coming out of the bushes along a trail, waving his pistol with his lanyard attached, and no hat on. He said "they are in there - they got John." (To me it was got, not shot). We bailed out of our police car and ran into the area that George indicated along a cow trail.

Soon we spotted a green unmarked Ford police car, and two men trying to get it going. It had a Standard Transmission and they were trying to start it but forgot to put their foot on the clutch, I guess they were getting used to their big stolen Oldsmobile. The three of us crouched down in various locations more or less surrounding the police car and shouted, "Throw your guns and come away from the car with your hands up". They stopped trying to start the car and got out on the far side -- little did we know that they were checking their guns for ammunition. I was behind a small tree closest to the car, later determined as 21 ft., 9 inches from the rear bumper of the car, and then one man got in the back seat of the car and shot twice at me behind the tree.

That started it --- We all started firing -- and they started running and we chased them - firing as we ran. I noticed one bullet hitting in the trail ahead of me –it had to come from behind. I took careful aim at one man disappearing into some bushes and fired and then saw the other bandit further on and he seemed to be getting away. By this time the other police car turned up and there were four members in this party, one of them being a Corporal who had a rifle, (25-20) and the furthest bandit seemed to slow up. I ran up to him first and he had thrown away his gun and was throwing away money, cash, out of his jacket and shirt. (There is a charge in the books for possession of stolen goods, and he knew it) He had a gunshot wound in his foot, but it went in through his sole and came out through his laces. The Corporal had aimed between his shoulders but for this distance a 25-20 dropped to his foot. What a lucky shot to get him when he was running, in the sole of his shoe.

Another Constable came up and said to the fellow "What is your name" and he gave him a fictitious name, but the constable knew his mug shots and said "No, I don't think so, its Zakopiac, I can tell from the scar on your face. " He had a long scar over the bridge of his nose, from a fight he was in while in the home for boys. Upon searching ZAKOPIAC, he was found to have $1680.77 in his possession and a further $1760.00 was retrieved in the bushes where he had thrown it.

As more members turned up I decided to go back and see the wounded officer. On my way there I almost tripped over the other bank robber who was taking his last few breaths, he had been shot through the lungs with what I would suspect a .45 Colt shell. I understand that just previous to me getting there he was up on one elbow aiming at another member but found his weapon empty. I carried on past the police car with the broken rear window to find the wounded officer lying on the side of the road and to me it looked as though he had passed on. His eyes were rolled back, but open and blood was trickling out of the corner of his mouth. His neck had turned dark blue or purple but signs of a lot of blood were not evident. Someone hollered, we need an ambulance and the radios would not work because we were out of range. I jumped in the police car with the broken window and headed for Vivian. That was a fast ride and the road ended in a 'T' and I almost went in the ditch, but that was the main grid leading into town. I went to the C.N.R. station and the agent was on hand. I told him what I needed and he said go ahead and use the railroad phone. I got the dispatcher in Winnipeg and it was someone I knew from my railroad days. He got the instructions right, for two ambulances and advise our headquarters that we have a wounded member lying out in the bush.

Then I went back to the scene, only a little slower. The boys had checked out the deceased bandit and found that he was Albert PROULX, alias John ZAHARA, and had $3456.21 on his person. They, of course, were making our wounded member as comfortable as possible, but it sure did not look good for him. I am certain that we all said a silent prayer. We heard the wail of sirens off in the distance and knew it was the ambulances. With them came more police cars and of course, some very high ranking officers. The scene was cleared very quickly and left some of us younger fellows to take the shot up police car back to Winnipeg along with the dead bank robber. He was placed in the trunk of the car and taken to Cook's Funeral Home in Transcona. They asked a few questions; like how do you know he is dead. Well, I said "He has a bullet hole in his chest" and I guess with us all being in uniform he believed us and took the body inside.

A fellow member was on the ride into Winnipeg with the ambulances and he said it was one to remember. Police cars and five Winnipeg City Police motorcycles met the ambulances at the outskirts of the city and went with them to Deer Lodge Hospital. One motorcycle took a tumble and one police car had a blowout. There were street car tracks down the middle of Portage Avenue in those days. Speed was important to our wounded member and because of that and a Doctor who was familiar with gunshot wounds (Korean War Doctor) his life was saved. We visited him in the hospital next day and other than a bandage on each side of his throat, he seemed in good shape, except he said he had a sore throat!!! Lucky man. The bullet, a .38 caliber, had passed through his neck missing his juggler vein by a papers width. He explained what happened.

The two constables saw these two men standing under a tree, west of Vivian about a mile, down a side road on a trail in what you call scrub pasture. They asked them what they were doing and the answer was they were just getting out of the rain. (A shower had just passed through the area). The policemen got out of the car and went over to them, a matter of some 75 feet. The suspects explained that they were farm hands and lived over that way, indicating the south west. The Constables were not convinced and one went to the road the summon help, believing there was another car in the area. No sooner had George left and the suspects jumped John, and grappling they fell to the ground. John rolled over on top of one of the men and had him pinned to the ground. The other raised his revolver and shot point blank at John, estimated at no more than 9 feet distance. John fell to the ground and culprits then proceeded to try and steal the police car. That is when we came on the scene at the beckoning of the other constable.

Subsequently, ZAKOPIAC appeared before Chief Justice E.K Williams in the court of Queen's Bench, Winnipeg, Oct. 29th, 1952. This was a red serge event being the Court of Queen's Bench. ZAKOPIAC elected to be his own defense, but had a Priest in attendance with him. He was charged with two counts of attempted murder, one being of the constable shot in the neck, and the other being of myself. Also one charge of robbery while armed and one charge of having a stolen automobile. The trial progressed quite well with members testifying and evidence being presented. I learned that the bullet holes in the six inch tree I was hiding behind were about an inch apart. The two had been fairly good shots, having done a lot of practicing in their basement at a home in East Kildonan. When it came to my turn to give testimony, all went well except for a slight knocking of my knees. Chief Justice Williams then addressed the accused, asking him if he had any questions for me. And he did!! ZAKOPIAC asked me "If I believed in the Bible" I said "Yes, I did" wondering what he was getting at. He said " Don't you know that it states in the commandments that " Thou Shalt Not Kill " and yet you deliberately shot my companion in cold blood. My face, turned about the same color as my Tunic , and then the Chief Justice came to my rescue. He said "Mr. Zakopiac, this is no time to be going into this man's morals. When the case was over, ZAKOPIAC was convicted as charged and sentenced to 30 years in prison.

In hindsight the two robbers were given ample opportunity to surrender, but they choose to fight with guns. Zakopiac was right beside his partner, Zahara, when I shot and he then went on the run through some scrub bushes. My shooting was good, as I got 198 out of 200, for my crossed revolver insignia, but I could not get a clear shot at him. Many years later, I got the file on Zakopiac, 1500 large pages of his record, and he started getting in trouble at age 9, and was in shoot out situations before, one in Los Angles and one in Vancouver.

The two bank robbers had stolen the Oldsmobile from a Doctor in River Heights, and had made a tent camp in the bushes south west of Vivian. My partner and I drove to that area one afternoon shift looking for the camp and we were probably within a stone's throw of it, but did not find it. They had drove the car right into the small poplar

Enfield (left) was expecting a cup of coffee, not armed thugs Proulx (centre) and Zakopiac, when he responded to the alarm.

saplings and then got them to stand up afterwards, completely concealing it. I even went up for a ride in a Beaver aircraft, owned by the R.C.M.P, with Sgt. Beaumont, the pilot, to look for the camp, but after all the tight turns all I saw was the bottom of a plastic bag while I was throwing up. When the camp was located - an additional $6.00 was found at the camp site for a grand total of $6902.98, just $17.69 short of the amount stolen at the East Kildonan Bank. Well, so much for that bit of excitement, back to routine patrols.

A month or so later, the first two Constables involved in spotting the culprits received notice that they would be presented with gold watches from the Bankers Association at a special ceremony. The rest of us that were directly involved received commendations from the Commissioner of the R.C.M. Police, to be placed on our file. The member shot recovered and spent the rest of his career in the service. Two or three of us ended up on plain clothes duty in Winnipeg for a period of time.

That would probably be the end, except that after two or three years, I decided to take leave of the force and try to make my living in private industry, and one night while on the midnight shift at Winnipeg International Airport, working for Imperial Oil, I heard on the news that ZAKOPIAC had escaped. There had been veiled threats that the Judge and a few more were going to get done in by Zakopiac or his friends... Apparently, Zakopiac had done 5 or 6 years in Stoney Mountain Pen and had ended up on a work gang on which he did a lot of queer things, one of them being he painted himself green in the paint shop. I guess that he passed the test for being mentally unbalanced and was placed in the Selkirk Mental Institution, were after a time he escaped by climbing down the drain pipe from the second floor. A few days later he was picked up by the Winnipeg City Police riding a bicycle over the Redwood Bridge. The rest of his time was spent in Vaughan Street Detention Home under close scrutiny. One Winnipeg resident, Mrs. Janet Laing, has seen fit to compose a poem entitled, "The Manhunt at Vivian" - the text follows:

> *The police car speeded eastwards,*
> *And scarce a word was said,*
> *Each man thinking grimly of - The task which lay ahead,*
> *The bandits had been sighted,*
> *The manhunt had begun,*
> *And who could tell,*
> *What fate might bring.*

"Twas in the bush at Vivian,
That they, their quarry spied,
And quick to apprehend them,
The officers had tried.

In the bitter fight that followed,
One gallant Mountie fell,
While a desperado's mortal soul,
Went plunging into Hell.

The Manhunt was now over,
Another job was done,
Soon an anxious Mother sped,
To the bedside of her son.

But miracles still happen,
They heard with bated breath,
The Doctor says "By a paper's width,
He has escaped from death.

The sequel to this story,
In a courtroom was told,
How Mounties always get their man,
As in the days of old.

With his life one bandit paid,
The greatest price of all,
Thirty years will the other serve, ---Behind a prison wall.
Never shall wrong triumph,
In our battle for the right,
And ever the truth will conquer,
No matter how grim the fight.

Chapter 10

Many years later, I was having coffee with an Ass't Commissioner who lived in my area, and we talked about this incident and the fact that we had received a commendation from the Commissioner of the R.C.M.P and he told me that they now had a medal or service ribbon, for members who were so recognized, and that it was retro-active, so I could apply. I did that, and after paying a fee I received this service medal, and it was made of Gold. It has two R.C.M.P. buffalo heads on it, signifying I have two letters of commendation.

I was one of the members picked to go in plain clothes, called the Criminal Investigation Branch, C.I.B. This meant wearing a suit and dealing with crimes committed by criminals who cheated people out their money by fraud or other illegal activities and I guess a lot of being told what to do by more senior members. The first day on the job I was paired up with two detectives who had to go to Headingly jail to interview an inmate but on the way there they dropped me off at the Kirkfield Park Hotel. The reason for this was - they had heard there was a bum cheque artist supposedly staying at the hotel and that he had been seen in the area. I took a seat in the lobby with a clear view of the stairway going to the rooms and made acquaintance with the clerk on duty, which happened to be the owner, George Dangerfield. I sat there all morning, reading the paper and talking to the owner. Noon came, and the members came back to the hotel to see if anything had transpired and told me a bit about the circumstances. His name was Joseph N. Calton, and he was an American, and he had a sand colored cocker spaniel dog, and had given the local veterinarian a bum cheque on a previous trip to Winnipeg and now the veterinarian had spotted the dog in the car at a store when the owner was inside. The vet called the RCMP and told them of this and they figured he might be staying at the Kirkfield Park Hotel as it was the one in the area. They told me you might as well stay at the hotel and we will pick you up later in the day. Who was I to argue, but it was a little boring.

Along about 2:30 p.m., a man came in the hotel carrying a cocker spaniel dog and had a girl on his arm. They went directly up stairs. He was dressed in a leather buckskin jacket with tassels and had a Stetson hat on. Mr. Dangerfield gave me a nod to let me know that was him. I ran out back of the hotel to check his car, and found it to be a big Buick with New York Plates on, and blue in color. That checked out with my information. I thought now I am going to have to arrest this guy and I have not been issued with a revolver, as yet. I sure did not want him to get away. On my way back in the hotel, I noticed an RCMP patrol car going by, so I flagged him down. Turned out to be the constable from Headingly Detachment and he was carrying side arms. We went in the hotel together and up to the room of Mr. Calton. He came to the door when we knocked and opened it, but when he saw the uniform; he tried to close the door. But Big Jack, put his foot in the door, and he was told that we want to take him downtown. Of course, the girl came too. That was the end of a long criminal career and as time went on, and evidence was collected from other detachments and the United States, the full extent of his exploits became known.

His right name was Joseph NIGGEL, and he was born in Butler County, Pennsylvania, U.S.A., but after getting married he moved to Atlanta, Georgia. Early in 1950, he separated from his wife for a short while, returning before the end of the year. However, in December , NIGGEL, deserted his wife and two children and set out for Miami Beach, Florida, where he remained for about four months, taking over the manager's job of a hotel.

After spending a third of a year in this winter resort state, Niggel pulled stakes for Washington, D.C., and here gained employment as a salesman at a clothiers. After three months, , however, he was bitten by the wander bug again, and this time set out for St. Louis, Missouri, once more becoming associated with the clothing business. It was while he was in St. Louis that the "complications" set in.

Niggel found it worth his while to write out worthless cheques and after about two months, earned himself approximately $1000.00 over and above his normal salary via this method.

In November 1951, he figured he had spent enough time in St. Louis, and packed up for Evansville, Indiana. Once more he entered the clothing business, this time as credit manager of a chain store, and changed his name to Jones. As Samuel J. Jones, he again took to writing out bogus cheques, and cleared another $1000.00 during his three month stint at Evansville. While there Niggel took a room at the Y.M.C.A., and had as a room-mate a man by the name of Joseph N. Calton.

Niggel left Evansville around the middle of January, 1952, and from there began jumping around so fast that he had difficulty remembering where he had been. Using his own name, and that of Jones and the name of his Evansville room-mate, Calton, he circumnavigated the U.S.A. and called in at a few locations in Mexico en route. Among the places he visited were Asbury Park, New Jersey; Rochester and Minneapolis, Minnesota; Denver, Colorado; Oakland, California and Washington, D.C. In all, he collected nearly $10,000.00 from the time he started writing these cheques in St. Louis.

In passing worthless cheques, Niggel represented himself as being a Deputy Sheriff, exhibiting both a badge and a .38 caliber revolver carried in a shoulder holster under his left arm.

Then in March 1952 Niggel decided to test the vulnerability of the Canadian people. Entering Canada at Sault Ste. Marie, Ont., he made his way straight to Montreal, Quebec, and once again used the "rubber" cheque racket to his advantage with the result that he netted himself between $600.00 and $700.00 in only three weeks. At the end of this period, he walked into a U-Drive agency and rented an 1951 Meteor convertible.

Niggel liked the vehicle and had no intention of returning it, so he decided to take it back to his native country. He first headed for New York City, but did not stay there long enough to even write out a cheque. From New York, Niggel drove to New Orleans, Louisiana, and using the name of Joseph J. Calton, wrote out cheques to the value of $400.00. After two weeks in that southern centre, Niggel decided to head for California, but en route stopped off long enough at Moorhead, Kentucky, to pull a rather smooth business deal. Selling the Meteor for $1800.00 cash, he turned right around and purchased a 1948 Buick sedan for $1600.00, thereby gaining $200.00 on the deal which actually cost him nothing. He then licensed the Buick in New York State, and while passing through Boise, Idaho, en route to California, re-registered t in that state. Meanwhile, he kept the Canadian plates off the 1951 Meteor. On Dominion Day 1952, he re-entered Canada, this time at Fort Erie, Ont. From here, Niggel went on a real cheque –passing spree which took him from coast to coast. Starting in Ontario , he worked eastward through Quebec, New Brunswick and Nova Scotia, and then decided to try the west coast, eventually reaching as far as Vancouver, B.C. Returning east again, he paused in Alberta and Saskatchewan long enough to pick up some extra cash, and then concentrated on Manitoba. After coming to Canada, he added the aliases of Joseph N. Cotton, Callan, Nelson and Samuel Jones to his string.

Niggel maintained practically the same modus operandi on each occasion. Here is an example of how he cashed his cheques:

On October 7th, 1952, he walked into a grocery store in Selkirk, Manitoba, and inquired of the woman clerk if she carried any dog food. When he received an affirmative answer, he requested ten tins. When the woman compiled, Niggel pulled out a cheque book and tore one out, already signed and made out in the sum of $30.00. The dog food came to $1.50, and Niggel tendered 25 cents in coin for the exchange when the woman handed him back some change, thus gaining $28.25 through the transaction. He told the woman he had a black cocker spaniel, and then paused to talk to some men in the store about the World Series game. Then before leaving, he purchased a 37 cents package of dog biscuits.

Niggel visited several towns in Manitoba carrying out similar procedures in each, but made the mistake of remaining in the province too long. The worthless cheques were beginning to show up regularly, and the victims were all able to supply RCMP detachments throughout the province with good descriptions of Niggel. Police radio broadcasts spread the descriptions and modus operandi around and concentrated inquiries began at various towns and cities.

Then on Nov. 27th, 1952, the RCMP received information that this man passing cheques under the name of Joseph N. Calton had registered at the Kirkfield Park Hotel in St. James, Manitoba. This is when I was dropped off at the hotel with the hopes that Calton (Niggel) had not skipped town. With Niggel arrested and taken down to Headquarters,

1091 Portage Avenue, the charge under Section 405 of the Criminal Code was laid. He was arraigned in the Provincial Police Court in Winnipeg on January 7th, 1953 on 15 counts of false pretences, for which he received from three months to two years, all sentences to run concurrent with his initial sentence of two years in the Manitoba Penitentiary at Stoney Mountain.

In all, Niggel obtained nearly $8000.00 through his worthless, cheques in Canada. Following completion of his sentence in Canada, he was deported to the U.S.; to face similar charges at points ranging from coast to coast.

From November, 1952 to January 7th, 1953, Niggel would have to appear in court numerous times to be remanded while all the information was being forwarded to the court officials. On some occasions the job of taking him to court became the duty of me and a partner. After court, we took him to the Salsbury House for coffee, before he went back to Headingly jail. He was handcuffed to one of us, I think. Anyway, he told us that he thought if and when he got caught it would be in Canada by the RCMP. He also told us about a wild chase he had in Iowa, running from the local authorities. He was checking out of a hotel and had his two suitcases at the front desk. He paid them with a bum cheque, only they wanted to check it out and phoned the local Sheriff's department. It took a few minutes, so he told them he was just going to put his luggage in the car and would be right back. They agreed and out he went; only he did not stop at that. He started the car and took off. He knew they would have road blocks up pretty quick so he took to the secondary roads heading out of State. He had a police band radio in the car so he could keep track of them... Pretty soon he was out of state and on his merry way, but it was close. Another time, he was washing his car out behind the hotel he was at, and a colored guy came out and told him that there was two men at the front counter who wanted to see him. He did not want to make any new acquaintances so he just left his luggage in the hotel and was long gone. We tended to believe him because what did he have to lose now, he was locked up. Actually, he was a real nice guy, but a person cannot help thinking about all the ordinary people that he cheated out of their hard earned money. And I knew one of those persons. Joe Cholosky, owned the Quality Store in Selkirk, and he was a real nice guy, and would give a guy a break if he needed it. This was one of Niggel's victims.

Things were pretty well hum-drum during the winter, except I went on a drug raid with the drug squad on Juno Street in Winnipeg. They went up three flights of stairs and broke the last door in, and grabbed a suspect around the neck and choked him until he brought up the drugs that he had just swallowed. My job was to stand outside the window in case he through them out the window. They knew their business.

Chapter 11

Sometime in the spring, we heard that other members were complaining that these young guys in plain clothes need to get some detachment experience. I guess they were jealous. I got moved to Selkirk and another guy got moved to Portage la Prairie. This was back on town patrol and some rural work.

On July 1st, there was limited staff on and I was told to go to the Indian Reserve at Scanterbury because of a suspected deceased woman at a home where there had been a party. I found the house and behind a bench lay a woman who did not have any vital signs. I called the office for an ambulance and proceeded to ask some questions. All I could find out is there had been a party in the house the previous night. We will call her "Irma" and she did not appear to have been stabbed or shot. The ambulance came and she was transported to Selkirk and Doctor Reid stated there would have to be an autopsy. This was done and it was suggested she could have alcohol poisoning. Her stomach was removed and put in a large cellar jar with instructions to take it to Winnipeg. Then I was told that I would have to take it to Regina to go through the laboratory for analysis. When there is something of a criminal nature being checked it has to remain in the possession of a member so he can swear to that in court. I put the jar on the Sergeant's desk and was waiting for my ticket to be prepared to go on the train to Regina. The Sergeant had some medical training and he said to me "You are not going to make it there with this;

it is going to blow up, look at it fermenting." He instructed me to go to Crescent Creamery, nearby and get some dry ice. I brought that back and had it packed tightly with the dry ice, in a cardboard box. Then I went off the catch the train to Regina. It was an overnight run and I had a berth. By this time the box was frosted up and when the porter was making up my bed he told me that I had to put that box in the express car. I said "No, I can't" The Negro porter insisted, so I had to show him my I.D. and tell him what it was. His eyes got big and he moved on. I put the box in the hammock over my berth and we arrived in Regina the next morning. As I got off the train, the same porter was at the steps to the platform. He said "Mister, when you have something like that again, tell me, and I will get off." Anyway, the jar was taken to the lab and checked and found to have an excessive amount of alcohol in the contents.

Back in Selkirk, we conducted a number of raids to see if we could catch the person making illegal spirits and selling it to the native people, and "Irma" finally got a decent burial, without her stomach.

Patrols, stolen bicycles, and a number of drunks were pretty much the order of the day for me. One Thursday afternoon, a call came in saying there was a drunken woman staggering down the main street with her dress half open. I was told to pick her up, get her off the street, put her in the cells and later on we will let her go. We kind of knew who it was. I took her to the town lockup, in the same building as the civic offices. I told her to go into the cell and lie down on the bed and have a sleep. She said in a loud voice, "I'm not going to go in there and lay on my back for no damn Mountie bastard." By this time a couple of the girls from the civic offices had come to the door to see what all the commotion was about. It took a long time to live that particular statement down. Anyway, the cell door was locked and she eventually had a sleep and the other shift gave her a ride home.

Another time, the Lisgar Hotel bartender called and said there was a belligerent drunk person that would not leave and he needed help. I went there and the big man in question was at the door trying to get back in. I needed help, and the owner of the other hotel was walking by and he asked if I needed help. I said "Yes" and the two of us put the fellow in the back seat of the police car and drove him to the cells. We still had to carry him out of the police car and up the short flight of steps to the cells. He did not seem to want to come too. I called Doctor Reid who lived nearby. He came over and pronounced him dead. This was a friend of mine's father, and I felt pretty bad about this but an autopsy proved that he had a heart attack. He also had a habit of drinking a little too much.

I often wondered when I was going to get punched out, seeing as I had been pretty handy with my fists. On this call, it was a domestic argument and sometimes they can be dangerous. I knew the particular couple and went with another member to their house. The wife had called and said her husband was drinking iodine with his beer, supposedly trying to do himself in.

The wife wanted to come with us and go to her sister's house and got in the back seat of the police car. The husband had been in the bush hiding but came out and went to try and talk his wife into staying. He was partly in the door of the car and after we could see that this was not working, he was told to go to the house and behave himself. He turned and nailed me right in the mouth and I went head over heels into the ditch. I swear I could see stars. We then arrested the husband and the wife stayed at home. I went to the Hospital and got eight stitches in my lip. So much for a knowing a guy, I guess my guard was down.

The Sergeant was a real square shooter. You did your work and you learned. He was strict but fair. The Corporal in charge drank too much and had his own circle of friends that got special treatment and was not a nice person to get along with, as far as I was concerned. We went on a liquor raid out on McPhillips Road and the Corporal stopped at the Liquor Store to buy a mickey of rye. He said he needed it. To me this is no way to conduct police business. On the way back, he drove recklessly and scared the pants off two of us in the back seat. A few years later he got killed in a traffic accident.

Selkirk is a real hockey town, and I happened to know a good player. Only once and awhile he would get drunk and this particular time he crossed the barrier of good judgment. He had a meal at the local Salsbury House and left without paying for it and creamed three vehicles with his car on the way down the street. He went home and was walking across the road when I got there. I said "Give me the keys" and he refused. We kind of hand wrestled for the keys and we heard a crack. He said "Now look what you done" but he dropped the keys and his sister came out of the house and said she would look after him. I told him he had to make a report on the cars in the morning and pay for his meal. He came to the office in the wee hours of the morning to play our usual game of crib but his finger was sore. When he saw the doctor the next day, it turned out to be broken. He had trouble wrapping that finger around his hockey stick that winter.

The golf pro at the Selkirk Golf Course decided I should learn how to golf and arranged for a set of clubs and a time to take me out and show me the finer points of the game. We teed off at the top of the hill and I gave it my best powerful swing and we all looked down the course to see where the ball was going to land. Someone noticed the ball rolling down the hill and stopping in a soft area about 15 paces away; so much for my fancy swing. We gathered our equipment to-gether and went down the hill for another try. I set the ball up on a tee with a few instructions what to do this time; correct posture, elbows and hands just so, and another powerful swing and we could not see the ball bouncing down the fairway. In fact, we could not see it at all. We noticed a little disturbance in the mud and dug around there and found it buried about six inches in the mud, actually to more solid ground. We all laughed and I said "Let's go have a beer" and we trundled on up the hill to the club house. That was the end of my golf lesson and I never tried again, but it made for a good story.

On one of my night shifts, I was told about a car in the ditch near the Old Stone Fort not far from Selkirk. I went out to have a look and the car looked familiar, and after I checked the license plate out, I knew for sure whose it was, my hockey playing friend. I figured the next shift would handle the matter as it was not impeding traffic any and may have just run out of gas. I found out later what happened. The driver was coming back from Winnipeg in the wee hours of the night, like 5:00 a.m., and fell asleep at the wheel and drove into the ditch. As the car hit the rough stuff, the driver had a bowel re-action and as he could not get out of the ditch, elected to walk home, about four miles. He stunk pretty badly and when a car came along he would run and hide in the ditch, not really wanting a ride. He finally got home and needless to say had an extensive clean up job to do.

There was a lot of water skiing done on the Red River in Selkirk, mostly promoted by Dr. Reid and family. They had a fast boat and also a ski jump near the bridge. I was asked if I wanted to try it and as I had done a little water skiing before welcomed the chance to show my skills. After a short run to get my balance the good Doctor sped by the ski jump

A learning Experience

and indicated with a wave of the arm that I should try it. The jump could be raised and lowered, depending on the proficiency of the skier. It happened to be at six feet, the highest level. I went up and never let go of the rope but at the highest point I was upside down, skis in the air and low and behold they got a picture of me, which I still have. After a couple of weeks, when I had healed, I tried it again at a lower level and mastered it, but never won any competitions.

Hunting trip to Saskatchewan

Funny circumstances, sometimes lead to a good solution. In this case a fellow from Middlechurch reported his Chevrolet Sedan Delivery stolen and it was found near the Stefanishyn farm on Highway No. 9. Mr. Stefanishyn phoned the office and said that someone had broken into his summer kitchen. I went out to investigate. I went to the Stefanishyn farm and took a list of what was missing. I then had a look at the Chevrolet Sedan parked on the road in front of the Stefanishyn farm and decided that I should drive to Middlechurch to tell the owner to come and pick up his vehicle. Mister Stefanishyn came with me. I knocked on the door and we were invited in. As soon as we went in Mr. Stefanishyn said "There's my boots". Turns out that this was the robber and he almost got caught so he found a ride home, and then reported his vehicle stolen. With further investigation it was found that this man had broken into many places in the St. Andrews area and all the charges netted him time in Stoney Mountain Penitentiary. Crime does not pay.

Good fishing trip

I had been thinking, when I started in this outfit (RCMP) I was making $108.00 per month and they paid my board and room and now I was making $270.00 per month and I paid my board and room. I was fortunate in that, I found a place to stay and it cost me $45.00 per month, and I ate my meals in café's. Mind you I got a few free meals. I asked a fellow who had been in 10 years, was married and had a little child, just how he made out. He said he paid $55.00 per month rent on a small house, drove an Austin car (small) and budgeted everything. He had to take $10.00 per month out of his bank account to live. He would not have had the bank account if he had not been up north for a number of years. Seems like we were not getting paid enough money, but who was going to be first to start a union? It was a good life, especially if you were single. I dreaded the idea of going to a small town on detachment, like two members. I don't know why, I was from a small town.

I met a nice girl who worked at the theatre in the evenings. I used to drop in to her place on my evening break for coffee. One night, just coming out I noticed a car at the stop sign with plates on 4 D 89 and I remembered this as a stolen car. It did not take me long to get the police car from around back and take off after this car. It went south on Main Street, west of Mclean and then over the tracks, west past the Mental Hospital. I had caught up to him by now and pulled in along side of him, and tried to force him off the road. We hit, not once but twice and he would not give an inch. Then it was just high speed out the graveled Cloverdale road, 85 MPH, even 90 MPH, dust and snow, coming up, I could hardly see. At the intersection, near the Cloverdale Church, I found out there was another car ahead of him that did not want to be passed, and pulled over at this point because the driver lived nearby. The stolen car driver decided he wanted to turn left at this intersection and stood on the brakes. I could not stop and hit him in the back end. He went down the road and into the left ditch, and the driver's door came open and the interior light came on. He was lying over the steering wheel. I got out of the police car with difficulty, the transmission was up inside and the doors were jammed. He came around and we ended up on the road and three fellows were walking down the road to see what happened. I thought they were with him and I guess he thought they were coming to help me, actually they were the fellows from the lead car and they lived nearby. My stolen car driver broke free and started running west down the road. My knees were sore and I could not catch him. He went over the fence and ran away into the bush. I never had my .45 pistol on me. You usually do not wear a gun to go visit a girl. I might have fired a warning shot or worse. I then went to the closest farm house, as I knew the owner. I asked for a gun, and then thought better of it.

I phoned into the detachment, and they got a crew out to help look for him, including a dog. One of the policemen who came out was someone I knew pretty good, and I said lets go to this fellows house, I think I know who it is. We drove over the Lockport Bridge and went north on Henderson Highway to his folks place. We were sitting in the yard with the lights out and we saw him coming up from the river. This time he decided not to run, as he had already run about seven miles. He ended up in hospital, then jail, and then court and then a longer time in jail.

A couple of days later the Sergeant took me around to see the police car in Doug Gordon's garage and he just shook his head. This used to be his car that he drove around on duty and I guess he was sorry to see it in that kind of shape, and besides that he had to make reports up so he could get another one.

A number of years later, I was getting a plane ready to fly up to Grand Rapids for the Hydro, and this fellow came up to me and asked if

I recognized him. I said "No" and he related where we had met before, in a chase on the Cloverdale Road. He was the driver of the stolen car. It was nice to see that he had straightened out and had a good job and we had no animosity between us.

Chapter 12

This was too much fun, in a way, but I was thinking about getting a job that paid more money, and this is why I believe that I was born 20 years too soon. I happened to be talking to the Commissioner of the R.C.M. Police later in life, (he was from Broadview, Sask. next to my hometown) and I asked him when they brought up the pay so a person could live half decently. He said "in 1963 Diefenbaker doubled our salary and two years later they gave us another good raise." That sounded good to me, but sort of reminded me what Ted Lindsay and Gordie Howe where going through with low pay in the hockey world, not that we were in their league.

Another thing, I was in the Detective's office of the Winnipeg City Police, with a more senior RCMP officer than me, and we were talking to a 28 year veteran of the city police. He said "you know I am thinking of retiring, I have spent all this time dealing with the scum of the land, and I am just about feeling like they are the only ones I know, I want a change". Along with the fact that I have seen a couple of NCO's in the force that were complete drunks. I could see were this came from, because this one member worked on the liquor squad and probably had too much time on his hands and not the will to stay away from drinking. If you are inclined, it will happen.

And one more thing, when you join up you are just happy to get in the force, no one explains the benefits to you, especially the pension fund. When I joined, the pension fund was Part 4, and being changed to Part 5. What did that mean? To take one example, Mrs. M.I. Burke-Johnson's husband, a retired member of the RCMP with 24 years' service, died on April 11th, 1967. Almost immediately, she received a telegram ordering her to return $159.00 of the money the family had received for that month because his pension had died with him. The telegram further advised that because he had died before 7:00 a.m. on the 11th, she was not entitled to his pension for that day. She was determined not to go on welfare, even though she and the kids had to eat popcorn and puffed wheat towards the end of the month. Part 4 pension funds, the constables and NCO's put in their own money, not the governments, not the RCMP's, and did not even get interest on this money. The officers had a different pension fund. No wonder they did not want to talk about it when I joined. Sgt. Harold Clark worked on this injustice for years and even wrote a book about it. Members of the force seem to be doing well now, and maybe those officers who controlled the pension fund do have something to answer for. I suppose I was looking around for something else to do, and generally had my options open, and one opportunity came up with Imperial Oil Ltd. This was to be a sales job and with responsibilities to check on oil agents for the company that were mainly in small towns in Manitoba. They needed six people and where starting to advertize the job. I requested a discharge from the RCMP to take effect immediately but they were not interested and said I would have to wait six months, which was in the contract. I left my request in and waited the six months. At that time, I took an Honorary Discharge and still started with Imperial Oil, only six months later. The positions in question were filled but another way was found to get there, only it would take time. I started out at the warehouse on Knox Street cleaning 45 gallon drums and painting them. This was dirty job and I wore cover-alls, but it was a beginning, and I made slightly more a month, than I was making in the RCMP. Then I went to the main office at 100 Main Street to work in the transportation office where I learned about the delivery of gasoline in tank cars to various locations in Manitoba, including the Winnipeg International Airport. I worked at this job until spring, and then they transferred me out to the Airport to learn about re-fueling airplanes. There were quite a few men on the job and we worked 24/7 on different shifts. It was interesting, meeting the pilots of itinerant aircraft, coming in from many locations. They seemed to like their jobs and got a pretty fair salary. I guess this perked my interest. I had gone for a ride in a small aircraft a number of years ago and I do not think I was impressed, maybe the pilot tried too many tricks. There seemed to be a lot of jobs around flying because the Mid-Canada and DEW line where both being built in Northern Canada. Next thing I knew I had signed up at the Winnipeg Flying Club to obtain my private pilot's license. The flying club was just at the end of the street I was working on and it was convenient to get a little time in each day the weather was good. There was a good bunch of instructors, including Hoffman, Allen, Wherle, McDougal and others. Some fellows where taking their commercial license and had hopes of getting a job immediately after they finished. Two fellows bought a small Taylorcraft after they had their private license, loaded it up with gas and sandwiches, and took off for Florida for the winter. When they came back in the spring, they had about 200 hours each in flying time. It was not cheap, but I kept on plugging away and we all seemed to be in the same boat. I can remember doing spins in an old Aeronca aircraft, CF-GAM. It seemed to creak and groan going down, and I am sure I left my fingerprints in the cross bars on that aircraft. We did tight turns, lots of landings and take-offs, spins, stalls, and simulated forced landings. There were books to study and night ground school classes to attend. I guess this all took about a year and then exam time came to write for our private license. I passed and then I was on my own to rent an aircraft to do some local flying. There was also a bit of social life around the flying club, as they had a bar and a lot of armchair pilots seemed to be occupying them. Of course, we had to hear the stories of the really experienced pilots, who came in from up north, and had graduated from a school a few years previously. All of this kept our interest up, and we kept on putting in flying time as money would allow. I continued to work for Imperial Oil at the airport, and visit with a girl from Selkirk.

I was getting to the point where I might just as well finish this commercial license off and get a job in the flying business. I still had some instrument and night flying to complete, and then there was the exams that I would have to do at the Ministry of Transport office. From the information we received from other pilots, the jobs on the Dew line and Mid Canada line, where coming to an end because the job was almost done. Spring was the best time to start looking and I should be done in time and then I could quit my boring job at Imperial Oil.

I finished everything, got my license and then took a trip west to the hub of bush flying in Saskatchewan, Lac la Ronge. I first visited with Floyd Glass of Athabasca Airways and saw a Cessna 180 come in from the north on wheels with a tail ski on the back and landing on the grass. Oh well, we never did that at the flying club but I would be learning lots. He did not make any promises and said I could hang around if I wanted to. I decided to go to The Pas, Manitoba and check out Lamb Airways. I got a job sweeping the hangar floor and helping around. I did a trip with Tom Lamb out to Moose Lake at about 20 feet, and also a trip to Thompson with Doug Lamb in the Norseman. They seemed to think that things were going to be a lot quieter, not as much work, and that is not what I wanted to hear. On making a phone home to southern Manitoba, I heard that a fellow with a Cessna 170 on floats wanted a pilot. He was a commercial fisherman and worked up at God's Lake, and the surrounding area. His previous pilot got a different job and I should come down and get checked out on floats. I left after a week and got this job but it would take awhile for the ice to clear out of the lakes. I guess that I was really anxious. I got my float endorsement and did some local flying from Connie Johanesson's Seaplane Base.

Frank - Lifting his sturgeon net off the Pontoon of the aircraft

Cessna 170 and a new campsite

Chapter 13

The owner of the plane, Frank Lindal, was a fairly short man, of Icelandic descent, who along with some of his brothers, spent many years in the north. He was an experienced commercial fisherman in winter and summer fishing. He had licenses for sturgeon fishing on the God's River, Stull and Hayes River, all north of God's Lake. In the winter time he fished east of Elk Island, at the Manshead. He did not fly himself, but needed an aircraft to get around to his fishing sites and haul the fish he caught to the railhead, or south to Selkirk. He was fluent in the Cree language and always had a number of Cree workers around. His actual home, with a wife and one boy was in Winnipeg, but he had cabins at God's Lake Narrows, Manitoba. We got to know each other and then I was told when we would be leaving and for where. Little did I know that my accommodation would be a tent and cooking would be over an open fire for the summer, rain or shine? Some people will do anything to get flying. I got some maps of the area and some emergency supplies, including a sleeping bag. God's lake is in the north east part of the province, about 400 miles north of Winnipeg.

The first day out, after we loaded the plane with what we could carry, was a flight from St. Andrews to Berens River, and our lodging was a "Ma Kemps Inn". Some log cabins at the settlement of Berens River and Frank seemed to know quite a few people, from fishing there previously. In the morning he wanted to know if I wanted to go straight to God's Lake from Berens River, or go around via Norway House. Norway House way seemed to appeal to me more, as there were more lakes, and I kind of wanted to see the settlement, of which I had heard a lot about. We arrived in God's Lake late in the afternoon, and Frank made preparations for a couple of native workers to start out by canoe for a camping spot they both knew, about 52 air miles down the God's River. We would fly on ahead of them and wait for them to come. Now we were really getting into unfamiliar country, and a place where no mistakes were to be made because no one was around to help you, for miles. This of course meant, watch your gas and oil, as there were no service stations, nor bulk dealers in the area. We landed on a good straight stretch of water and pulled into a shore area that Frank indicated and pitched our tent. Then we lit a fire and cooked something to eat. This was to be my first night out camping for a long time, and this was in a pretty remote area. We went to bed and listened to the sounds of the night, beavers slapping their tails on the water, fish jumping and the odd wolf calling his mate. In the morning everything was a little damp from the dew, but no rain, at least the first night.

In the morning, after breakfast, we assembled a fiberglass boat that was in eight pieces and it had a canvas bottom. It was about 12 feet long, a regular car topper, and seemed to float alright. Frank rowed out a set a sturgeon net. We were anxiously waiting for the two helpers to turn up in the canoe, mind you, 52 air miles would be about 75 miles by river, and they also had to cross God's lake, from God's Narrow's to the River, which would be about 20 miles. It could also get to windy on the big lake to travel by canoe. They did have a motor, a 5 H.P. Johnson, but then again they could have had engine trouble. It became overcast, and soon started to rain. With nothing to do we went to bed.

Sometime during the night, Frank heard a noise outside, and got up to see that the canoe had arrived, and they talked in Cree, which of course I could not understand. They were going to sleep outside, rolled up in a tarp, but Frank brought them into the tent and said "We might be a little crowded to-night". Spent a miserable day as it continued to rain, but cleared up late in the day. I figured, seeing as we were so crowded in the tent, that I might as well take the seats out of the Cessna 170 and make a bed inside. This worked pretty well, so I continued to do that for the summer, also it was pretty mosquito proof. I got used to the gentle lapping of the waves on the pontoons, but not the beaver who came to inspect.

Charlie and a Sturgeon

Charlie Chubb was the Indian's name and his partner was Benjamin Spence and the fish is a sturgeon. They were seasoned trappers and fishermen, and talked a little English. They all got busy and started to set more nets for sturgeon. Frank sent me to Ilford, a settlement on the Hudson Bay Railroad, to get supplies. It was about 110 miles and this time I would be on my own. I got my maps out and drew a straight line on them, marking it off in 8 mile segments, an 8 mile to the inch map. Frank said "Don't cross the railroad and to circle town and someone would come and pick me up at the lake". It sounded pretty straight forward to me. After I got in the air, I saw 'Brassy Hill', which was about 300 feet high, and a good land mark. It was just off to my left going to Ilford. Good job the weather was clear. Found the railroad, found Ilford, although it was pretty small, circled, and landed in Moose Nose Lake and pulled up to an open dock. Pretty soon, an older fellow, on a Ford Ferguson tractor pulling a trailer came to the dock area. He said his name was John Hatley and wanted to know if I was going into town. I said "Yes" and paid him the $5.00 taxi fare into town, and also gave him the $5.00 to bring me back with my gas and groceries. It was about a mile in and we stopped at Oliver Lindal's store, Frank's brother. After introductions with Oliver, I got on with shopping. I also found there was a hotel in town, the 'Gold Trail Hotel' and a railroad station, and a few houses, and an Imperial Oil agency where I got my gas. All this took about 3 hours and the taxi turned up and took everything to the lake. I borrowed a gas pump and filled the aircraft up and loaded my groceries. The 170 was no Super Cub on floats; just make sure you had lots of room ahead and right into wind. A good aeroplane to learn to fly on floats because from then on, you learned to have lots of room to take off in, something like a Husky, as I learned later. The flight back was, although there was lots of apprehension, uneventful, especially when 'Brassy Hill' showed up on the horizon. At the camp, everyone was pleased I made it, and we had something different than fish for supper. The usual food fare was a pot of sturgeon with potatoes and onions, put on and taken off the fire, until it was gone, and lots of tea.

The next day another aeroplane turned up on floats, a Blue Fleet Canuck, owned by Garth Monkman. He was also a commercial fisherman and was going to go to the Stull River to fish. We would meet him there on occasion, about 30 miles to the east. As the fishermen caught the sturgeon, they would tie them up to stakes along the shoreline with sideline through their mouths. This was to keep them fresh for a few days, and when they had enough in pounds for a plane load they would dress them, and send me out with a load to Ilford. After we caught quite a few at one location, we would pack up and move to another river. This would be on the Hayes River, below Brassy Hill.

From Mountie to Bush Pilot

George Solberg, caretaker, Gods Lake Mine

Dave – Hudson Bay Clerk

Part Wolf/Husky at campsite

Frank – Prospecting

Frank's 12' boat made of eight sections of fibre glass and a canvas cover - easily transported in the CESSNA-170

One day a moose turned up in camp on the Hayes River, and Benjamin shot him with a .22 rifle. Mind you he was close, but it was a big animal for a .22 rifle. After dressing it, and I helped him, we had meat for a few days and then he smoked the rest of it. Benjamin took the moose nose off the head, put it in a pot and boiled it. That I did not try, but he thought that it was good. One day, I saw Benjamin and Frank in the 12 foot boat bring in a big sturgeon, and it weighed 125 lbs. Also, it had a lot of ripe caviar which they had provisions to look after as it could be sold for a high price. Only thing is, they almost flipped the boat out in the middle of the river. With this fish and the others, it was time to make another trip to Ilford. I had been going in and out quite a few times by now, but the railway agent, had an interest in the local air service, and came down to the dock on this occasion to chase me off. It turned out the community owned the dock and he was just sounding off. After awhile, I sort of bumped him, and he fell in the water. The old guy that hung around the dock said "Good for you, he had that coming". No more trouble after that. I took off for camp and we had a few fresh vegetables for supper along with some milk that Frank seemed to like. Little did I know that he had a stomach problem?

There was a sport fishermen cabin nearby owned by Elk Island Lodge where they flew clients in to fish for speckled trout. The guides would travel to the camp by a big square stern canoe and would arrive a day or two early, just so they would be sure to be there. In the evenings they played cards, actually poker, and I got in on one of those games one evening. The stakes were not too high; actually we used wooden matches, which translated into money at the end of the evening. We had a problem though, in that they did not speak English, only Cree and I could not tell if they were discussing their cards to gang up on me or not. So we made a rule that you could not talk once the cards hit the table, only to say 'raise' or 'I'm out". This seemed to work okay as I left with a few dollars, but then maybe they were just getting me ready for another night, which did not come as we moved to the Hayes River.

I learned a little about the Hayes River from Frank and the Indians who were working for him. The river was the original route that the settlers took from York Factory to the Red River settlement and now I was camping on the shores just as they had done. Benjamin Spence told me about some poles that were along the shore at Berwick Falls, and that is where the men working on the York Boats pulled the boats up and around the rapids at Berwick Falls. We were camped just a little way upstream from Berwick Falls, and I spent a little time looking around for lost items. One time at York Factory I found a cannon ball along the shore, all rusted and dirty, which I left there. I also went looking up a little stream that came out of the hill, Brassy Hill, and the water was so clear and the stone and gravel just looked like a place where you would find gold nuggets. I imagine the early travelers on the river would do the very same thing. Someday I am going to travel this river by canoe or whatever and spend more time looking around and learning about what took place here in the 1800's, but now it is time to build up some hours flying.

After a couple of more trips to Ilford for supplies it was time to move to the Stull River to see if we could catch a few sturgeons there. Garf Monkman was trying his nets out on the Stull and one day he landed his plane in a strong cross wind and it tipped on its side and damaged the wing on the water. The wing was bent up slightly and Garf, being a very capable person, fixed it by pulling the ribs straight and patched the hole with his undershirt and amberoid (glue).

I saw this story about Garf Monkman in Northroots Magazine and asked the writer, Clarence Thordarson, from Norway House, if I could use it and he agreed. "A True Story of the North.."

Island Lake Rescue

Story by Clarence Thordarson

In the 1960's Island Lake, located in northeastern Manitoba, was a remote community. There were no roads in to Island Lake. There were no flat areas where an airplane could land, no runways, no airports. Normally the local rivers and lakes provided natural runways for the airplanes which were the community's only link with civilization. In the summer the airplanes landed on the water on pontoons; in the winter on the ice on skis. Between seasons when the forming or melting ice was not strong enough to support a landing, no airplane would fly in the North.

It was the mid-1960's. It was between seasons now --- late October. The house had burned to the ground overnight. Everyone was out, but the little girl was severely burned. Unless they got medical treatment soon, she would not survive. She would face a slow and painful death on the remote reservation in the northern Manitoba.

The call came in from Island Lake to the Norway House hospital pleading for rescue: "Could you please get someone fly a mercy flight in to pick up the girl."

There was no airplane at Norway House. Calls were made to the northern air operators - Lamb Airways, Ilford Air, Cross Lake Air Service.

All were contacted. They all had nothing ready to fly. The float planes had been all pulled out of the water and skis had not yet been put on.

The southern operators were contacted - Selkirk Air, Riverton Air, Northway Air. They all asked the same question, "What are landing conditions like?" The reply was, "Island Lake has completely frozen over with a thin ice cover. Norway House is mostly ice covered but there are a few areas with open water." Their answers were all the same, "No, our planes are still on floats, but as there is no open water - we can't go. It's too dangerous." It looked like there was no chance of a rescue.

Max Paupanekis said he had a friend who was a bush pilot and had been flying this areas for years. He would give him a call and at least get his advice on what to do.

Max phoned Garf Monkman, Garf, his wife Gladys and six children were living in Grand Rapids at the northwest side of Lake Winnipeg, Garf said there was still open water where he lived, on the banks of the North Saskatchewan River, and he said he would at least go and have a look at things. So he flew out to Island Lake to have a look. As he set his compass east, he was thankful that the weather was fine.

On arrival over Island Lake, Garf circled the lake looking for open water. The report that was given was correct, it was all ice covered. No open water.

After circling Island Lake, Garf made a major decision to land his float plane on the ice. He knew the risks. If the thin ice broke, it would rip into the floats and the plane would be lost. He may even lose his own life. But he had to try and save the little girl.

He circled and flew low over the lake. He landed his airplane on floats on the ice. The floats slid smoothly alone the ice and did not break it.

The landing went well. the little girl was loaded onto the plane and with a push to get going - the take-off from the ice was a success.

As Garf flew over the hospital at Norway House, he could see Playgreen Lake was ice-covered, but there was some open water as well. Directly in front of the Norway House Hospital was a short stretch of open water - too short to land in by itself. He assessed that the only way would be able to land would be to once again take the risk of landing on the ice with his pontoons and then sliding in to the open water. Once again he did this and safely delivered the little girl to the Norway House Hospital.

I Fought The Law

And now for the rest of the story. At least as it was told to me.

The airports were now built all over northern Manitoba. The float operators were starting to feel the pinch as more and more business went to aircraft flying on wheels. At Norway House there was Lamb Air, "Fly-a-long", Selkirk Air, Northland Air - all on floats. No one was flying too much except for Garf Monkman. He was flying a lot. This did not sit too well with the other operators. Garf was building a fly-in fishing camp east of Norway House at Washihagan Lake. So he was coming and going for supplies, picking up his workers, etc., etc.

The other operators complained to the RCMP that Garf was flying commercially and did not have a business license to do so. So the RCMP set up a "sting operation". They had an undercover RCMP offer Garf money to fly out to the lake and then pick him up again later. As Garf was going that way anyway, he said, "Sure, jump in."

Consequently Garf was charged with providing an air service without the proper license. He would have to go to court. The fine could be up to five years in jail and a $5,000 fine. The court was held at Norway House.

The judge was His Honour Max Paupanekis, doing his first court case after being appointed judge. All the important judges from the provincial court were there to watch Max perform for his first day in court.

His first case was his best friend, Garf Monkman. Garf said, "Guilty".

The charges were read and the crown recommended a harsh penalty or a stiff fine for such a serious crime. Max then told the story of Garf saving that little girl when no one else would even try. He said no one even said "thank you" to Garf, let alone pay him for that trip. Max said, "So today Garf, I will say thank you and pay you for that trip and although a stiffer fine would be expected, I'll only fine you $50."

All the important visiting provincial judges were impressed.

Garf Monkman (centre) on a visit to the North with his boat

It was getting into September and the geese were starting to fly south coming out of Hudson Bay. What a noise they made at night when a person was trying to sleep. There must have been 10, 000 in our area. The nights were getting colder and the metal floor of the aircraft was not as comfortable for sleeping, an air mattress just conducts more cold air. Maybe I need to move back into the tent --- no way.

One day Frank sent the Indians home and that seemed to signal the end of sturgeon fishing. Now we would be doing a little prospecting to different lakes that Frank had in mind. We would fly around a little and then land, and Frank and maybe a helper would walk in the bush for a couple of hours and break a few samples up and put them in a bag. Elk Island, on God's Lake was an old gold mine, so the logic was that there must be more gold in the area. There were other prospectors in the area and one was Pete Burton, who was also involved in the sport fishing business with Barney Lamm. They liked to pull tricks on each other and one they pulled on Frank was planting a bunch of magnetite rocks out on an island and kind of talking about it in hushed tones until they got some interest and sure enough Frank fell for it. Out he went by boat to a certain area on God's Lake and brought a bag of the rocks back in. Sure, they were pure iron ore; a small piece would spin the compass on the airplane. What he did not know was Pete had some American fishermen bring a bag of iron ore from the iron mines in Eveleth, Minnesota, along the south shore of Lake Superior. They had their laughs and Frank did not find out about the trick until the following summer, as a matter of fact neither did I.

Pete Burton came to the God's Lake area in the early 1930"s and worked in the gold mine for awhile and also trapped and eventually got involved with the tourist business. He married a local native lady, Aggie, and raised four boys. One became a pilot, Jack, and was flying a Cessna

185 commercially and on one trip never got back to base. It is reasoned that he went into the water on Island Lake and has never been found. Gilbert married and lived in God's Narrows, doing various things to make a living and finally got a tourist hunting business going, especially on Red Cross Lake, near the Stull River, where the geese came in on their way south. When the mine at Elk Island closed, Pete got some local help, and fixed up the foundations on a number of log cabins that the mine had and made a deal with Barney Lamm to take them over and promote the sport fishing business. Barney Lamm owned Ball Lake Lodge in the Kenora Area and was involved with flying. Pete lived until his 90"s and had a good knowledge of the area and guided many notable people, including General Mark Clark, and Clark Gable. Pete came from Cape North on Cape Breton Island, so he really came from "away".

Another local character in the area was George Solberg who was the caretaker of the mine site at Elk Island. He had spent his days prospecting and even had a friend of mine out on the rivers east of Gods Lake for a summer. "Pot" would get to know him pretty well during the summer of '48. I think that they were outfitted by a geologist "Mark Smerchanski" and were mainly interested in gold properties, such as Favorable Lake and Elk Island, God's Lake, two mines that had flourished for a number of years in the '30s. I knew him as he just lived near the dock on Elk Island and I would see him working in his garden. He grew some great potatoes in a patch amongst the rock, as a matter of fact; Gilbert Burton told me he had one potato that was seven pounds. Oh well, even the fish have been known to grow in size in God's lake area. I am told that he used fish guts from the fish shed for fertilizer that could be the reason. George liked to drink whiskey and would order six bottles of 'Imperial' every two weeks and have them delivered by mail plane. When he drank he would make a big pot of 'bully beef stew', a mixture of square cubes of "Kilk or Spork" and boiled potatoes and vegetables. This would stay on the stove during his week of drinking, as he said you have to eat once and awhile. Then he would open one bottle and hide the rest, and when he was drunk he would have trouble finding where he hid the next bottle. He never offered a drink to anyone, it was for him. Anyone that came around, well they might be "bums". The following week he would work in the garden and do other chores. He was wrote up in a book called "North of the 54th" and the story goes that he and a geologist paddled in a canoe on "Herb Lake" to see who was at a campfire they had seen and to socialize. They stayed into the late evening and on the way back the wind came up and tipped the canoe. George was a powerful man and a good swimmer, he had huge hands. The geologist went down a couple of times and George grabbed him and put him on top of the canoe, then he tied the lead line around his shoulders and started pulling the canoe and man to shore. He would look around periodically to see if his friend was still there. He had about a mile and a half to go. One time he looked and his partner had disappeared. He swam around but could not find him. So he unhooked the canoe and continued to shore. Eventually the canoe drifted into shore, and George made it to his arranged meeting place. I lost track of George over the years and I was told he went south and died in Winnipeg after a number of years of drinking in the local establishment.

The Cessna seemed to be a little sluggish, not taking off as quick as before. I took off the cowling at the dock near George's place and was looking around for something that might be the cause. Another plane landed and taxied in to the dock, and the pilot was an aero-mechanic as well. I told him what I was looking for. He said "try that big nut on the carburetor, there is a screen attached to it, and it might be plugged." I got a ¾ inch socket and opened it up. Sure enough it was full of fuzz, from the gas chamois. I blew it out and put it back to-gether. Over the summer as I used the chamois, it actually is a felt, little pieces of fuzz came off and went into the gas. I was told to singe it when you start a new chamois and this would stop the fuzz from coming off. Sure enough when I put the cowling on and cranked her up I had new power.

It was getting towards the end of the season, but Frank had one more little visit to make and that was to the East End Camp, owned by three fellows from the United States. The camp was a previous Hudson Bay camp and these fellows took it over, CBS, Coulson, Busch and Stefanick, and they were planning big things for their camp. Other planes started landing to; "Pete" came in and then a Cessna 195 on floats, with "Castleman" and then a Stinson Reliant with "Aime Mann" – it appeared as though this was a fall party, end of the season bash. Of course some whiskey was brought out and it did not take long for everyone to get jovial, lots of talking. Pete took a stroll down the dock, it was a long one, because of the shallow water, and met 'Aime' by the Stinson. It was covered with oil and Pete spotted a loose nut on some part of the Stinson, actually Pete owned the Stinson. Aime was an air engineer as well as a pilot. Pete said "Aime, why don't you tighten that nut and clean up the plane". Aime replied " Well Master, when I fly this plane I fly it as though I don't own a nut or a bolt in her" Aime was a bit of a character as I was to find out. He wore a suit jacket but he still wiped his oily hands on it to clean them. I heard a story about Aime' later, and it is worth repeating. Aime was flying in Ontario, taking Moccamans (American Sport Fishermen) out to the various camps in the area. (Moccamans) is the term the guides have for the Americans, and it is a throw back from the days of Custer,(it means long Knife and refers the swords he and his men carried.) Anyway, there were six of them loaded in a Norseman at the dock, waiting for the pilot to turn up. Down the dock came this guy leading a supposed blind man, dark glasses and white cane, in his soiled business man's suit jacket.

He was tapping the side of the dock as he walked, then as he got to the Norseman, he stumbled and just about fell in. The fishermen were looking worried and started to talk about this fellow who by this time had got in the pilot's seat. Aime continued with the act of fumbling with the controls and actually got it started. By this time some of the fishermen were ready to get out and then Aime took the glasses off and poured the coal to the Norseman and got airborne. I think that some of the fishermen were in on the act, just to get the junior ones worked up.

That same day, a little later, Ivan Castleman, came down on the dock, drinks in hand and wanted to know if I wanted to get checked out in the Cessna 195. I declined and he had some unpleasant things to say about green pilots. However, a few years later, Ivan took off from Pascal Lake, in the Little Grand area, in a Seabee and was headed east, possibly McGuiness Lake, and was never found. So much for my visit at the East End Camp and the owners, although I did meet them in Chicago during the sport show season.

It looks like this visit ended our summer and fall flying, so we went south to Rivercrest and had the Cessna pulled out of the water and serviced. It seemed like a good idea to stick around and get some ski flying in and Frank said he would need me in the winter.

Chapter 14

The girl that I mentioned before and I were getting serious and she stuck with me through the change of jobs on two occasions and this seemed to have what I wanted. An interesting and possibly a rewarding job, and not a ho-hum type of existence like at Imperial Oil. We decided to get married in November and find a place to live in Selkirk. A suite in a house was rented near the river and within walking distance of where I was going to park the aircraft on skis after the river froze. I made arrangements with Booth Fisheries to be able to plug in to keep the engine warm and gassing up off the dock seemed to be no problem. I got a few poplar poles to have for running the skis up on so they would not freeze into the ice, and the fisheries were happy to help because they would be getting the fish that I brought in. Now we just needed some cold weather to freeze the lakes over up north. Frank would be fishing at the Manshead, a group of islands just east of Elk Island on God's Lake. I wondered about this as it was 370 miles north-east of Selkirk, quite a run, but I was to haul supplies in, groceries and trade goods, and fresh fish south. I did not make any return trips in a day until the days started to get longer. The weather was also a problem with very little in communications to find out what I was going to have to contend with. Manitoba Telephone System had radio communications with most of the settlements up north and as long as the signals where okay a person was able to get the present condition from a local person who more or less took a guess on what it was going to be like in four or five hours. Be prepared to spend the night, anyplace, and maybe in the bush. Airways weather people gave a prognosis of what you may be expected to encounter but that did not always turn out in your favor, and who was to know when you were coming back.

A lot of unanswered questions in this bush flying, as I was to find out, but people enroute were marvelous, just treat them with the respect they deserve, and bring the odd gift from town, be it fresh fruit or milk, or whatever. I am still in touch with some of them after all these years. One of my best friends was Brother Leon Cartier, who was a working man with the Roman Catholic Church, in the settlement of Berens River, Manitoba. He did what was required to keep the Berens River Hospital and Mission functioning properly, which included keeping the roads open and graded a large field to cut hay from and store it in the barn for the cattle they kept, so they could have milk and also make butter and cheese for their consumption. The hospital served the local community and was run by up to sixteen Grey Nuns, some of them nurses, some teachers, others cooks and administration staff. A Priest and a couple of retired Priests or Brothers looked after the spiritual needs of the community, which included weddings and funerals. More will be told of these good people as time goes on.

My good Friend, Brother Leon Cartier, of the Oblate Mission meeting aircraft with his bombardier.

Other air craft visiting Berens River

The trips I would be making with the Cessna 170 took me east of Berens River but it was more convenient to put a gas cache in Berens River, than try and get it into God's Lake and I choose to leave the gas at the R.C.Mission. I also had another place to leave gas and that was at Pine Dock, which was accessible by road from Selkirk, Man. I used to leave my gas at Bill Selkirk's place and it was always there for me. All I had to do was roll my 45 gallon drum down the hill to the lake and pump the gas into the wing tanks, or use a 5 gallon bucket, with a funnel and chamois. I always strained my gas; you cannot be too carefully with it. This made my 370 mile trips a little easier, taking into consideration for bad weather, and the need to have to stay over someplace because of darkness. For the most part I bought the groceries locally that where needed at the fish camp and some of my grocery lists and other requirements had some strange things on them. Seaming Twine, Conibear Traps, coal oil, lamp wick, and of course, flour, sugar, lard, (they did not use butter on their bread, but I could not get used to it) and some of the things I was told not to bring was liquor, beer, or beans, raisins and yeast, because the local people would make their own moose milk and the fishing production would slow down. Booth fisheries were pretty happy to see another source of fish coming in and I do not think they got very much trout, but they really liked to see the pickerel as it was a good price. I would bring about 650 or 700 lbs all wrapped up in a good tarp, in other words, loose fish, but I had to keep the heat in the aircraft on low or else it would cook some of the fish and spoil it. Anyway, I was dressed for the cold and I did not mind too much.

Chapter 15

As the trips started to mount up, I was beginning to like it more and more, maybe, just maybe, I found what I wanted to do. As time went on I learned from people in the area. Old Bill Selkirk told me about Garry Quirk, a pilot from Winnipeg, flying a Super Cub aircraft in wintertime and taking a local person home to Princess Harbour. That is around the narrows on Lake Winnipeg, and he flew from point to point, about seven miles, in a white out condition, in other words, he could not see the other side. They crashed on Lake Winnipeg and both were killed. The point is – Do not leave the shoreline, know where you are on your map, and if it gets too tough, turn around and come back to try later. The trips kept on piling up with fish coming in and groceries going out. Frank, my boss, came in with me on one trip and on the way back we stopped at Charron Lake to visit the Boulanger family. Charron Lake is just where the border of Manitoba and Ontario turns to go north-east, right on the corner of the Keystone province. There were several members of the family there, men, women and kids, and dogs. The primary reason for this visit was to buy furs when the trappers were ready to sell them as Frank had a fur buyer's license. The members of the family, with the heads of the families being Old Tom and Ian, then there was Wilson and his wife Florence. Then there was young

Garry Quirk's crash site
Photo credit / Al Nelson

Tom, who had a bad hand, and Harrison, and Istay, and Tom Charlie and their respective wives and children. In all there where quite a few cabins and of course, they were fishing and hunting to feed themselves and their dogs. This was the time before snow machines and the dogs where used to haul a toboggan and their supplies. They really did have some nice fish, medium sized trout, pickerel and whitefish, so Frank decided toward spring he would buy some of their fish and transport it to market. After a preliminary visit and drinking lots of tea, we were on our way north to God's Lake. We would be returning. I found out later that the Boulanger family lived in Berens River and fished on Lake Winnipeg during the season but Charron Lake was their trapping area and they either flew out or came out by dogs. We would have a close association over the following years.

On to God's Lake to see how the men were doing fishing and bring back another load to Selkirk. Believe me, there were days that the weather was challenging and one of them occurred on the next trip.

I suppose I was getting a little confident because things seemed to be going all right but today with a load of groceries, I headed north with a tail wind at about 4000 ft. I ran into trouble. North east of Berens River about 40 miles the cloud cover started to build up below me, fluffy clouds at first, and then more and more build up. Pretty soon I was on top of

Boulanger Trapping Camp on Charron Lake

solid overcast and it looked as though there was clearing ahead, but as seasoned pilots know this is just wishful thinking, and as I could not get a radio signal from God's Narrows I started to get worried. Finally someone came on the radio and said that "God's Narrows is about 500 ft. and a half mile in snow". I had flown for an hour with the tail wind but I knew I would have to turn around and try later. First I had to get down and see where I was at. I turned around and got the sun coming in the passenger's window and the compass reading south west, for a heading back to Berens River. Then I let down through about 1500 feet of cloud. All of this is like 'duck soup' if you have the proper instruments but with a needle and ball and compass!! I came out over Weaver Lake, which was good, pretty well on course, and a sigh of relief from me. I had gas in Berens River and with a better radio (HF) I could give them a call and let them know I was holding and would try again in the morning. It took awhile before I went back up on top.

On one of my early trips to God's Lake, Frank, my boss, was on board and we stopped overnight at Elk Island, at the sport fishing camp of Barney Lamns. I guess he knew there would be a few old buddies around and had brought a few bottles of whiskey. There was one log cabin with the heat on and the Hudson Bay Clerk (Dave) was staying in it. The "Bay" had a satellite store at Elk Island from their main store at God's Narrows, mainly for the trappers and fishermen. Well, as the winter brings darkness pretty early, and then the drinking began pretty early and by 8:00 p.m. the music started, and Dave then played a few jigging tunes and got the men moving their feet around. There were only four guys there, and one was Tom Ruminski who owned a lodge at God"s river. Tom was about 6 ft. 3 and Frank, my boss, was 5 ft. 6, and as time wore on and the whiskey was consumed, they started to dance. They called that "Bull Dancing". I was lying on the top bunk, space was limited, and this sure did look funny to someone who was not drinking, but I figured this was life in the north. I went outside to use the toilet, and found that it was very clear and cold, -40 below on the thermometer. The only sounds were coming from our cabin and there was only one other light on with a single occupant. The booze was running out and they all fell asleep with their clothes on, pretty well were they were sitting. It took awhile to get going in the morning but I used an "Iosol" heater to keep the engine warm after it was tarped up and it pretty well started right away, unless it was very windy.

Another character that I met was in Selkirk. I came in to Booth Fisheries in pretty bad weather, snowing heavy, and as I was tying up the aircraft, I heard and then saw another airplane landing more or less in my ski tracks. It taxied over and the pilot got out and asked if he could leave the plane there and pick it up in the morning. I said "No Problem" but noticed that this fellow was dressed like a business man, with an overcoat and top hat (a Stetson) and spats on. I thought his was kind of out of place for bush flying. He said he came from Moar Lake and that he was building a fishing lodge up there. It turns out that this was Mr. Ken Leishman, the famous bank and gold robber and I never saw him again. I guess he was busy robbing banks.

The winter went along pretty good but towards spring the weather seemed to be bad with fog and I ran into problems. I was coming back from God's Lake with a load of fish, mainly trout and north of Weaver Lake I was flying around 300 feet, and I knew there was a rock hill, called Thunder Mountain, on the south west end of Weaver Lake. I was following my four mile to the inch map very closely so I could avoid the hill and then I would only be 32 miles from Berens River. I managed to talk to the R.C.M.P. pilot who was flying along the Lake Winnipeg shore going north to Norway House. He said the visibility was okay but you had to stay low. I was low alright; I think I was going around tall trees. There was muskeg in the area and a few small lakes, I should have landed, but they seemed pretty small. Now I am starting to sweat and knew that I had to get down. The Leif River turned up and I started to follow it but the trees where pretty tall along the river. The first long stretch I figured I would land on the ice. There was not much snow on the ice, as it had been melting, and I probably would have been okay to stop if there had of been snow. But I was sliding along pretty fast and a bend in the river came up. I took one part of the bend but the second one I was too close to the shore and I clipped a tree with the wing. That spun me into the shore and that was the end of my flying for that day. I strung out my antennae for the plane radio into the trees and being that I was fairly close to Berens River I managed to get someone to talk to. I made a schedule time for calls as I knew that it may be awhile because of the weather. Then I went to work and made a camp site and using my engine tent for my tent and then I built a fire and got lots of wood. I did not know I was going to be there for three days. I used some of my emergency rations, and of course, I had lots of fish to eat. The wolves sure sound close when you are trying to get to sleep but none came around. It was still winter but not too cold. Morning came and it was a little crispy but I lit the fire and boiled the pot for some coffee. I was sure that there would be some action today, if only the weather would clear up. My radio schedule time was for 8:30 am and Brother Leach of the R.C. Mission in Berens River knew that there was a plan in progress to get me out after the weather cleared. Bruce Smith who was the number one pilot for Teal Air was to come out in a Super Cub on skis and have a look at the plane for getting it

Glare Ice on the Leif River

out and myself. I guess they were a little concerned with the thickness of the ice, as it was getting close to spring and the snow was melting, except at night. The day was spent watching the weather, getting more wood, and cooking and doing a little reading. Next radio schedule was for 5:00 p.m. and there was movement in the overcast in Berens River as they could see a clearing out on the lake. They figured someone would come out the next day. Come to think of it now, I could have probably walked out in about two days, following the river and then the lake shore into Berens River. I bed down for another night and clear sky greeted me in the morning. After breakfast of a couple of pilot biscuits and coffee, my radio schedule had the good news of an aircraft coming out and would be around in the afternoon.

By this time I had decided that the fish in the aircraft would be wasted, so I put it out on the ice. Too bad, there were some nice trout. I kind of got my things to-gether, at least my personal stuff, and secured the aircraft to the bank of the river. Then I was sitting around camp and a bush partridge wandered into camp and I shot it with my .22 rifle. I figured a change from fish would be a nice treat. I heard a small aircraft in the area but it did not land on the river. I figured I might as well cook my partridge for a late lunch, so I stoked up my camp fire and roasted it on a stick. A voice behind me said "Doctor Livingstone, I presume" and that really startled me. I turned and there was Jack Thompson, the chief

Sleeping quarters – in an Engine tent camp (LEFT) & Campsite (RIGHT)

engineer for Teal Airways. Bruce had dropped him off on a little lake 2 miles north of me and he walked in. He was going to check the thickness of the ice and mark out a landing strip for Bruce. Well, at least I was going to get out of the river and maybe get home today or to-morrow. Frank for sure would be worried about me, and the state of his aircraft. There was lots of room for take-off so the three of us squeezed in the Super Cub and flew out of there. I can't remember whether we got home the same day or not, but I know I was plenty sorry for the predicament that I had got myself into. They say that a pilot with about 6 or 7 hundred hours thinks he knows everything and that proved well in this case. If only I had landed on Weaver Lake which was quite large but I thought that I could make Berens River and then follow the shoreline south. Maybe I took some false hope from the RCMP pilot that I talked to on the radio. A person has to remember that it is still up to themselves, knowing their capabilities, to do the right thing. For sure I was not an instrument pilot, with the limited equipment and facilities that were available to me; I should have landed sooner, instead of flying at tree top level. Well, anyway, no blood or broken bones.

My Savior, a Piper Super Cub

Frank got out of God's Lake somehow and we called the insurance company and eventually Frank got paid off for the aircraft and negotiations were started to find another aircraft, preferably a little bigger one. It took about two months but a Cessna 180 was purchased with floats and skis and I believe the registration was CF-IXS. I got checked out in it and we started to look for a little extra flying work.

Cessna 170 with a broken Wing

Chapter 16

One of the prospector's that Frank knew was Jim Cummings and he had a few claims in the eastern part of Manitoba and required a bit of flying in the spring of the following year. Jim asked me to take him out to Cole Lake and he would pay us later. As there was room I asked if my friend, Wayne, could come along, and that was okay. Ski flying was just about over for the year, and I believe it was around the middle of April. Cole Lake is pretty well northeast of Selkirk. Jim guided us into the bay where the cabin was situated, only there was a creek coming out at the bottom of the bay, and that made for weak ice. On turning in front of the cabin, we sank on one side. Needless to say, we scrambled out in a hurry, and the aircraft hung there. Our best thoughts were to wait until the early morning, when the ice is stronger and build a tripod and use an old rope block and tackle that was in the cabin, and lift it.

Prospector cabins are usually very rudimentary, built from what is at hand, which is the trees from the bush. Log walls and small poles for the roof and in this case, on the floor. The two windows and one door are most often brought in, along with a roll of roofing material to keep the rain out. The one room cabin had a stove and table and not much else. Wayne and I slept on the floor. About 5:00 a.m., Jim started chopping blocks to make kindling to light the fire-- right on the other end of the poles that we had our heads on. This was a sure way to let us know that it was time to get up. Jim's friends, Jimmy and Johnny Chernoski, came along from their cabin at Gem Lake, with a pair of Newfoundland Dogs, named Windy and Brandy, hooked to a sleigh. They pulled out three stout trees for us, and we set them up as a tripod. The rope on the block and tackle was kind of old, so we took it easy and sure enough the one side started to lift. Then we made a basket weave type of support out of small trees to put under the ski, once it was clear of the ice hole. By the time we had it up, we were in about a foot of water, but the ice held, and we skidded it forward and away from the hole. It did not take long to get our gear to-gether and leave that lake. I do not know if Jim ever found his molybdenum that he was after, as a matter of fact, I never seen him again. Just a little wrinkle in the wing tip, but we were lucky not to get a bath.

Some of my fishing friends were eager to try out lakes that could not be reached by road. We had to be careful because we did not have a charter license so we could receive money for our flying services although we were trying to build up a case so the Air Transport Board would grant us a license. This had to be applied for through a lawyer and other existing airlines could state their case why we should not have it. The fishermen wanted to go to Bulging Lake, north-east of Gem for trout and then we went to a few lakes south of there, in the Whiteshell area. Echo Lake was a favorite, also Indian and Beauchimin Lakes. Over the summer I put a couple of wooden boats in Echo and Indian Lakes, ones that we made and flew in the pieces and assembled on the lakes. Frank did a little sturgeon fishing on the Pigeon River and we prospected here and there.

On one particular weekend we decided to go on a little private fishing trip to Echo Lake, with the girls and our friends. Some of us flew in from Selkirk and others drove to Dorothy Lake in the Whiteshell and I flew them in from there. We were standing on a rock and casting for fish and I guess I got a snag and flipped the line a bit to get it off with tension on the line and it came off alright and flew back and the hook ended up embedded in the back of my head. Of course, I don't like to see blood especially if it is my own. I am lying on the rock sweating and feeling sick to my stomach and the girls are putting cold cloths on my forehead. Meanwhile, Doctor Wayne is looking the situation over and decided that the hook was in there pretty good. He tried to get it out a couple of times but that is a tough part of your skin and I would more or less pass out when he tried. I guess maybe they started to think that they would not be able to get out of the lake, as no one else knew how to fly. Somehow, the Doctor got a hold of a pair off needle nose pliers out of a fish and tackle box and unknown to me he got the pliers on the fish hook. Maybe I was passed out at the time but I do remember him giving the hook a terrible yank and it came out okay. I am not sure but I think he ran down the shore after that because it really hurt and he was not sure what my reaction would be. However, a little swabbing and a bandage made seem to be okay and we flew out a couple of hours later.

Frank decided to go north and do a little commercial fishing. He got permission to fish on Colin Lake and was going to haul the fish to Savage Island, on Island Lake. There was some big trout in the lake and I believe one topped 50 lbs. The lake was very nice, but we lived in tents and I made trips when the fish made up a load. There was quite an operation going on at Savage Island with a packing plant and planes flying to other lakes. This is the first time I met the owner of the packing plant and looking back I wish that meeting had not occurred. I believe that Frank fished Sharpe Lake for pickerel as well but it was getting close to fall and we had to get ready for winter fishing on God's Lake.

At this time Frank still owned the Cessna 180 but the idea was, when the charter came through and that was a big IF, I would become half owner. The aircraft was fitted with straight skis and pretty soon it froze up enough to get on the ice. Booth Fish let us use an old warehouse at the south end of the dock, near the bridge. We had electricity and a place to store out equipment. Fishing started at God's Lake Narrows and Frank had an old house on the reserve to start with and then moved near the Hudson Bay Store. We acquired a Super Cub on skis and this aircraft was more or less based at God's Narrows and flew fish to Wabowden, the nearest railway point. Our pilot was Jack Maloney, and he was from Selkirk, had a commercial license and was the dredge master for the Dept. of Transport in the summer months, mainly based at the outlet of the Red River into Lake Winnipeg. The aircraft was CF-JMI and we bought it from the North West Territories, Ft. Norman, I believe. This aircraft was a pleasure to fly – It would just jump off the ground as it had a 150 HP engine. We got it modified to legally have a third seat in the far back and it would carry a fair load, even though the usable area was restricted. We got our Air Transport License, even though Trans-air and others opposed it and now we were going to have to keep track of what we were doing and obtain a few items, fire extinguishers, scale, and an office to maintain our records, which also meant billing out our revenue trips. I had developed a bit of work for the Cessna 180 in the south, which I mean Berens River, and later, Little Grand Rapids. We even got the Boulanger's from Berens River fishing and trapping at Charron Lake, after I flew of couple of trips with them out to the lake. I would also make trips to God's Lake Narrows with groceries and trade goods for Frank and bring back a load of fish. Flying seemed to be picking up and I was getting known in the north. Mind you there was other competition and one was Northway out of Arnes, and they were doing a good job with their customers. The owner commercial fished on Sasaginnigak Lake and later started a tourist fishing lodge there. He was flying a Piper Super Cruiser, CF-EFI, and we met in weather more than once.

Chapter 17

Jack Maloney was doing good flying fish into Wabowden and bringing back groceries. I have an 8mm movie film of him loading bread, loaf by loaf, in the back of the Super Cub in 40 below weather, and it looked like one of those old time movies, slow and jerky. We did a trip from Selkirk to God's Narrow to-gether, Jack in the Super Cub and me in the Cessna 180. I just slowed up a little and we could see each other. Around Elliott Lake it started to snow very hard and I lost sight of him. It was less than one-half mile visibility and I decided to turn back to Little Grand Rapids. I landed just before dark near the Hudson Bay Store but I had no idea where I was going to stay. I fellow from the store came down to see who I was. It turned out to be the manager, Wilf Cable and he invited me to come up and stay the night. I had my own sleeping bag but it was nice to get into a warm place. His wife, Genevieve, was just as hospitable. I had something to eat and visited for the evening. These wonderful people are still friends of mine, and are retired in Newfoundland.

Next morning, I took off and headed for God's Narrows, as it had cleared up. When I got there I asked where Jack was, but he had not turned up. So I unloaded and went for a search for him, checking at known settlements, but no one had seen him. After a full day of searching, I thought I had better alert the search and rescue team. They appeared that night in DC-3's with spotters on board doing a grid search and looking for camp fires. Two more days of searching and the grid got ever wider and now extended to the border of Ontario. Jack spotted them in the distance; he was on the Stull River, just inside the Ontario Border. He was trying to make black smoke with his signal fire and finally decided to take off his rubber boots and burn them. That worked but now he was in stocking feet and they could not land being on wheels only but they alerted me and I flew over and got him. He was none the worse for wear seeing that he had a load of groceries on board, except that he needed gas, which I had with me. The next day I was talking to Barney Lamm and Rex Kitely at God's and they had come up for an inspection of their tourist camp in a Super Cub on skis, and they knew Jack was missing and where looking for him on the way. On Elliott Lake, they saw a trapper's cabin with smoke coming out the chimney and a man standing on the ice waving. They thought maybe he knows something about the missing plane, so they landed. No, he did not know anything about a plane, but he sure was "out of snuff." They had a good chuckle about that. Jack pushed the weather a little too much and got off course, but then again who hasn't done that. Jack continued to stay at God's Narrows, hauling fish to Wabowden and also trappers out to their traplines. One morning a trapper turned up with his family, a wife and three kids, good job they did not have much stuff, so Jack piled them in the Super Cub and took them out to Sharp Lake, a short flight.

Charron Lake was producing some nice fish, but not too heavy, but they were only using dogs on the lake and not enough of them. They talked of getting a snow machine, and wanted to know if I could fly one in. I said I would find out what kinds where available and if they would fit in the plane. I remember taking off from Charron Lake one clear day, and started to eat my lunch and look at a book. I noticed the cut in the trees indicating the border between Ontario and Manitoba, but as I had not been paying too much attention I did not know if I was going into

Ontario or coming out of it. Further south I saw a bi-plane on skis taxing around to the fish holes on the lake and the pilot was lifting nets. I did not want to do this but I thought I had better, so I landed and asked what lake is this. Spoonbill was his answer and it turned out to be Henri Boulanger from Lac du Bonnet in a Tiger Moth plane. Whatever works, he did not need a snow machine or dogs. I then set course for Bissett and paid attention to what I was doing, as they say about flying "Hours of boredom followed by moments of terror."

Towards spring there always seemed to be a lot of trappers wanting to fly out to their traplines and then they would canoe back or make arrangements to be picked up on a certain day when the ice melted. Little Grand Rapids and Paungassi had the most trappers; there was little else to do in those communities to make money. I suppose my exposure to this way of life and the fact that Frank had a fur buyer's license made me think that I should have a license too. It was not too hard to get the license and to learn more about what to look for in buying fur; I spent some time at Soudak's Fur Auction in Winnipeg to learn from Maurice, one of the owners. They would even give you a cash advance, if needed, and you would bring all your fur to them to go on a large auction at a later date, and then you would get a final payment, as long as the prices stayed up. Long hair fur, such as Lynx and Foxes, and even Wolves where in demand and I can remember a trapper getting $700.00 for an exceptional good Lynx hide. Soudak's gave me a chart to go by and of course, I started very cautiously until a learned more. The trappers were happy as it gave them an alternative to the Hudson Bay Company. I can remember flying into Settlement and buying Beaver and Muskrat skins one spring day. The ice on Lake Winnipeg had not opened up and the people could not cross by boat to Matheson Island and sell to Tiny Monkman, another fur buyer, who also had a store on the Island. I took a load of groceries with me and a helper, Rolly, would sell the groceries and I would buy the fur for cash. The people were happy because they were short of groceries and it was almost like a picnic atmosphere, women, kids, dogs and trappers all milling around and we sold all our groceries shortly after dinner and left with a pretty good load of Beaver pelts, much to the dismay of the two local fur buyers, who lived about seven miles away. I also tried buying some muskrats that were trapped in the Netley marshes by local trappers but that did not work out as well because there was no trading involved. Mr. Rifkin, a Selkirk merchant and fur buyer, told me he once bought a pussy cat hide, rolled up and the trapper claimed it was mink. All kinds of tricks were thought of to take advantage of the fur buyer.

We had a new business going in Selkirk but I found out that many years earlier there was a bush airline also in Selkirk called Starrat Air- but had since moved to Ontario. A local fellow who was interested in aircraft told me about a strip of land north of town, down by the Red River. It was actually a river lot, just at the mouth of the slough. In the old days, the Red River settlers figured to have long lots (two miles long) with access to river as that was their transportation system. This proved to be an ideal lot for our purpose, with thoughts of building a hanger at one end, and be able to pull aircraft out of the water and change them over from floats to skis, or wheels and vice-versa in the spring. We bought it, I believe for $2700.00, and then added another piece beside it later on. A small log siding office building was bought and then a HF radio with a high antennae installed. We were ready for business, later hoping to build a hangar. Upon walking out in the back bushes one day, I spotted the fuselage of an aircraft, a fairly large one, but I never did find out the history of it. It seems as though we were in the right place, even had an old house next door that I had hopes of making it into a better place. Our flying consisted of mainly going north to, Berens River, Poplar River, and the Little Grand Rapids area, and flying in the local area and passengers to and from Selkirk. I could not believe how much the local Hudson Bay Company had a hold on the people, and it was all to do with credit. They advanced them credit each month to the extent of their known income, and then the next month would come and the credit would start all over again. There was not much welfare in those days and the people only got along from trapping, fishing, hunting, and working out for someone, but not usually on a steady basis. There was the odd government job around, working for the nursing station as caretaker, or some Federal Indian Affairs project that was started, i.e. a sawmill, or hauling wood, commercial fishing, and in the fall, picking wild rice. With the high cost of groceries and clothing, this kept the people in debt and they had a very meager existence. As time went on, it was decided to build a small store and trade with the people, and possibly another cabin to accommodate sport fishermen and hunters. This transpired over the next two or three years, and Wink Wheeler was made storekeeper. He actually hired the local Indians to haul logs to our site by dog team in the winter, and they cost us a dollar a log. The logs were peeled in the spring and four walls and a roof went up on two buildings. Plywood was flown in for the floor and a couple of windows and doors were installed. Boats and motors were brought in and we had a nice little satellite operation going. Most of the groceries were brought in on back haul trips, with passengers going and coming. Wink stayed in Little Grand and kept in touch with us by radio,

Little Grand Rapids Trading Post and Cabins

giving us the weather and advising us of local trips that could be made, either with trappers or people just going to visit in other communities, remember there were no roads at the time in that area. I called it "the convenient wilderness" as it was only 140 miles from Selkirk, a little over an hour in the Cessna 180. We sold everything in the store, flour, sugar, lard, bacon, eggs, candy, and of course, tobacco and snuff. Beans, raisins, and yeast were off the list, because the locals would make bean juice (alcohol) and then tend to cause a little trouble. We also traded for fur, and bought fish. We also got a little trading post going in Bloodvein on an Island, across from the reserve. Wink's brother Jake ran that store and later Bill Lewis was the operator. We sold a variety of items, mostly groceries but snow machines and items not readily available where acquired and transported to the area. I even had a bombardier and sleigh for winter hauling.

We were a Moto-ski dealer   A motorcycle for her son, brought in by Cessna 180

In the fall, wild rice was picked in certain lakes and hauled out to a processor in Lac du Bonnet. Whole families would go out in early September by canoe, and of course live in tents, and cook over open fires, some of the lakes that had wild rice on them where 30 or 40 air miles away from Little Grand. I went out with groceries and a beam scale and tied the scale to a stout branch on a tree and weighed the rice in cotton sacks. The amount over the cost of the groceries was paid in cash and then a usual grocery list was given to me and a date that I was to return was made. Some of the lakes were pretty small and taking off with a full load was out of the question. One year I bought over 25,000 pounds of green rice and other years the rice either did not mature or other rice buyers would be around as well. The people used a canoe and paddled through the wild rice with another person bending the rice stalks over the canoe and tapping the heads into a tarp in the canoe. Rice ripens from the top down and in another couple of days, the process would be repeated. On some of the bigger lakes, were the rice was more plentiful, related families would gather, and put two canoes in tandem, with poles between them, front and back, and have a tarp slung between the poles and actually make a swather type apparatus resting on a V made of poles on each canoe. Then a homemade crank would be attached to the swather, and a man would stand on the side of the canoe and turn it. To make it turn easier they would spread some lard on the moving parts. Keep in mind this was all made from bush material, no square lumber parts. They had good production and usually made a lot of money. This kept me pretty busy from sometime in late August to the middle of September.

Then came the moose hunting season with mostly American hunters. Harold and Stan had been up at the camp fishing in the spring and decided to come for a hunt in the fall. They liked our hospitality and had a lot of fun. First, they wanted to go to a picture show at the Roman Catholic mission hall with the guide's daughters. These two hunters were well over 50 years old and the daughters were in their 20's. They went and picked them up by boat and drove to the hall at the south-west end of the settlement. Lots of people turned up as the show was a big event, only the Priest did not like anyone to spit on the floor, or make a mess with garbage as he had to clean it up. Men and women both chewed snuff and it was necessary to spit once and awhile, so they spit in empty drink cans. Stan's girlfriend gave him a poke in the ribs and told him to get her a can and either he did not understand her or could not find one, so she pulled open his pocket on his parka and spit in the pocket. So much for learning about the local culture or customs. Anyway, they took them home in the dark and went hunting the next day with their dad.

It was late in the day before we finally took off for our hunting area – which was Whiskey-Jack Lake with the McPhail River below it. I landed at a nice rock point and told Stan to make the camp and put up the tent. I left with the plane, stating I would be back in a couple of days. Harold and the guide, William, would travel down the river by canoe to see if there was any sign of moose. Of course, it was in the rutting season, and a few calls from the guide should bring some attention if there were any around. Sure enough, within 30 minutes they had three Bull Moose in different areas calling back. The closest one was following them along the river, walking through the willows and every once and awhile breaking out in the open. Bear in mind that a moose has poor eyesight but can hear very good with his big ears. The hunter's stopped in mid stream and sat still and called some more. They could see the Bull Moose splashing along the side of the river, in and out of the willows, and getting closer. One more call and the moose turned and started to come out in the shallows of the river, towards the canoe. Harold was sitting in the front of the canoe and took aim and fired. The moose kept coming and Harold fired again. By this time the moose was splashing towards the canoe and obviously not hurt. Harold got excited and had his gun up but pumped all the live cartridges into the canoe and water without pulling the trigger. By this time, the guide had enough and took his wired up old gun and shot the moose, it was getting too close. Harold was really excited and had to go to shore. As he got close, he got out of the canoe and went beside a tree and had to wrap his arm around the tree to steady his arm, so he could light his cigarette. Harold said "That's the most excitement

I have ever had in my life time". After a break, they went and pulled the moose to shore and found two perfect holes in the horns, one on each side, and one in the chest were the guide had shot. A perfect hunt, as far as Harold was concerned. The moose had a 46 inch rack and was dully mounted on Harold's garage back in Minnesota, I know, I saw it on a visit at a later date.

Over the period of the summer, Frank had little to do with the operation out of Selkirk and had not paid anything on the flying account for the winter past. It was obvious that he was not really interested. So I went to a lawyer and had the ownership changed and settled his account.

Jack Maloney was pretty interested in what Frank was going to do for winter and went out and bought a Cessna 170, Registration CF-FBG, which used to belong to the Winnipeg Flying Club, and was kept for instrument training. Jack had it on floats and manual wheel skis. When winter came, Jack was finished his job as dredge master and was looking to do a little work with the aircraft. We used him on some trips and he developed a little work for himself. We still had a presence in the God's Narrows area through Frank as he was back fishing for the winter. Trappers still needed to be taken out to their traplines and Frank always needed provisions. The other areas, Bloodvein, Berens and Little Grand kept us busy as well. We had hired a mechanic by the name of Bruce and were in the process of building a 40 by 60 metal hangar to do work on the aircraft. Of course, the Ministry of Transport was monitoring our progress and made sure we were complying with all the regulations. Then disaster struck. Our Cessna 180 – CF-IXS, was already on skis and beside the uncompleted hangar and ready for an early morning flight. As we did not have the electric power to the building site as yet, we had to use the blow pot to heat up the engine in the morning. The flight was for 8:30 am and Bruce went to the hangar earlier to warm it up. He started the blow-pot and put it under the engine and as it seemed to be working okay, he went back to his car to get warm and must have fallen asleep. That type of procedure is a No-No. The passengers and I arrived to find the aircraft on fire and with full tanks of aviation gas. The aircraft fire was put out by the fire department but needless to say it ruined our day, and many more. Fortunately, we had insurance but it took awhile to get a pay out and buy another Cessna 180, which turned out to be CF-IEF, an old Trans-air aircraft. It was well into the New Year before we got established with our new number one aircraft. The little Super Cub – JMI – and Jack Maloney's aircraft carried the load for a time but we did not make as much money.

This is the type of aeroplane that Jack Maloney flew out to Lewis Lake to save a young boy who had burns from falling in a camp fire.

Chapter 18

Two new businesses had been started in Selkirk and I was sure we would be getting some flying activity from each of these. First, was the silica plant and they obtained their product (sand) from a pit along the shore of Black Island, just east of Hecla Island. They had equipment and loading facilities on the south side of Black Island but it was wide open to the south basin of Lake Winnipeg, and it was a difficult place to land, because of the wind and waves. But never the less, I got several trips with a Mr. Robertson of Winnipeg Supply and Fuel. One particular trip, I was to pick him up with the 180 on skis just below his cabin on Lake Winnipeg, in the Balsam Bay area. I saw him standing on the ice but I did not like the looks of the ice in that area and as I had no radio contact with him, I had to drop him a note, to basically move to another area further along the shore. So I wrote a note and put it in an empty Pepsi bottle for weight, and then flew over him and dropped the bottle out. He just had to make one step and he picked up the bottle and read the note, of course he complied. When he finally got on board the 180, he said, "You should have been with me in the war as my bomb aimer". Apparently, he was a bomber pilot during the war. I was not as good on another occasion. Princess Harbour, sometimes called Rabbit Point, is a small settlement (12 people) jutting out into Lake Winnipeg and subject to big winds and rough seas, but it is only about seven miles from the narrows of Lake Winnipeg. Ole Anderson and his family lived there, and had a trading store and fishing operation, mainly servicing the people of Bloodvein, a nearby Indian Reserve. I was supposed to land there with the 180, but a strong wind was blowing from the south and this made it too rough in the harbour. I needed to get a message to Ole, so I wrote a message out and again used a Pepsi bottle for weight. I flew over and threw it out and it landed in his front flower garden, just six inches from his picture window of the house. He told me about it later, so I decided to quit that practice.

There seemed to be lots of work around, it was a chore keeping the aircraft all running and finding good people to fly them. The other business that was just getting started was Marine Transport and they would be hauling freight on Lake Winnipeg. There was a Stinson Voyageur owned by a conservation officer in Berens River, but I think it was sitting at Netley Airport and we were asked to bring it to Selkirk. There was a young pilot by the name of Lynn, who wanted to go over to Netley and pick it up and fly it back to Selkirk. After getting bugged for awhile, I finally consented and away he went. There was some delay at Netley, maybe getting gas, and he came back to Selkirk a little late, the sun was down but still light. He landed from west to east and hit a hay coil on the side of the runway, and flipped over. Now I had to inform the owner, and in fact we bought this aircraft before it caused a problem and had it fixed up. One of the lessons learned was do not lend or say okay too fast, and the other was a pilot rule, no or little wind, and getting dusk, land into the west as you will have some advantage in seeing objects in front of you.

We used a Stinson, for hauling trappers in the Island Lake area and found that it worked fairly well. There was not as much room as in the Cessna 180 but the landing gear was very strong and it could stand the drifts a little better. Actually, Ron Michaluk was the pilot and he did not seem to mind flying it at all. The ice was getting around 6 inches thick on Island Lake and Ron was anxious to get going to bring the trappers back into the settlement. Ron was in Island Lake and I had a trip in the Cessna 180 to take Ed. Tripp into Savage Island on the east end of the lake. We met and were to stay in Pete's cabin (Owner of the Fish Shed) at Savage Island. Little did I know but Ed. had about a half dozen bottles of rum in his suitcase.

It gets dark early in December, about 4:00 p.m., and Ron and I found cots to sleep on in the living room of the cabin, across from each other. The manager (Ed) and the guy who stayed there over freeze-up (Johnson) started drinking the rum after supper. About 9:30 or 10:00 p.m., the manager was sufficiently inebriated, so he went to bed.

Johnson sat at the kitchen table and had a few more drinks. We were wishing that he would go to bed so we could sleep. He started mumbling about how he did not like Ron. After awhile, he got up and went to the cupboard drawer and pulled out a big butcher knife. That got our attention. Then he came into our room and was waving this big knife around at Ron who was by this time, standing on his bed in his long johns.

I was up and behind him; the guy with the big knife.

I motioned to Ron that I was going to jump him and I did – grabbing him around the neck and Ron piled on to and we put him down and gave him the licking of his life. We then took all the knives and guns out of the cabin and threw them in the snow.

Johnson staggered off to bed.

In the morning, as we were having breakfast, Johnson came out of his room and went to the wash basin. One eye was closed and his face was a mess. As he looked in the mirror, he said "From the looks of me, I owe someone an apology". At least, he was remorseful and he knew damn well what he had done.

No problem with him after that and he helped us dig 45 gallon drums of gas out of the snow and roll them down to the lake for the planes.

Ed Tripp, the manger, shot himself in the cabin later on that winter. I heard that Ed and his wife split up and that was probably a factor.

Ron stayed up there for the winter and did pretty good. As a matter of fact, he went back there in later years and started a store and his own airline. He was well liked in the area, and of course, got the flying bug, like many of us.

The ice in the Island Lake area stays a lot longer than it does down south and there was still some work to do when the aircraft came up for an 100 hour inspection, so Ron flew it in to get checked. We had no wheel skis, just straight skis or wheels. The aircraft was in the hangar for a couple of days, and then came out on the strip on wheels. I took it off and flew it down to the ice to change over to skis and then it would go north. Except, that I could not make a turn into the shore like I wanted to, no brakes, also because of the wind was blowing across the river and I ventured out too far on the river, were the current had worn away the ice more and made it weaker. I WENT THROUGH TO THE WINGS. I had a little trouble getting out and had to put my back to the door and push the opposite door with my feet. Fortunately, I got out and climbed up on the ice and while walking away from the aircraft I went through again. Again I got out and moved swiftly away from the area. The ice was rotten in the centre but seemed okay away from the current. I got to shore and related all my excuses to the rest of the crew. By the weekend we had a diving crew out there to hook on to it.

Even that turned out to be hectic, and almost disastrous. Pot, my friend, and I were around the hole in the ice watching the divers get ready.

One of the divers was sitting on the edge of the hole waiting for someone to bring his air tanks, and he fell in. The current was strong and he was swimming but not towards the hole. We could see him under the ice. Finally, he made it back to the hole, out of breath. Then they re-grouped and got the hoist attached to the aircraft and we kept on moving it ahead towards the shore and finally back on dry land. That spoiled our plans of going north to Island Lake with that aircraft; I think Ron settled for using the Super Cub for a spell. We drained the oil out of the engine, and changed some instruments, and cleaned it up and it was none the worse for the dunking. The Stinson is a tough old bird and I liked the 165 H.P. Franklin engine that they had in it, a little underpowered, but it worked pretty well.

The yellow pages or Trade-a-plane was like our Eaton's catalogue to us; it came from Crossville, Tennessee and was mailed to us every three weeks. There were planes, parts, instruments, radios, engines, floats, antique aircraft and old war birds, just about everything, even hangars, in this publication and we read it all the time. I had done a little crop spraying with the Super Cub and we had it equipped with a belly tank and spray bars. I went down to Roland, Manitoba and a friendly crop sprayer gave me some lessons, especially how to mix the chemicals. He was flying a J-3 cub so we did not spend any time on air work.

I noticed a PA-18A – for sale in Albert Lea, Minnesota so Bob, our maintenance expert, and I went down to look. It turns out the owner was in the crop spraying business along with his two sons who were the pilots. They were spraying a potato field and the one son had engine trouble and landed in the field and caught fire, the second son, saw what had happened and landed quickly across the rows in an attempt to get to him to help, he flipped and was killed. The first son perished in the fire. That was enough for the father, and he sold his remaining Super Cub.

This one had the tank inside, behind the pilot, and had a quick release mechanism, to dump your load in case of trouble. It also had a few other safety features because it was made the agricultural business. The spray bars had a fold up feature, and had wire cutters mounted on the undercarriage. We bought it for a decent price and flew it home. So I was already for the crop spraying season, which was coming soon, and it would be busier if we had wet conditions. Norm McRae was already doing some spraying in the Stonewall area and I believed there was room in the Selkirk Area and even to the east, Lac du Bonnet, and Ladywood area. I put my shingle out and started to get some calls. I don't know if I ever perfected my stall turns at the end of a run but I got around okay. We used a flag man to indicate the next run, he would take 21 paces from the last place he stood, and would show his flag.

One of the nicest fields I had was Bruce McIvor's field north from the hangar about 6 miles. It was over a mile long and had a good gravel road beside it to land on and no hydro lines at one end, just low brush. The field was pretty wet and needed to be sprayed, and I had help from the hangar with a water truck and gasoline for the cub. Another field that I did in the area was Kicking Bill McCrae's field, Eldie's father. Then to the east, around Ladywood, was Walter Cryplevy"s field, he was in the construction business and had no time to spray. His dad had only one arm and was my flagman; also he could not speak English, only Ukrainian. I was spraying a field that had a roadway and hydro poles at the end. He would take his 21 paces but would not move over enough when I wanted to go under the hydro lines, a few times I came pretty close to him but he would not move. I was also landing on a road that had high grass on the sides, and I caught my spray bar and kind of turned me towards the ditch. Good job for the brakes but it was another wake up call.

I was spraying near Libau and I got thirsty and taxied up to the Red and White store to go in for a drink. The owner came out as he heard the plane and as I was getting out of my shoulder harness, and crash helmet he had a look in the little cramped quarters I was sitting in. "Yep" he says, I had a lot more room in the planes I flew overseas" and he pulled out a Airline Pilots License, and showed me. Ray was his name, and I had a new respect for that store owner. I did some spraying for another McRae, Jimmy, west of Selkirk, in the bog area, also, for Denny, I am told, as I guess he was my flag man and he claims he lost his hat. It was getting a little windy at Jimmy's place and I wanted to quit near the end of a field but he wanted me to continue. He said the next field, a flax field, was his relation's and it would be okay. I sprayed and about 3 weeks later, I got a letter from T.P. Hillhouse, a lawyer, claiming his flax in one corner was stunted, and that I owed him $675.00. I went to Jimmy and showed him and he said don't worry about it – I don't know how he settled it.

I sprayed for Stanley Popowich in the Fort Garry area on a beautiful morning, early, no wind, and he had lots of mustard, and that is what I was to spray for. I noticed as I went along that once and awhile my wheel would come up with a bit of yellow on it, from the mustard, and I thought what a good job I am doing here. I went back a couple of weeks later to look and I noticed an even swath about 3 feet wide down each row and I realized that being as calm as it was I should have been 15 or 20 feet high. Oh well, Stanley did not complain. I had a close call with a dead tree in the middle of brush land I was spraying with a heavy dose of 2-4-D. They call those trees widow makers, so I guess other sprayers have had trouble with them as well. I never liked getting too close to the hydro's high tension lines and in the Lac du Bonnet region there are lots. I had to wiggle between two steel bases on one occasion with a full load on. Sometimes, it is better to go under the wires of tall hydro poles, and I have been over the telephone poles (shorter) on one side of the road and

This aircraft is now in the museum in Calgary

I will let you guess what this one is

Last trip, for the Good Old Ship

Our base in Selkirk, with a New Hangar

under the hydro poles on the other side. This maybe only my preference or that I did not know any better. Anyway, I crop sprayed for about three years and then the Pawnee sprayer came into being, and was the aircraft to have but other things were happening so I decided to concentrate on that.

The "Keenora" boat used to travel up and down Lake Winnipeg carrying passengers and freight, and was now going to be retired. I have a picture of it on its last cruise to Lake Winnipeg with a load of Passengers going past our base in Selkirk.

In the spring of the year, May and June especially we had lots of sport fishermen going out to the different lakes. They always think they are going in a half ton truck by the amount of gear that they bring, especially beer. One party had 22 cases of beer and then their food and equipment. I left, telling them to pare

Jack Collison from Selkirk, enjoying himself

down and then phone me and I would come back. One of the lakes that we went to was Harrop Lake, and we stayed in an old wild rice warehouse that had a few steel bunks in there and a stove to keep warm. The fishing was really good for big pickerel, and some big jacks, (walleye and northern) The guys had a great time there and the cost was not too much, then some guy decided to build a tourist camp there and we had to close down, as it was not licensed accommodation in the eyes of the tourist branch.

Les Dodds, our pilot and a happy fisherman

Doug Grant and a stringer full

Eddie Balcaen and Barney Wilson with a catch

I hope they can fish and hunt where they are

During the summer, an emergency call came into the office and the word was that a man was injured at the end of the road, across from Matheson Island. Apparently, a construction job was in progress, building a wharf, and a gravel truck and a loader squeezed a man in between them and injured his insides. Our float planes were away and one was getting serviced, so I phoned Jack Maloney to borrow his and it was out at the mouth of the Red River, where he worked, about 10 minutes away by plane. It was made available as soon as possible and I flew up to "the end of the road" to pick up this man, because they feared for his life. We laid the man out in the aircraft, having taken the passenger's seat out and I was off with him, headed for Winnipeg, St. Boniface Hospital, because I knew that it was on the river. The sun was beating down on him through the front windshield and I held up a book to give him relief from the sun. I told the Winnipeg Air Traffic control what I was doing and they gave me clearance to land over the Norwood Bridge and pull in behind the Hospital. I did not know how difficult it was going to be carrying that man up the bank and to the emergency of the hospital but by this time I had some help. I do not think that this has ever been done since, but the man is still alive and living out at Fisher Bay on Lake Winnipeg. Thanks to Maloney for lending me his aircraft.

We heard about a Cessna 206 that had a bad landing in Winnipeg and broke its back, just behind the seating arrangement. It was up for bids from the insurance company and we put in a bid and got the aircraft. Bob was qualified to fix this machine and he did along with his helpers. It was a real good aircraft on wheels, lots of room, but we had to put it on floats and got a pair from Wiplinger in Minneapolis. The aircraft worked pretty well but it was best to trim it off the water. The Hydro came down with a couple of panels for Oxford House and asked us to deliver them. We took the wooden case off and got them in the 206, thru the double doors at the back. They were pretty long and weighed only 250 lbs. It made our day as Oxford House is at least 360 miles one way. This aircraft was also good for hauling coffins, which we got some of, returning people to their home communities.

Yes, we got the Hydro panel in!

I am not sure which way the pup was going, north or south

Our Cessna 206 in Berens River, Man

Another job that we got from Indian Affairs was flying the youngsters from their community to the residential schools in the fall, also home at Christmas and back again in the spring. Other charter companies got their fare share but it was good business. A lot of the sick people went to the hospital in Pine Falls, and were invariable dropped off at Virginia Fontaine's overnight stopping place in Fort Alexander, which was just up from the Winnipeg River. We also fly different people from Indian Affairs to the communities that they worked with. I remember Tom Reeves, was the Agent in Selkirk and we stayed overnight at Little Grand Rapids, in the basement of the nursing station. I think he only slept about 3 or 4 hours a night and then he had the light on reading. He said it was something to do with the years he spent in prison camp overseas during the war. I sometimes flew Joe Stefanson – He was known as Indian Joe because he worked for Indian Affairs and had something to do with the people starting commercial fishing on their respective reserves. There was another Joe Stefanson who was a commercial fisherman. I also flew Hank Mitchell around to the communities and he had expertise in the building trade, especially in building houses for the people to live in. Then there was Lloyd Jonasson, who worked with Hank Mitchell and finally took over from him when Hank moved on. Lloyd had his brother, Jack, go out and start sawmills in the communities, so they could have their own lumber, for docks and houses. And then, there was the HERO to us all, who was a bomber pilot during the war, spent time (Lots) in a prison camp and never talked about it, and never once criticized my flying even though he probably could have flown circles around me. We had a get to-gether every winter, when the five of us would curl in the Selkirk Bonspiel, (4 and a spare, in case someone was out of town) and we always won a prize, not the big one, but at least we won something. Many years later, Herb, who died at 86 years old, wrote a book "To Hell in a Halifax" which detailed his war time exploits in the Halifax bomber he flew and time in prison.

During the winter months, Herb, Lloyd and I went moose hunting up near Kinwow Bay with the Cessna 180 on skis. We parked at a camp and then walked south into the wind and one of us shot a bull moose. We had it rolled over and Herb was on top opening up the belly. The knife slipped and he cut his leg. He did not think too much of it at the time, but later on he felt uncomfortable and took his pants down to see the wound. It was just spurting blood out and his underwear and pants had blood on them. We did our best to stop the flow but realized that we were going to have to get Herb some better care. I went as quickly as possible to get the plane and brought it down to the area near Lloyd and Herb. We helped him out of the bush/muskeg as best we could so he would not have too much undo exertion on his leg. The closest place we thought to get to was Bloodvein and figured Brother Leach would have some wise old idea on what to do, as we all knew him. He put a pressure bandage on Herb's leg and that is when I noticed all the scars on the inside of his legs. He said "That was during the war, when they got me with flak and shot the controls of the plane out of his hands." We then proceeded to Selkirk and had proper treatment at the hospital. Herb and I met in the spring at a sport show in Omaha, Nebraska and we had a good visit to-gether, even went to the bomber command museum at the Air Force Base.

Brother Fredrick Leach - the weather/radio operator in Beners River

Lloyd and I also had an interesting and lucky experience moose hunting at another time. We flew out to the Hay Bay area, which is north of Hole River, along the east side of Lake Winnipeg in a Piper Super Cruiser on skis. After a couple of hours walking in the deep snow and getting nothing we decided to leave. We got off okay but I noticed that we had gone through some slush and, of course, it was hard going, full throttle for sure. We flew towards Victoria Beach but were planning on going to Selkirk. Lloyd's brother, Jack, lived at Victoria Beach and it was decided to stop and visit and maybe put some gas in. Jack lived on the shore along the east side and it seemed I was having a problem getting my depth perception to be able to land. Therefore, I went out further on the lake and landed beside a pressure ridge which gave me a better visual reference. Lloyd and I stopped and got out on the ice. We both had headaches and walked like a couple of drunks. Then I noticed a piece of the bottom cowling of the aircraft hanging down, one near the end of the exhaust pipe, must have tore it open in the slush. It was directing the exhaust up into the aircraft, near were my feet would be. No wonder we were having a problem walking, we got gassed. Jack's wife, Jo-Ann, was watching us through field glasses from the house and she said to no-one in particular, "look at those guys, they are drunk". We made it to the house and had a sleep for a couple of hours. Good job we landed when we did, or we might have had a worse problem.

Every year, for five years, I had the pleasure of taking Bud Grant, the Bombers football coach, out for a moose hunt in the late season. Apparently, the meat was used for a sports- writers' dinner sometime in February and our hunting was considered a legitimate expense. One year we got a big bull north of Bisset and gutted it and took the hide off but it was starting to get late, so we had to leave. We knew that the birds, magpies and ravens, would be there, practically as soon as we left, so we put the hide back on the moose to keep them from causing damage to the meat. Next day, we could not fly, due to weather, and that night it turned very cold. When we got back, the moose appeared to be okay as the birds spent most of their time on the guts, which we left handy, but what a time we had trying to get the hide off the second time. It froze solid. We could not pull it off, so we went to the bush and cut a couple of stout birch poles and sharpened one end. The sharp end we put under the skin and both pried to-gether. It took a long time to get if off and we were both perspiring profusely. Only then were we able to quarter the moose and haul it out to the truck.

Another time we were more or less in the same area, and a moose was in some dense willows. I went around behind it and made it run towards Bud, who was up on a high rock. I heard a shot which seemed to be over my head but he got it. Then we stopped for our sandwich and frozen 7-up. To make conversation, I said "pretty foggy in Toronto at the game" He said "Yup" – a man of few words. (That is the year they had to delay the Grey Cup game until next day to finish.)

The next year we had help and went hunting in the Hay Bay area, one of my favorite areas. We, of course, fly to the area and leave the plane far enough away. Our additional crew was Charlie Sheppard, Cecil Luining, and Bud and I. We shot a moose and had two toboggans to haul out the quarters, one short 3 ft. one and an 8 footer. We loaded a hind quarter on the small toboggan and told Bud to go ahead and break trail with it. Then we loaded the rest on the bigger toboggan, tied it down, and each of the other three of us had a different length rope and tried to stay in the trail and pull as hard as we could. These fellows had just come off a season of playing football and were in good shape, but I attempted to keep up to them or get run over. I developed a Charlie horse in my leg and flopped in the snow. They knew what it was and massaged it out of my leg. We got out to the aircraft and covered the meat over in a snow bank and took off because the weather was starting to get bad in snow. We flew south, but could only make it to Fort Alexander, and landed in a field because now it was starting to get dark, along with the snow. Then we caught a ride to the Manitou Hotel to wait for a ride to come from Selkirk. Of course, we went in the basement to the beer parlor, no more flying for the day. Everyone looked at the strangers coming in and the bartender came over and said to Bud "You look like Bud Grant" He said "Yeah, everyone tells me that." And we did not tell them any different. Pretty soon our ride came along, and next day I got the aircraft and went out and picked up the quarters of moose.

Not every year was a success, and one year we failed, Bud was away scouting and did not leave us much time to hunt. Not to be outdone, he went to St. Boniface stock yards and bought the oldest cow he could find and had it cut up and served that to the sports writers. The only comment he had was it was a bit tough.

Someone thought it was a good idea he have some of the Blue Bombers go up to Norway House for the Trappers Festival. We were slated to fly them there and it certainly was an experience. First, there was a steak dinner out at Hecla Island, in the old fishers shed, which had been made into an accommodation unit. There were a few 26 oz. bottles consumed and a little bit of devilry followed – such as borrowing Helgi's bombardier and getting a barb wire fence all wound up in the tracks – and having a fight inside the building with dry Ansul fire extinguishers but no one got hurt. Next morning, three aircraft took off for Norway House, and our rendezvous point would be the Playgreen Inn on the Jack River. The Jack River is like a highway in Norway House, snow machines, people walking, dog teams, and aircraft landing. I landed and one thing you can say about the river, it is smooth from the traffic but there is not much room to make a 180 degree turn. The answer to that is to drag a rope off the tail ski and someone can grab the rope and pull it sideways until your turn is completed. I had to make a turn and Charlie Sheppard was near the rope and he was told to pull it. So he grabbed it and held on, I opened the throttle and was going nowhere, so I stopped and opened door. Charlie had his heels dug in and he had snow in his eyes, no hat and was wondering what was wrong. We told him he had to pull sideways so I could turn – then he caught on – being from Texas and all, he was unfamiliar with this kind of procedure. Mr. and Mrs. Lowe ran the Playgreen Inn and had a beer vendor, but no beverage room. After we checked in, everyone was standing around looking out the window towards the bushes. A lot of local people were out in the bushes drinking beer. They could buy a case of beer but could not take it on the reserve so they just drank it outside and then went and got another case. As we were watching, Mr. Lowe noticed that the pail a day bathroom at the top of the stairs was full and overflowing. As he could not carry it downstairs, he opened an upstairs window and threw the contents out, into a tree in front of the window we were watching from. We were sure glad we were not standing outside. However, we had a nice supper at a large dining room table and then everyone dispersed to the Trappers Festival festivities. It seems like the last guy home did not get a bed as he was sleeping on the chesterfield in the dining room. Ray Jauck had a broken leg and it was in a cast but he still came, what a good bunch. About noon, all our crew was accounted for and we flew home, to Selkirk.

Someone at the base must have been reading Trade-a-Plane when I was away, because they found a good buy on an Aeronca Sedan with a 145 Continental Horse Power engine in it. We bought it, thinking that it would be a good plane to haul trappers with in the winter time on skis, there was lots of room inside. One day, I had a load of meat to take to Alix Store in Berens River, and the total weight was 875 lbs. I got off okay and landed in the smooth area in Berens River, maybe I left my gas down at bit.

Another fellow had a similar type aircraft, although I did not know him, but he had a sawmill in the Wabowden area. One winter day, he was going to Wabowden and flew right up the centre of Lake Winnipeg but it was blowing hard and the ground drift was reducing visibility. Around Georges Island he was too low to the ice and clipped a wing tip on a snow drift and spread pieces of his aircraft over a wide area, but he was okay, still sitting the pilot's seat. He got out and took the compass out of the aircraft dash and took his good Arctic down sleeping bag and a little grub and headed south east for the closest settlement. It was 25 or 30 below, with a strong Northwest wind blowing. He spent two nights out on the ice and the third day, some fishermen from Berens River, actually Harrison Boulanger, found him near the north-east corner of Swampy Island and brought him in to the hospital. Much later, we hired Harrison, his bombardier and sled, and went out and picked up all the pieces for the insurance company and took them into Selkirk. I guess this pilot had not learned the rule of not leaving the shoreline in bad weather because of white out conditions.

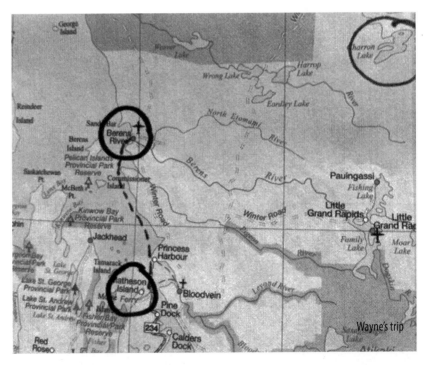

Chapter 19

We were still dealing with the Boulanger family of Berens River and Charron Lake on fish, but they were having trouble getting around the lake to their nets and wanted to have a snow machine as there were a few on the market at that time. The Skidoo had not appeared as yet, but there was a reasonable machine called "The Bozak" made in Beausejour, Manitoba and it appeared to be a good workhorse. We bought it and then started to figure out a way to get it to Charron Lake. If we took it apart, we may be able to get it in the Cessna 180, but there would probably still be two trips and could be combined with some of the Boulanger supplies or people going out to Charron Lake. But how to get it to Berens River, there was no winter road as yet and the tractor trains had finished their runs up to that settlement. There was a fellow named Wayne, actually Doctor Wayne, a hockey player, who had some time on his hands and just might drive it up to Berens River from the end of the road. He was game for the trip and someone taking a half ton truck to Matheson agreed to carry the Bozak to the end of the road. Everything seemed good, until a severe storm closed the road at Washow Bay, north of Riverton and several cars and trucks were stranded, including the truck with the Bozak on board. Some people were looking for a place to stay

No problem, Wayne would do it again

overnight and one guy decided to go back to Riverton. Wayne and the driver of the truck followed this guy and found a place to stay in Riverton with an Auntie, of Wayne's wife. Next day turned out beautiful and not too cold, so they went north as soon as the snowplow cleared the road. The trip from the end of the road north, was uneventful, and Wayne was not scared of the wolves I told him about, as he was packing side arms. It started to get dark around Pigeon Point and Wayne was checking his map when I flew over and then landed in the bay, the other side of Flat Head Point. He knew were to go then, and I was waiting for him. We stayed overnight in Berens and went home the next day.

In a couple of days, I had time to take the snow machine to Charron Lake, but I had to take it apart, and the engine had a gear shift on it that I had to bend into an upside down U with a torch, so I could get it into the plane. I think that it is still up in Charron Lake, and it worked well.

Jack Maloney was in Berens River and Sigfusson Transportation had their tractor train cabooses on the ice near the Hudson Bay store. They asked Jack on the radio to check on the caretaker in one of the cabooses, as they were waiting for other freight and tractors to arrive, and the caretaker had not checked in on the radio for a couple of days. Jack went in, no fire on, and found the guy dead in his bunk. He reported to them and had the nursing station personnel give an official report and was told to take the body to Winnipeg to the Health Science Centre. Fortunately, Jack had his friend, Jim Want with him along for the ride. Now Jim was able to help load the deceased caretaker in the Cessna 170 aircraft. It was difficult because rigor motis had set in and his knee would not go down. Also, one arm was stuck out straight - besides the body was frozen. They covered him over with the engine tent, and because the passenger seat was taken out, Jim had to sit on the deceased knee. The flight south to Selkirk was a little more than an hour, and they landed at the air base for

From Mountie to Bush Pilot

gas. It was a good thing as Jim was getting a sore behind and Charlie, the deseased was starting to thaw out and Jim was losing his perch. After a break and gas up, they continued their flight to Winnipeg and delivered thier cargo to the Health Science Centre. The passenger seat was put back in and Jim had a better ride back to Selkirk. The official outcome was the caretaker died to heart failure.

We had hired a pilot by the name of Les Dodds and he was a wartime bomber pilot who was tired of his mundane job at the CNR express shed. He had his commercial license and wanted to work – he was a short person and the mechanics talked about putting a couple of blocks on the rudder pedals, so he could operate them properly. He took a load of groceries into Little Grand Rapids and then the storekeeper (Wink) had a trip for him to Stout Lake in Ontario with a couple of trappers, sons of Whitehead Moose Owen, whom I knew quite well. Les loaded up and took off and should have been back in two hours, at the most. He did not show up that night. Wink called me on the two way radio and advised of the situation and I made plans to go north, once the weather cleared up a little in the area. Les turned up at Paungassi, a settlement, 12 miles north of Little Grand, just after lunch the next day. I think the Search and Rescue went out that night, but as it was overcast, they could see no signal fire.

Wayne has a smile on his face, he knows he is going home

Les related what had happened. As he went east with the two fellows, he ran into heavy snow and tried to go around it to the north, but the weather did not improve and he made a landing on a lake, and ground looped. He probably landed down wind. The two fellows did not speak English and just got out of the aircraft and put their snowshoes on and headed east, going home, and left Les there.

In awhile, a dog team went by on the far side of the lake, it did not stop. Les went over and followed the trail to the hole in the ground type of cabin the trapper had and spent the night with them. He asked them to take him back to Paungassi and they said to-morrow. They did not offer him anything to eat; maybe they did not have very much.

So, I picked up Les, at Paungassi, and had a look at the aircraft and went back to Selkirk. The leg on the Cessna 180 had buckled under and the wing tip was touching the ice, and bent up a little. Within a day or two, I took a mechanic out to the site, and to-gether we got it ready to fly out. The propeller was not damaged and after we got it back on both skis it looked better. We took the wing tip off and shoved a couple of birch poles through the ribs and then took a nylon rope and tied it to the poles and then to the ski. Then I twisted a pole into the nylon rope and tightened it all up, so ski would not fold back in. It was ready for flight, and I took it out a couple days later, when I could arrange for a drop off at the aircraft for myself. As I got going along the east shore of Lake Winnipeg south of Manigatogan, I hit a bit of bad weather, but toughed it through and got into Selkirk. I had a little trouble keeping that wing up, but it had a lot hanging from it. We had a wing jig for Cessna's and it was repaired in due course.

Our small store at Little Grand Rapids was a beehive of activity in the summer time. Lots of groceries to be sold, people staying there and sometimes workers in the area as there was little in ways of accommodation. One such person was Fritz Metzcar, a German fellow who was making a living around the country, especially Berens River,

Fritz Metzcar- A real old transplanted Northerner

where he lived with his wife. This man was exceptionally good with carpentry, building his own house with tree slabs, and dimensional lumber that he cut on his saw mill. Now he was over at Little Grand showing the native people how to set up a saw mill that Indian Affairs had provided and he was staying with Wink at our store, and of course batching-cooking their own meals. I had brought a load of groceries in and Les Dodds, our pilot was also staying there with the Super Cub aircraft, doing a little local flying for the people of the community.

Fritz had brought home a little caribou roast that the local people had given him. Apparently, the caribou was out swimming across the lake and they went out and caught it and drowned it. This is in the middle of July and hot weather. Fritz announced we were going to have caribou steaks for dinner (lunch) and started cutting up the roast and cooking in a flying pan. I fixed the table and opened a can of beans, and went over to see how the meat was doing. I lifted the lid off the frying pan and they were sizzling okay but the top of the meat was covered with white maggots, just crawling around. I called Fritz to come and have a look and he said "Oh, that's okay just turn them over they will be really tender." Well my desire to eat caribou meat just vanished and I had a lot of beans. I never mentioned to Wink or Les as Fritz figured it was okay, and actually nobody was and worse off for eating it. Life in the north, go with the flow, I guess, and I will be returning to Selkirk for my next meal, at any rate.

I came to work one morning to find that Maloney was missing on a trip from God's River Lodge. I guess that he had arrangements with the Ruminski Bros. to pick up a couple of mechanics and bring them south after they had finished repairing the light plant. I started calling around on the telephone to see if there was any news of him. A fisherman and resident of Victoria Beach could see an aircraft out on the lake near Ironwood Point and he called the R.C.M. Police in Beausejour, their closest detachment. Lake Winnipeg was actually breaking up with open leads and shifting ice, so it was very dangerous out there. Then a report came in that there were men on the ice, not far from the plane, and they wanted to know if I could fly there and pick them up from the ice, by landing in an open lead. The winds were gusting to 52 miles an hour and we had a Super Cub on floats, but it was a risky venture to say the least. But I am sure Maloney would do the same for me. Just as I was getting ready to leave, word came in that the men were moving and some ice flows had come to-gether allowing them to get closer to shore. The fisherman watching with field glasses from his house seemed to think they were going to make it. The police were at the scene and a small boat would no doubt help. I got the story from Maloney later and it went like this – He took off from God's River late in the day heading south and climbed up on top because of the low ceiling. This aircraft had ADF and gyro, etc in it as it had been an old instrument trainer at the flying club, and he did not mind being on top. After a couple of hours he dropped through and found that he was over Bisset but he knew that he had to land someplace before he got to Selkirk because he had roll on wheel-skis and the wheels had to be cranked down into place, manually, before landing on the runway as there was no snow.(Fly-light type) He elected to land out on Lake Winnipeg, away from shore, as the ice should be stronger out there. The ice had candled and was starting to move around because of a strong north wind, as well, it was dark. The aircraft went through on one side and then the other, but they were able to salvage the suitcases. I am not sure if they turned the ELT on. (Emergency Locator) They had to spend the night out on an ice flow, which was drifting in the wind. The only thing they had for shelter was an open suitcase that they all tried to get behind, and a few extra clothes. To say they were cold is an understatement. They prayed and sang hymns as they thought for sure it was their last night ever. In the morning they could see shore and if they could only get to the next ice flow, and then possibly there was a way to get to shore. It was quite far, but Jack tied a rope around his waist and then took a run and a leap and did not make it. The other two fellows pulled him back onto the original ice pan. Now, for sure, he was cold and wet, but you got to know the guy and he sure is not a quitter. The wind switched a little to the north-west and pushed the ice pan they were on towards shore, still about a mile out but going in the right direction. Who says Prayers do not work. Testing the ice and they went and taking their time, they made it to within hollering distance of the crew who had assembled onshore, with a boat. The last hundred yards or so the boat brought them in. They were mighty thankful. Dory, one of the mechanics, said "Good, now I will be able to spend my cheque" He had a cheque over $900.00 on him, and he went straight to the Gimli Hotel to re-live his night on the ice. Being a bachelor I guess it was allowed, most of his friends were around the hotel.

At the hangar, we welded a couple of loops on a ten gallon drum and painted it orange. Jack went out with a helicopter and attached the drum to the lifting rings on the aircraft with cable. There was no helicopter around big enough to lift it and Jack figured he could get it onto a barge in open water. We were wrong with the drum; it should have been a stout post that would bend over with the ice movement instead of getting under the drum and forcing it off the cable or breaking it. We lost the aircraft and it is still out there. Jack got a horrible cold and he seemed to have a chest condition for the rest of his days. He was a fine man and a heck of a good piano and accordion player.

Again, I guess we were looking at the Trade-a-plane, and got an interest in a Maule Rocket. According to their advertizing they were a four place and took off like a Super Cub and the price at the time was around $15, 000.00, also it was adaptable to floats and skis. Bob and I decided to go down to the factory in Jackson, Michigan and we flew a Super Cub down and back to Selkirk. We were impressed enough to tell other people about it and eventually sold one to a tourist camp operator in Ontario. A tourist camp on Moar Lake, that was first started by Ken Leishman, the infamous bank robber, was eventually taken over by a group of people who had connections to the daily newspaper business in Winnipeg. We were doing a certain amount of flying for them and the manager, who finally took the business over, showed an interest in buying a Maule on floats. So the manager and I flew down to the factory, and he liked what he saw, so bought it paying by cheque once we had it imported to Canada. Then we bought and had it mounted on a set of floats.

We enjoyed flying for this tourist camp and met a lot of nice people, even the one that got a fish hook implanted in the top of his bald head by another fisherman standing too close to him and casting dangerously. We cut the fishing line and he put a cap on and we flew to Selkirk and had the doctor take the hook out. A real doctor.

Reminds me of a fishing hook story I was told from another camp, one in Ontario. Two fishermen and a guide were out in a boat away from the camp on Manitou Lake. One fisherman was basically casting from the boat towards shore and the other was busy sorting out the hooks in his fishing tackle box. He had some hooks spread out on his partner's seat while he re-arranged his box. The casting fisherman decided to sit down and as he had been facing the other direction did not think twice about sitting on his seat. A treble hook implanted in his rear end and then the hollering started. The guilty one cut away his partner's pants and attempted to work the hook out but it hurt and he jumped and another part of the treble hook ended up in the fisherman/doctor's finger. The guide had enough of this and started the motor and head for camp. A float-plane was at the dock and they loaded up in it, mind you standing, and went to Dryden to the doctor, about 20 minutes away. It was an uncomfortable walk from the float-plane base to the doctor's office, about two blocks away, and just as uncomfortable taking the hook out. I don't know if they still fish to-gether or not.

There were a lot of good pilots around flying fish with twin Beech aircraft on floats, and they had two Barkley-Grow aircraft, which looked

Beech on skis

Old faithful, Cessna 180

Picture of Beech 18 on floats at the dock

like a twin Beech but was more solid. Some of the pilots were Jim Hoglander, Ralph Birch, Matt Kirby, Ted Coates and Rudy Schonert, and others.

There were at least two Canso flying boats and I had the pleasure of being co-pilot on one or two occasions. Other aircraft turned up when a good purchase was made and they included two Huskies and a Howard on floats. I was asked to learn about the Howard so I could demonstrate it to a potential buyer. So I got in and flew it, but I found that you had to be going about 90 MPH to get off the water, and then it flew about 110 or 115 MPH. Not a good aircraft on floats, but I learned that Howard Hughes built it to go in air races, and it was fast on wheels.

One guy I was checking out on floats just about done me in, when he tried to pull the aircraft out of the water before it was ready, and the right wing stalled and we just about hit the water. I checked an air force guy out on a Norseman, and he had been flying Otters all the time, and I had not been in an Otter. Coming to the water on the Red River, he had the nose down too much and I had to reach over and pull the control back quickly and add power, no control wheel on my side. With a Norseman, you have to pull back until you can hardly see the horizon. We went to the dock and he got in his car and left and I went to the can and checked my shorts. I checked out a guy by the name of Fred G. on the Norseman, and he was an older guy with a brand new commercial license, came from Montreal. He wanted to change careers and maybe impress his wife, but he seemed Okay after the regulation number of hours. He went north and I heard that in about 3 weeks or a month, he was pushing weather, I believe, in a late snow storm and crashed and got killed.

Another fellow, Tage, was checking out a pilot out in a Norseman, owned by Northland Fish, and flying a canoe into a new lake to fish and he banked too close to the water, and a gust of wind caught him and they crashed in the lake. Tage was a good swimmer, he had the life jacket, but he gave it to the other guy and left to swim to shore because it was so cold, early in the spring and the other guy did not make it. The owner of Northland Fish and I went north and picked up the body at the nursing station, as he had been recovered. He was wrapped up in a tarp and we put him under the bench seat in Northland"s Beech and Jimmy Hoglander flew us to Selkirk. The body was shipped back to Ottawa. I was firmly convinced that the best new pilots were about 22 years of age, with the necessary qualifications and as much pilot time as possible. I checked out a lot of guys in my time and a lot of them went on to a career with the airlines and did well.

A humorous incident happened at the Burntwood base in Thompson when a pilot had a trip flying the new teachers out to their respective schools to start the year term. Of course, it is good to know the teachers and nurses because sometimes they invite you in for coffee, and it is nice to break the monotony of just sitting and waiting for your passengers as they conduct their business in the various communities. This particular pilot wanted to make an impression, and combed his hair and checked his appearance in the mirror before he went out to fly the Otter that had the passengers already seated. He smiled at everyone and took his place in the pilot's seat. He hit the starter switch; nothing happened, again, nothing happened, Oh Yeah, the Master switch, now it started. So turned around and smiled at everyone. He warmed it up for a few minutes and then applied more power expecting to go out in the river. The Otter did not move, oh yeah, it is still tied to the dock, so he signaled to the dock hand to cut her loose. Then he moved out in the river, and as he was checking to see if things were well behind, he ran into the tail of a Cessna 180 that was parked in front of him. He shut her down and the current took him out further in the river, and into a back eddy that kept turning him around and around until the dock hand came out in a boat and rescued him. On shore again, the pilot went up to the bunk house and got his suitcase and put it in his car and left. He knew that he did not have an option.

Bellanca Skyrocket after mishap in Bloodvein

Showing damaged Wing Tip

Mishaps, accidents, whatever you want to call them are part of the northern flying scene and you just have to re-group and carry on, hopefully learning from the past experience. Flying in the north got better when the air strips were put into each community and we did not have to rely on unimproved landing conditions. One mishap we had was utterly ridicules, in that the pilot was going to overnight in Bloodvein at our little trading post, only he did not have any beer to treat the manager. He was flying the Bellanca Skyrocket on skis and went to Berens River, 45 miles away, to the Inn and bought a dozen beer, late in the evening, too late. On his landing back in Bloodvein, late, he struck a large rock with the ski and knocked it off and the machine came down on its wing, damaging it. Mechanics were taken north from Selkirk and they salvaged the airplane and had it flown back to base. The wing was made of wood, glue and fabric, and by much work, the men in the hangar patched it up and got it flying again. I think that was the end of that pilot.

From Mountie to Bush Pilot

Family Holiday going to Saskatchewan

Nice little boys

Chapter 20

On the home front, we had purchased a house, and two boys were born, John in 1962 and Michael in 1965. They would probably see many trips to the base. It was not always work, and we had a flying trip west, probably to Whitewood, Saskatchewan, to visit with Family.

Okay, Dad, Take me for a ride

Our Super cub and Les made a trip north and on the return picked up a Grey Nun at Berens River who had to get out due to family problems. This was the spring of the year and we were on straight skis, wheel skis are expensive and do not work very well in deep snow, not enough load bearing area to be advantageous. Les had to land on Fey's slough, north of Selkirk, instead of the strip, but he landed alongside the bush close to the river, and low and behold there was an underground spring weakening the ice and he went into it. They both got wet but the Super Cub wings held it up and we got it out the next morning. The Grey Nun was taken to our house and got dried out and recovered from her dunking, with some hot tea that my wife provided. You know, I always landed on the other side of the slough, close to where I park the plane, or it could have been me. I never landed on that side close to the river, probably because sometimes the trees that were there play tricks with the wind and give you unexpected drops in your landing pattern.

We were always interested in getting salvage jobs on aircraft from the insurance company and we knew one adjustor particularly well. A Cessna 180 pilot was taking off with a load on the ice at Wunnamin Lake and he hit a foot path that was just packed snow, turned to ice, and the landing gear leg broke, along with all the other things that happen – bent propeller, wing and tail damage, and of course, the pilot's pride. We bid on it, got the bid, and went to Pickle Lake, by train to Dryden, Ontario first, and then by bus, taking the necessary tools and parts to fix it, or so we hoped, as we had not seen it. When we got to Pickle Lake, the air charter outfit people told us, you had better fix it, because this is our last day on the ice, as there was a lot of water on the ice. Bob and I got some pretty good co-operation from the Hudson Bay Manager, and were able to use his shed to fix the tail and store our stuff, also got a radio to the listen to the Stanley Cup playoffs. The repairs took a day or so, but soon we were ready to go. We got full tanks of gas and took off, staying away from the foot paths. The trim was a little off and we had to push forward on the wheel all the way home, some 350 miles. A landing place was selected at Riverton, on the ice, out from Sandy Bar as we were still on straight skis. Next day, we got the wheels and made a 3 point take off early in the morning when the frost was still in the ice. The aircraft was repaired by the capable crew in the hangar and returned to the owner.

One of our pilots was slated to take three people out for a fishing trip to Shining Falls, near Little Grand Rapids for the day. They left early in the day and around 2:00 p.m., I heard that they were in Little Grand Rapids without the plane, came by canoe. What happened was, Paul, landed up above the rapids, instead of below, and the current caught him and took the plane into the rapids, actually Shining Falls, which has a drop of 20 feet, overall. They clambered out of the floatplane and into the water and made it to shore. We usually landed below the rapids, even in a marsh area, and taxed through a little fast water to the shoreline below the rapids. I guess I should have given better instructions, but I do not think I was even there when he left.

Not a good place to park an airplane

So we had our own salvage job to do, because the insurance company would not pay us off, saying we cannot help it where you park your plane. We flew out and had Ezra Bouchie meet us at Shining Falls with his boat. We wanted to put a good nylon line across the river and then work a rubber boat downstream to the plane and tie onto it. Sounded good, and Ezra made it across the river, bouncing off a few rocks as he went. We secured the ends of the nylon rope to stout trees and then put another good rope in an appropriate spot to be able to work ourselves downstream to the plane. We asked for volunteers to get in the little rubber boat and one new pilot looking for a job decided to have a go at it. As he played out the rope and the little boat got a bouncing in the rapids, he had a change of heart, and by the time he got back to the cross rope, his eyes were as big as saucers. That destroyed plan one, back to the drawing board.

But we had lots of flying to do, and did not get back until late in the fall. We thought if the insurance company won't pay us out we will give it a little nudge with a rope and a barrel and it will go over the rapids, and then they will pay us. That did not work; maybe it is a good thing. We then decided to get a diver, even though he did not have to go under water. Gill came out with us, put on lead bottom shoes and a lead belt and walked out to the plane. He had no air tanks on and went under once but the water had gone down a lot since the spring, next thing I knew he was on the plane and pumping the floats out, and it shifted a bit. He secured heavy lines on the floats and we had a winch on the far shore and pulled it into that shore, which was closer. Then we had to cut a portage trail down the island to the water for an airplane. It was starting to get real late fall but the pontoons got a patch-up job, just to get it out of there and we tried once but it was too late, the ice had started to form. It was February before we could get at it again; we were too busy around Christmas time.

We chipped out the ice from the pontoons and tried to take off on the snow but could not get enough speed to fly, the snow was too deep. One more try coming up. On a good weekend, weather wise, we took two airplanes on skis, and plenty of help, plus a snow machine, and we packed a good runway and got all set up to have our final go at it. I tried it after I got the aircraft engine warmed up and it went to the left into the deep snow. No amount of right rudder could hold it. One more trick so all the wise ones decided. I got the floatplane facing the right direction, Jack Maloney, in another Cessna 180, created wind ahead of me, and a big aircraft (550HP engine) with poles in front of the skis, sat at the side of the runway with the throttle on full and I got the biggest lift into the air that I ever want. I circled a few times and I could see everyone, cheering, and waving their hats. The engine was running a bit rough, so I leaned it out a bit and then it ran better. Then I headed towards Selkirk and about the mouth of the Red River the oil gauge started to flicker, meaning it needed oil. I guess the rings where seized up from sitting in the moisture all summer. I could not land and pushed it another 10 minutes and landed on floats on the grass strip and was thankful it was finally back at home.

The boys in the hanger did a top overhaul on the engine and fixed the floats, and it was back in service for the spring. So much for our favorite fishing hole, someone put a tourist camp above the falls, and someone else put one below, about 5 miles below. Paul went on to be a Captain for Air Canada, and I met him at the Doctor's office one day, when we were getting our pilot medicals, and I said "Paul, were are you based now" He said " I fly out of Toronto, to Rome and Frankfurt." No doubt with fairly big aircraft, I thought he said 747, but I am not sure Air Canada had 747's. No more bush flying for that chap, and a very nice fellow. If he only knew how much in lost revenue and rescue work he caused us, and I estimate it to be in the range of $30,000.00.

We had a phone call, out of the blue, from a Mr. Bond in Nova Scotia and he wanted a aircraft on skis to take part in the seal hunt. He told us about the potential to make money and it was being done by other carriers, some private, and after checking Mr. Bond out (No, he was not the James Bond in 007) we decided to go. Ron went and it was at Tignish, P.E.I., and a day and a half to get there and met the sealers. I was on the phone with Ron every time I could get hold of him and he said everything was good. The sealers were good hard working people and Mr. Bond seemed okay, just keep track of the money and make certain it is in the bank. Some of the rules were; Do not leave your sealers out on the ice overnight and of course, be careful. Smooth areas on the sea ice is where the sealers would gather the pelts and you would throw in as many pelts as you thought you could get off safely with and bring them back to shore, gas up, and go again, until just before dark and then get your men off the ice. You do not want them to be caught out there in a storm. There was lots of blood around and everything got covered with it, so you had to wash the aircraft down once and awhile. The sealers used a stick to hit the pup on the head and the hook on the stick was used to haul two or three pelts at a time to the plane. They worked fast, and the pilot had to work fast. Sometimes the sea ice would be glassy and sometimes kind of rough and the mileage to and from would be about 20 to 30 miles. Anyway, in three and one-half days, Ron made $7000.00 and that was pretty good money back then. I think Ron met a friend down there, and maybe he has some relations.

Seal hunters on the ice near the herd, of near 500,000 animals

Ron Michaluk on the ice, off Tignish, P.E.I.

When he came back he brought two seal pups with him, and one had a broken flipper. One day only, flying in a Super Cub from Montreal to Selkirk, pretty good. I did not know what to feed those pups, who were changing color, from white to a motley grey. I tried sardines, but that did not work. I called the Assiniboine Park officials, to see if they could keep them. They had no facilities to handle them but said that Calgary did, and we got them ready and put them on a Air Canada schedule flight to Calgary and they were more than happy to have them.

We went again the following year to the Magellan Islands and this time we worked directly with the seal hunters, and our take was 65 %, but we had a problem with the Cessna 180 and it sat for a week out on the ice. Bill Brady was the pilot in the other aircraft and now he is retired after being Captain on a 737 for Canadian Air Lines. Bill became a helicopter pilot after he flew for us and this took him away from home a lot. His wife did not like this, and told him to quit. He said okay, no more, but he got a call stating he was needed in Jenpeg, Manitoba and did not tell his wife. He got out of bed quietly and went to Winnipeg and the twin Otter was waiting for him on the taxiway. His wife missed his presence in bed and knew what was up, so she went Winnipeg in her little car, saw the Otter starting to taxi out and pulled in front of it and stopped the plane, and had a discussion. I do not know the outcome of that discussion but I understand he has a different wife. Bill was certainly a good pilot and from 35,000 feet over that northeast country in a 737, he could pick out the little lakes he used to land on and call me on my hand held VHF radio and tell me where he was.

Ron started his own airline out of Island lake area and was doing well, until he too met with some bad weather on a flight in an Aztec from Island Lake to St. Andrews, and both he and his wife were killed, in an accident at Long Lake, just off the Berens River. His son took over the airlines, and he too pushed the envelope, and had an accident at Little Grand Rapids on a medivac flight and did not survive.

I used to deal with Peter Chenkie who owned Selkirk Motor Products and sold me at least three new trucks. His son, Gord, was around the garage, sweeping the floor and doing things as his Dad requested, but Gord seemed to think he was destined for better things. He talked about flying and how to get started and I told him what I did. I said I will try and get you a job at St. Andrews Airways and I did. Gord started and I went to see him a week or so later, and there he was "sweeping the hangar floor and loading aircraft for trips." Maybe it was the young fellows around and the comradeship he found, but Gord had a plan to get his commercial pilot's license, and he did over time.

This next part may be a little out of place, as it happened a few years later, but Peter is gone now and I am sure he would not mind. I used to take Peter and his wife, Ella, out fishing at a shack we had on Eardley Lake. A couple of bunks in there, a cement floor and a place to cook and sometimes other people around in tents, but there were boats there and the fishing was good. It was nick-named the "Sugar Shack" We had a pair of Bilko's pants (Walter Skrupski) hung from a pole for a windsock, that's when he was overweight. Everyone had fun and they did not know for sure when they were going to be picked up and how, but they always got out. I had occasion to fly an Otter, hauling lumber out of Berens River, for a school to be built in Paungassi and on the return I stopped in and picked up Peter and Ella, and other fishermen that they knew. As we were flying along, and Peter was sitting the co-pilot's seat he noticed something hanging from above that looked like a communication device, a microphone, maybe. He got it down and it had a flexible hose or wire attached and decided he could make an announcement to the passengers in the rear. I said "Go Ahead" and he is telling them what lake they are over and when they would be landing in Berens River. They are all laughing but I am sure they could not hear him and it was sometime later that we told Peter that was a pilot's urinal or relief tube. Anyway, back to Gord, and he did get flying, got his commercial license, went to Island Lake and built up experience and maybe had a mishap up there, but that I do not know much about.

When Peter was getting low, a bunch of people were around talking and visiting and Gord was asked when he went to the North West Territories. "Well, he said, I'll tell you what happened" I was flying the Twin Otter out of St. Andrews and they sent me to Red Lake to fly about a million pounds of freight to Pikangikum. Ken Leishman had arranged for this freight and hired us to do it. Ken was the famous gold robber who was now the manager of Tomahawk Airways and the President of the Chamber of Commerce; he really changed his life around. Ken lent me a truck and we were working off a dock in the bay at Red Lake. It is around 80 miles to PIK,(Pikangikum) and we were really working to get the job done. After about three weeks of steady slugging, we loaded our last trip about dark and then decided to take the night off. We went to the Red Lake Hotel and met some friends and ended up closing the place up. The people we met had gone home earlier, taking a case of beer with them. It seems as though we were not done celebrating, and as we knew where our friends lived we went to their house. The lights were out and even loud knocking did not get them up. So, I backed Leishman"s truck across the road, put it in 4 wheel, then popped the clutch and went across the road, through the fence and up the steps and when I hit the door it did not take too long for the lights to come on. I think we got some beer but no welcoming committee. The fence belonged to Norman Heglund, owner of Sabourin Airways, and probably the house too. Leishman turned up at my hotel room next morning and he was crying as he kicked me out of town. We made our last trip, and then went back to St. Andrews. Shortly after I was called into the Boss's office and he had got a complaint about me, and the outcome was, I was suspended for 3 weeks. I figured I would use the time and go up to Yellowknife and see what was going on up there. It was a wise move and I never looked back." Gord worked for North West Territorial Airlines, and flew Hercules aircraft in many parts of the world and I am sure could fill a book of all his experiences. Now he has over 28,000 flying hours and is flying a Boeing 737 on Schedule flights for First Air. He also looks in great shape, an Arnold Schwarzenegger physique, and he figures he will be still flying when he is 108. I don't know if all his muscles have developed like his upper torso but I understand that he does a lot of hiking in the mountains, as well. His love life has finally meshed and this truly a success story. He forgot to tell me about the bottle of Crown Royal that he borrowed from the boss's office desk in St. Andrews and filled it with tea when he returned it. His complete story of his early flying experiences are following in this book.

Gord and supplies for the pilot's cabin

Chapter 21

I got a call from Marine Transport, our neighbors down the road, and they said and insurance adjustor was coming from Cincinnati, Ohio the next day and they wanted to go to Playgreen Lake. I knew that the tug boat, Teddy, had sunk in the area when it was overrun by the barge, trying to make a turn in the channel. I also heard that the Captain was in the washroom at the time and came out standing in a foot of water on deck. They arranged for another barge to take two cranes up and get ready to lift it, as they had it located. There were two passengers and we landed in Playgreen Lake near where the tug had gone down and tied up to the barge. After coffee and conversation on board the other tug, they said they were ready to lift it, the sunken tug. They had a cable attached to the bollards on the bow and one on the stern, only as they began to lift the rear cable came off. The guy that put the cables on was no longer there, so Captain Roberts said "A hundred dollars for anyone who will go down and attach the cable". No one seemed to offer, so I said "I'll go" I went and took off my shoes and jacket; it was overcast and 55 degrees Celsius, not a good day for a swim. I dove off the barge, which was sitting about 12 feet out of the water, and swam over to a pike pole the men had stuck into a rubber tire on the stern of the boat. All I had to do was go hand over hand down the pike pole and put the cable loop back on the bollard. I suppose it was down 12 to 15 feet of water but I got it on and came back and climbed back on the barge and then to the washroom of the other tug, which was parked on the other side. I wanted to have a hot shower as it was cold. Half way through my shower, it came off again. They were not being careful enough on tightening the cable to pull. I went in again and did my thing, and back for another shower. This time it worked and they lifted the tug up and placed it on the barge. The Teddy tug was smaller, about 60 feet, I presume. We took off and headed for Selkirk and I could feel a cold coming on. The Captain came through with his $100.00 and I think I spent most of it in the Legion trying to kill my cold with single malt scotch. That did not work either.

Another time, the company lost a barge in a big sea in the north end of the lake and the Captain and I went to look for it. We found it off Marchand Point, near Poplar River, drifted up on shore. The Captain called the tug on my radio and told him where it was and to come as soon as possible. That meant we were going to have to spend the night at George's Island and the wind was blowing from the south and I could not get into the harbour. Therefore, I landed on the north side and pulled up on the sandy beach, but if the wind changed to the north overnight, we would be in trouble. So then I decided to pull it right out of the water by manpower only, as there were no tractors on the island. We cut some green poles and pulled the floatplane out of the water and in the morning, sure enough the wind had changed, but I got out of there early and went in the harbour. Finally, the tug arrived and because of the wind change, it was able to pull the barge off the sand. Then we were able to go home.

George Island lighthouse and keepers quarters

George's Island is the only manned light house on Lake Winnipeg and it is 11 miles off shore in the north end of Lake Winnipeg. It has seven beautiful beaches and lots of nice trees, at lot of Birch. There is a commercial fishing station there, mostly for the whitefish boats to work out of, and return their catch to the packing station. There is also Little George's to the west about 2 miles, but it is rocky and mostly a hangout for the birds, gulls and cormorants.

Willard Olson was the light house keeper, and, as lighthouse keepers can be, he was a little eccentric. I had taken some contractors in there to do some renovating on the house, etc. and I went to visit Willard. I knocked on the front door, Willard opened it and at the time the contractor was walking by and saw a snake in the grass. He had a stick with him and he flipped the snake at me, I stepped back and the snake went in Willard's front room. He thought I had thrown the snake in and he was very mad. It took a long time for him to get over that, and of course, the contractor disappeared around the corner, having a good laugh.

Many years ago, when the Keenora was operating, a fellow went over the side during the night and could not be found. A few days later, he drifted up on George's and as no one claimed him, he was buried on the island. Someone came out later, and put up an iron cross at his grave site.

Later on Willard asked me to bring his mail out to him. Again, the wind was blowing too hard and I could not land so I dropped the mail to him in a mail bag. A few days later, he asked me again on the radio, if I would bring his mail. I told him about dropping it before, so he went looking for it. Low and behold, it was up on the top of the tallest tree, near his house. Willard thought it was a bird's nest. He climbed the tree and had to have a stick to get the bag loose.

Another time, Willard called and said his little dog had a swollen neck and he feared poison. He really liked his little Sheltie dog and he asked me to come and get him and fly him to Anderson Veterinary in Winnipeg. That is over 400 miles return, but he wanted it, so I took the dog in. They said the dog had got a bone in his throat and it caused a swelling but in a few days the dog died. Willard stayed on the island for a few more years and then the Federal Government automated the light and he was no longer required. A few years later, Willard died, and I was at his funeral and luncheon at the Legion in Selkirk. George's Island is where they should have buried him, and then the lone grave would have company.

I spent a lot of time working with Marine Transport. I took them to Big Grand Rapids when they first bid on the Hydro contract and they were successful and got the contract. Later, they were bidding on the 8 mile channel and the 2 mile channel at the north end of Lake Winnipeg, and we went again. I showed them were to put a temporary airstrip at the 8 mile channel. They then decided to cut pulpwood on Playgreen Lake so they would have a back haul for their barges. I flew the men in and out on their time off.

Harry Gooseheads trappers Cabin

They also started a pulpwood operation of the Pigeon River, near Berens River. Harry Goosehead, was their semi-official caretaker, as he lived nearby, and one fall, Alvin Tyndal, the camp manager, left three drums (45's) of gas at the camp and told Harry wanted to have that when they came back. So Harry, knowing there would be lots of hunters and trappers around, took the gas out of the red gas drums and put it in black diesel fuel drums. No one touched it, and some people thought Harry was a little behind the times.

Three of us decided to go hunting caribou at the camp on Playgreen Lake, as the season was open in that area. We stayed at the camp and flew south on the lake in the morning. The herd of about 20 was inland a mile or so and two of the fellows were going to walk in on a south east direction and I was to go around and make sure they did not go further away. My snowshoes were tied on the wing strut of the ski-equipped aircraft and as I had been in slush the day before, the lamp wick ties were frozen tight and I had a heck of a time getting them off. I thought I was going to be late getting in front of the caribou. The area was muskeg with a few small spruce trees and the snow was deep. I finally got into the area, and they were starting to get a little nervous. I was pretty close up to them and the other two guys were walking fast towards them, one short guy and one tall guy. I figured they were going to run, so I started shooting and dropped four of them, one for each of us and one for Alvin, at the camp, who also had a license. We dressed them and went to camp to get Alvin and a bombardier to pick up the carcasses. We had a good meal at the camp that evening and then Alvin said it was time to go.

He was leaving with his snow machine and jumper (sleigh) and taking a couple of animals, along with Victor, one of the hunters, across the lake, about 20 miles, to his half ton truck. It was dark and they were getting ready on the ice, down the bank from the camp. Pretty soon, Victor, came walking back in to the cook house, he said "Alvin left without me" A couple of hours later, Alvin came back. He thought Victor was on the sleigh. Alvin had a habit of not looking back and had gone right across the lake to the truck. They decided to go again and were going to drive in the truck all night, to Selkirk. This time Victor made sure he was on the sleigh. Half way across the lake, Victor was uncomfortable in his position, and was in the act of shifting, when they hit a drift, and Victor flew out of the sleigh. Knowing Alvin would not stop and his hollering would not be heard, he grabbed the handle of the jumper and slowly, pulled himself back on the sleigh. He was right; Alvin did not stop until they got to the other side. We flew south in the morning, after an enjoyable hunt.

As I mentioned before, we had the Super Cub set up for a third seat and I liked to use it for hunting, as it was fairly reasonable to fly, and had lots of power. I took a couple of guys from Selkirk, the milkman and his friend, who were both from the same church. We went to the area around Manigatogan and were going to walk through the bush near a certain point, and push out to the lake. On landing in the river, I found I had hit some slush, but we went and did our hunt and when we came back it was getting late and time to get out of there. I loaded the men and tried to take off, but slush again and lots of it. This time I could not get out, the skis were covered with snow and ice, we pushed and pulled and run the engine hard but to no avail. It was getting dark and all we could do was leave the aircraft there, and walk into Manigatogan. It had to be about 6 miles and our boots were covered with slush and we were pretty well pooped. (Played out) As well, the temperature had dropped and it was about 25 below, and that's before Trudeau's time, so it was Fahrenheit. We started to walk and a mile took us forever, it seemed, and my religious friends wanted to go in the bush, light a fire, and pray for someone to come and find us. I was having none of that, and had to use some pretty strong words to keep them moving. We kept plugging along and pretty soon we saw a light in the community and that gave us hope and encouragement. I am sure it was around 8:00 p.m. when we finally got to a house and got a ride down to the hotel. We stayed overnight, and the next day got a ride into Selkirk. I came back in a couple of days to get the aircraft out, after the frost froze some of the slush.

I took a load of groceries into the trading post at Little Grand, by this time Wink was selling pretty good and I got a good buy on a large amount of flour in 20 lbs sacks, so we always had freight to go north. In fact it was a carload, like in trains. At Little Grand, they told me to go to Paungassi as there was a woman in labour who needed to get to the hospital. The missionary told me that I had better pick up a nurse in Little Grand and the lady in question was very close to giving birth. I took his advice and then headed south, and around Manigatogan, the nurse started to move around quite a bit in the back and asked "How much Longer" She said to "Hurry" - How do you get an aircraft to go faster, it is not like a car, the best way to go faster was to start descending, but we weren't there yet. To please her, I added a bit of throttle. More movement in the back, and finally we went over the mouth of the Winnipeg River. We were headed for the Pine Falls Hospital, and I would land on the outskirts of town, by the nearest place to get a phone and call the hospital. This I did and the Doctor said he would come in a taxi. I went back to the aircraft to see what I could do and she said "Here, take this little guy to the hospital" He had no clothes, so I took off my parka (it was new too) and wrapped him up in it and ran to the closest road. The Doctor had just arrived, so I got in the taxi and went to the Pine Falls Hospital. Then I went back and helped carry the woman to the ambulance that had been dispatched and the nurse went along as well. She had done a fine job, sure a good job I had an engine tent in the back, and you know, I don't even know the woman's name or what she called the little guy, but I think Cessna would have been appropriate.

I made a deal to trade a Stinson and some money for a Seabee. The Seabee arrived and the Stinson left, with the seller, a pilot. I did not like flying the Seabee and returned it and said "No deal". But my Stinson did not get home, so I located it in Sudbury and went for it. I flew it home in the winter time on wheels, no heat to speak of. I landed in Armstrong, Ontario and went to the hotel. I got a room on the second floor and was lying on the bed about 5:00 p.m., reading a book and a mouse poked up through the covers. I swatted at him but missed. Then I took the bed apart to find him, and I found a whole nest in the box spring part. I complained to the management, but they said no more rooms, so late that evening I took my mattress out in the hall and slept on the floor. I left before daylight, and took a taxi to the airport, it was 40 below zero. An Air Force Otter was getting the Herman Nelson treatment, and I guess they felt sorry for me, and put three heat tubes in the Stinson to warm it up, even in the cabin. I made it the rest of the way home, hitting a bit of weather in the Whiteshell area, but determined to push through. I froze left side of my foot, closest to the cabin exterior and was glad to get the trip over with.

Three aircraft were coming back from Island Lake on a Sunday, and by this time we had some new pilots. The weather was bad around Selkirk but had cleared up in the northern area. About Grand Beach the snow was coming down really heavy, and two of the aircraft followed the shore into the strip, but the third one came straight across the lake towards the mouth of the Red River. It did not make it and wiped out in a whiteout on the lake. The passenger got shook up pretty good and spent some time in the hospital. This was our worst mishap so far, and in the forty years that I had anything to do with aircraft, this one was the most serious. The pilot was not too bad but decided to quit flying after that and became a ski instructor in B.C., his home province. We cleaned up the mess on the ice and had more work to do in the hangar, repairing.

What I liked about this flying business is the interesting people that you are able to meet and the cross-section of jobs that people have, one day a Doctor, next a trapper, then a fisherman, then a well off businessman, trades people and that, with the odd bit of excitement, which was about to happen very soon.

I had just flown a load of government people into Island Lake and was on the way back south, empty, flying at 4000 feet, and I even pulled out a Readers Digest to see if there were any good stories in it, when bang, and the engine stopped. There were a few lakes around and being on floats it should not be a problem. One particular lake below was big enough, but had a few rocks poking up here and there. I was not about to change my mind about the lake, and on the way down I called on my HF radio. I picked up Al Nelson, who was coming south from Ilford, and at 10,000 feet, with a good tail wind. He was reluctant to lose his height and the tail wind but he agreed to stop and pick me up and I told him the lake I was on. I landed okay and drifted back into shore on a bit of a sand beach. I tied up to the trees and by the time I had finished all this I heard the Cessna 180 of Al's coming. I think I was an hour late getting home, and it could have been two or three days.

We found a new engine and my friend, Doug Grant, came out with me to put it in. We also got hold of and AME (mechanic) that we knew to sign out the engine. His name was Al, and from his reputation the rest of his name was Al-cohol. We flew this load in with a Norseman and unloaded the engine onto a big tractor tube that we blew up with a manual pump and placed it on piece of plywood and floated it to shore. The Norseman left as the pilot had other work to do. It was either get the engine put in or sit and wait to get picked up. We got three stout poles out of the bush and placed them over the engine area of the aircraft, and took the damaged engine out. Then we stripped the components off the old engine and the engine mount and built up the new engine. Now it was ready to mount but that would be done the next day and we made camp and ate. Somebody flew over us and checked on our progress. After an early morning start, the engine was hung and now the propeller and cowling. When I tried to start it, the battery was dead. So, the prop was spun by hand and fortunately, it started. We ran it for quite awhile but people were anxious to leave. So we shut it off and turned the aircraft out facing the lake, tied it to shore and this time the battery was charged up enough to start. We left most of the tools, engine, there as it could be picked up later when there was room. An uneventful trip south and I did not even pick up the Readers Digest.

I was in Little Grand, and Wink was telling me about the two bear cubs the kids were playing with, well teasing. They had them in a garbage burning barrel, and were poking sticks at them, and making them wicked. I went to see them and they were all dirty in the burnt barrel and I told the kids I was going to take them. They did not seem to mind, someone had already shot their mother, and I figured it would just be a matter of time before these little guys succumbed to the punishment they were taking. It was a chore to get them out of the barrel, their claws and teeth were very sharp, but I eventually got them into a bag and flew them south with me. They were transferred to a large box and given some water and food. They were not friendly by any stretch of the imagination. Then I built them a bit of a pen under the basement stairs at home. No one was too impressed with that arrangement, even the bears. News spread and the game warden got hold of me, and asked me about the bears. I told him, but he said it was illegal to have wild animals in captivity. So I turned them over to him and he (Mr. Tommy Schindler) got a home for them in the Zoo and told me later that one was going to Germany.

Every year in Selkirk, there is a celebration, with lots of water sports. Water skiing was one of them, Dr. Ian Reid, was front and centre in this sport. He said; give me a ride behind the aircraft, on floats, of course. We found an area that we not too busy with boats, and attached a ski rope to the pontoons. I had a little difficulty getting it up on the step, but when I did we were going along about 70 MPH, and was just about ready to lift off and stay close to the water, and I could feel that he let go. On talking to him, he said it was the fastest he had ever gone or ever wanted to go. Sprays, just like pellets, were hitting him in the face and he could not keep his eyes open.

We spent the rest of the day giving aircraft rides out of the park and lots of people came. Sure had to keep your eyes open for boats, as there was lots of boat traffic.

When it quieted down, I decided to fly under the Selkirk Bridge, the lift bridge. I think Wilfred Helgason came with me. I went under the centre, first taxing slowly, and then on the step, and then in full flight. This was with a Cessna 180 and I do not think it has been done since, but don't try it.

We had the job of taking a politician around his constituencies by aircraft and flying low over the town and cutting the engine and hollering through a bull horn "Vote for Joe Slogan". He was doing the talking and one day he got mixed up and said "Vote for Slow Jogan" I doubt very much if the powers to be would let us do this now. One day we got the Conservatives and NDP arm wrestling in a coffee house to see who should win, all in fun.

My two sons, John and Michael, would come with me to the base and this particular day I was driving a Dodge Station Wagon, with a push button selector for the automatic transmission. I parked on the top of the hill by the office, and those little guys, pushed the selector to take it out of park and went down the hill towards the water. Fortunately, they stopped or hit something before they went in the water.

Our family dog was a little Terrier, Mickey, I think was its name, and if he got left at home he would hitch hike to the base. He would be running along the side of the road, and someone would pick him up and drop him at the base. That is where he wanted to be and so did I.

One morning, about 6:00 a.m., I got up and went out to my truck, an International Traveall parked in my driveway, and a guy sat up in the back seat. It was Harry Goosehead, a trapper, from the Pigeon River area; he did not want to miss his ride home and had slept there overnight.

The other company starting up in Selkirk was Marine Transport and they had a mandate to haul freight to Big Grand Rapids, which is at the outlet of the Saskatchewan River, on the north end of Lake Winnipeg for the Manitoba Hydro as they were going to build a hydro electric dam at the location. This was to be a four year project and promised to make us pretty busy. It would appear that we were getting established in what I would call an interesting business but it also had its ups and downs. One of those downs was to occur during the coldest part of the winter.

Frank was fishing at God's Lake Narrows and I was slated to take a load of trade goods, groceries, etc. in to him. For some reason or another, Doug Grant, was along. Doug was an aircraft mechanic during the war and still did a little to help, along with his car garage in town. I think he went into God's Narrows with someone else and was going to come back with me. After the Cessna 180 was warmed up in 48 below zero weather, Doug and I took off empty (No load) and were headed south over Beaverhill Lake and the oil cooler froze up. The procedure was to land and cover the engine up with the tarp and in a short time it would thaw out. The landing was made in a fairly good area but the ski leg broke and went under the aircraft and punched through the bottom and narrowly missed Doug, and of course the aircraft came down on the wing and a little damage to the tail feathers as well. Good job we had our HF radio and we were picked up without too much delay. I believe that I probably cracked something the night before with my load on, and the landing area in God's Narrows on the ice was none too smooth. No one ever got around to packing the runway and taking the wind drifts out. We went back to Selkirk and got the necessary parts to fix the aircraft, a new leg, and tools, hydraulic jacks, etc. and in a few days went back and fixed the aircraft and flew it out. Fortunately, the repairs could be fixed in a shop in a couple of weeks with the right guys working on it. We did have a couple of very good sheet metal people, Ed Kirton and Ian MacKenzie. Both of these guys were tops in their business.

Chapter 22

This seemed to be around the time that I made a very serious mistake. There was a fish monger around who thought that he controlled the north. Anyone who tried to move in on a lake for commercial fishing was met by untold difficulties. A fellow by the name of Carl started a fish station at Island Lake, (Gardenhill) and just as soon as he could, the fish monger started another station right beside him. We had a piece of land in Selkirk for a float plane base and he bought a piece of land similar to ours just a quarter of a mile away. All I could hear from my friends, those who knew him, was he (the fish monger) was going to put us out of business. I even got this from his right hand man, Percy and he should have known his thoughts. It certainly made me concerned, as if I did not have enough to worry about.

One day, towards spring, he called me on the phone, and said "Let us have a talk". I went into his office and by the time I had left he had convinced me to sell half of my business to him for some worthless land up north and the promise of co-operating to-gether to make a bigger and better seaplane base and air service. There was some merit to the proposal if he had of put a little money in to expand and buy more aircraft, etc. He already had numerous aircraft, larger than the ones we had, for hauling fish up north and the fact that he had a contract to haul a lot of Hudson Bay freight on his back hauls. We also had a bit of a conflict, in that, we had a small store in Little Grand which was in direct conflict with the Bay. That probably did not fit with him as well. We also had a better seaplane base, nice sloping bank out of the water, up and across the road to a runway that a person could take practically any aircraft off on. His piece of land north of us, had a high bank and no room to maneuver on. He may have put in a couple of docks but did not offer any money to help with the operation or even help pay the taxes. I did get a good aircraft mechanic from him, but we still paid the wages. I guess he wanted to see that he had some control. So all I could do was ignore him, and go on my merry way. Lord knows, I could make enough mistakes on my own, but now as I look back that was one of the biggest ones.

I had a trip to Big Grand Rapids, late in the day, with some badly needed parts and the only Cessna 180 around was a green one, that my so called partner had parked at our dock. I loaded it up and went to the Hydro site, Big Grand, on a quick trip. They gave me mail to take back and said I should stop at McNamara's camp, the road building contractor, and pick up their mail to. All the camps were in touch with each other by two-way radio. I did, but it made me a little extra late. Southbound now and following the trail that was going to be a road north, Number 6 highway, and actually dark, not getting dark, I heard a bang coming from the engine area. Then I could see a white glow and it had something to do with the cowling door. It seemed to be running okay, so I continued on and landed at Selkirk in about an hour. I found that the cowling door had come partly open and the white glow was the exhaust lighting up the inside of the cowling door. Nothing that a better catch would not fix but it sure got my interest.

I heard about a larger aircraft for sale in Thunder Bay, one that O.J. Weiben had been flying with his air service. It was a Bellanca Skyrocket on floats, and with wheel and ski gear. This aircraft had the same horse power as a Norseman and could carry the same load. The Norseman that I found were about $25,000.00 and this one was only $10,000.00. Mind you, there would probably be some repairs that we have to do, but it seemed like a good way to get started. There were only 16 Bellanca Skyrockets made, and that was by Northwest Industries in Edmonton, Alta. This one was registered CF-DOF, and in the end I spent a lot of time in it, over 2,000 hours total. We nick-named it the "Yellow Bird" as that song came out about that time and it was yellow with red piping. The one problem with it was once you put a load of freight in it, you had to crawl through the window to get into the pilots seat. I guess a good reason to stay slender. There were 48 square feet of lift in the wing struts, but I never did like the gas indicators on each side, under the wings. Boiler type gauges, and the rougher the air, the harder to tell how much gas you had. Anyway, it was moored to a buoy out in a bay on Lake Superior and the chief pilot of the outfit that was selling it took me out to it and came with me to a tourist camp about 100 miles west from Thunder Bay, where the owner was. I guess that was my check-out. We tied up at the dock and went inside the office to complete the paper work and pay of course, and get insurance on the aircraft. When we had this completed, I was ready to leave but the aircraft seemed to be sitting a bit lower in the water on the pilot's side, in fact I think that it was getting ready to sink. No wonder they were keeping me in the office, feeding me coffee, and making conversation.

They consented to pump the floats with an electric pump on the dock but said I should be ready to take off when it was done. I could see the reason for the cheap price now. I phoned the base in Selkirk and told them to clear any aircraft away from the ramp because I would be taxing right in, no delays. I took off from that lake and I could see a steady stream of water coming out from behind the float and then it stopped. With full tanks of gas I should be able to make it home, God willing and the west wind does not come up. It took the boys in the hangar a week or so to fix the floats and check it over. It flew like a Norseman and I am sure would do us well, seemed to use a lot of oil though, we always took a 5 gallon pail of oil on all trips. I was told it was because of the chrome cylinders, but it purred along good until the engine was time expired, or maybe until we had enough money to buy a new engine. After a few 400 mile return trips, I was getting used to it. The flap leaver was over head and of course, this took some adjusting to.

One Saturday, I had a trip in the morning and I knew that this was beer day for the boys in the basement of the Lord Selkirk Hotel. The usual crowd was there when I came walking in about 3:00 p.m.. Our crew, Balcaens plumbing men and Goodbrandson's truck drivers etc. There were 18 guys around a couple of tables, as I was to find out. As I came down the stairs someone said "Jack, how do you put the flaps on in the Bellanca" Not thinking, I just showed them, with a circling motion above my head, but that also caught the eye of the bartender, (who they had already clued in) and it cost me beer for 18 guys.

A call came in one evening, I think it was already dark, and they said a fellow cut himself in the arm and was bleeding profusely. The call was from Poplar River, about 200 miles north of Selkirk. Apparently, a fellow, Berens was his last name, was drinking and he went home and the door was locked. So he smashed the porch window to get in and cut a vein on the inside of his arm and it was just pumping blood out. There was no landing strip in Poplar River at the time, floats only. We knew that Poplar River had numerous reefs in the landing area but we got assurances that the local fishermen would light a fire on each of these rocks, about 3 of them, to guide us. Jack Maloney said he would take the trip, in our Cessna 180. The night was black, no moon, but the fires were out on the rocks as promised and a safe landing was made. It was getting after midnight when they got loaded and a nurse came along to tend to the injured person. On the trip south the patient, got delirious or something and kicked and bent the throttle control. Jack said the next time he was going to crown him with a pipe wrench. They made it back okay and he made a safe landing on the river, and the patient was transferred to the hospital. Sometime, near early morning, he passed away, probably from losing so much blood. We took him in a coffin back to Poplar River, in the daylight.

One evening, a contractor from the Hydro site came to me and said he had to get to Big Grand right away. He had a problem that had to be fixed before morning. He was not kidding, he was serious. So we gassed up the Super cub on floats, and took off heading north, in the dark. I really was reluctant to go but he was a good customer. It was not too bad going north until we passed the last town and then no more street lights. Also, the smoke that was lingering around from forest fires did not help the situation. I turned around and went back to Selkirk, arriving about midnight. We just slept in the caboose near the dock, and took off again about 5:00 a.m., still dark. An hour north, we hit a bit of rain, and I had to land. I knew we were near the Mantago Marsh so I let down into it, with ducks flying out from under my wings. We waited an hour and then took off again. We made it to Big Grand before 8:00 am, and he was able to catch his crew and correct the problem before the inspectors turned up on site.

We acquired a Mark IV Norseman for $14,800.00 and it was registered CF-BFU and Manley, our most experienced pilot, used to fly it for us. He nick-named it Born Friggin Ugly and it was probably because of the small floats it had on. They were 6470's and most Norseman had the bigger floats, maybe 7850's or something similar. We used to heel this aircraft up on shore on the mud bank, load it and then Manley would take off. Not that he was really overloaded but the small floats made it sit pretty low in the water. Once you got used to it, then it felt better.

Manley took a trip into Little Grand and was going to overnight there. About dark, someone came and told Manley he was needed at the nursing station. He went over and found that a man had been cut with an axe in the foot and needed better medical attention than they could provide there. He loaded the man in the Norseman and headed south. Around Manigatogan, the weather turned bad, it was fall and snow was pretty heavy. He turned back and by the time he worked his way out of the snow, on needle and ball, and not much else, it cleared and he recognized Poplar River. Then he worked his way down the shore to Berens River, where there was a hospital. Berens is about 48 miles south of Poplar River. The man was put in the hospital and next morning his flight was continued. We spent some anxious time waiting for him in Selkirk as we knew he was on the way but did not hear from him until he landed in Berens River. He said he could not get through on the radio. Manley was a good pilot and grew up with bush flying in his veins from his days in North-western Ontario.

That winter we found a Mark V Norseman, in Prince Albert, CF-OBD and I believe that Rusty Myers, from Fort Frances, Ontario, owned it but had it leased out. It was sitting floats, on the airfield in Prince Albert. We made a deal and Manley, went and picked it up. Took off on the packed snow and landed at Selkirk on the ice in the river, 400 miles straight through, with a slight tail wind. That was a good machine, on big floats, and we did a lot of work with it.

Another trip occurred in the spring when the strip had no snow on it and we were on skis. A call came in from the Little Grand nursing station and they had got a call from the missionary, Henry Neufeld, at Paungassi saying a fellow was badly burnt. A trapper had walked in, some 30 air miles, and said that Willie Crow had an epileptic fit and ended up in the camp fire at Lewis Lake. He was still there and needed medical attention.

We got the Super Cub ready and went down the runway with shovels and threw snow onto the strip from the fence line and that mixed with water, was enough for the Cub to get off.

Again, Jack Maloney took the trip and he found the ice at Lewis Lake okay, which we suspected. Willie, because of his epilepsy, had spent a lot of time in the St. Boniface Hospital, and talked pretty good English. He was now about 12 years old. Sometime in the afternoon, Jack came back and made a landing in the field next to our place, in a slough about a foot deep, of slushy water. He carried Willie from the Cub to dry land and then we got him into the hospital in Winnipeg. The Cub was rescued a day or two later.

The commercial fishermen were all getting to their stations in the north end of the lake and one particular one was in poor shape. I got a call to go to Montreal Point, and pick up a man that was coming out of the DT's. I think that Booth Fisheries had phoned us regarding this. Montreal Point is on the east side of Lake Winnipeg, in the north end, not much shelter there for a landing, with only a fish station. I got in because the wind was not too strong, and picked up a fellow, who was obviously very distraught.(DT's) Then he decided to act up. So I tied his arms behind him and strapped him down in the back on the floor. This is the way he stayed, all the way in, two hours. Actually, he fell asleep after awhile and I did not have to watch him as much.

Actually a similar type incident happened at Rabbit Point, when a chap had an epileptic seizure and they phoned to get him out. The pilot took a helper with him and they tied poor old Felix in the back seat and had a crescent wrench handy to give him a bonk on the head if he acted up. We had a store in Bloodvein and this chap used to come into the store all the time. He never gave us any trouble and I liked him, too bad he had a problem.

The tractor trains that travelled in the north, taking the yearly supplies to the Hudson Bay Posts, and other places, were having a tough time because it was starting to melt. They got as far as Big Sandy Lake and could not carry on into Round Lake. We went up there with 3 aircraft on skis, and flew 45 gallon drums of gas and other freight to Round Lake until it was all finished. There was about six inches of water on top of the ice by the time we had finished. When the water goes off the ice that is when you got to start worrying, because the water has drained through the ice, making it weak, and the ice candles. The aircraft were then flown to the Winnipeg Beach area and landed and parked behind the old break-water that was there. Then I would fly them to Selkirk on skis on the muddy strip with a bit of water, but I always put two fish boxes full of sand in the far back of the cargo area, to keep the tail down when landing. Someone else tried this and they turned the aircraft over and it caught on fire and burned. No boxes of sand in there, but it was not my aircraft.

The tractor trains did not get the beer into Ma Kemps, Log Cabin Inn, in Berens River, one spring; maybe the order was not put in soon enough. There was like, 12 hundred cases of beer and we had it delivered to the end of the road and stored. I found two guys; Harry Shead was one, who liked beer, to look after it and help load the Cessna 180. There is no way these two guys would let anyone steal beer from them, they were responsible. I flew all this in for the rate of .06 cents a lbs, 1000 lbs. per trip, 45 miles, or 90 miles return trip. In those days, 45 cents per mile was considered standard rate.

I was headed to Little Grand with a load of groceries, and it started to snow steady and I could not make it. Being that it was fairly late, I decided to stop at a trapper's cabin on Sasaginnigak Lake. I knew they were there, as I had flown them in. I put the aircraft up on poles and was making ready to put the Iosol heater in the engine compartment. I was in the cabin getting the heater ready, filled it, and lit it on top, and it flared up a bit. One fellow watching jumped back and hit the can full of fuel (Iosol) and it spilled on the floor. It was not long before the whole cabin was on fire. We all got outside and used shovels and snow to put out the fire, but not before it had burnt all the moss out from between the poles. The moss was used for chinking and it was very dry. We saved the heater and pretty well everything else, but we could see the stars through the walls that night, and it got quite cold.

I was getting familiar with the "Yellow Bird" but I had not been on a real long trip with it to see what the fuel consumption would be, could it be as much as five hours. Now I had my chance, I was going to Sachigo Lake, close to 375 miles one way with plumbing material. Full tanks and 2-5 gallon pails of oil and away I went. Sachigo is just behind a row of hills, called the Sachigo Hills, in North-western Ontario. The lake itself is not clear water, and hard to spot any reefs unless the wind is blowing. I delivered my load to a new nursing station site and left for home. All the time I am flying, I was trying to steady the aircraft so I could watch those fuel gauges; it is hard to look at both of them at the same time. Around Stout Lake, on the Berens River system, it appeared as though I would need gas. I was hoping to make Bisset, another 90 miles. I knew some trapper-fisherman on Stout Lake so I head for their little island and cabin. No-one home, but they had an aluminum boat and a 5 h.p. motor but very little gas. Some white gas for lamps and used oil was found, and I mixed it to-gether and started out for a cabin that I knew of at the outlet of the river. It belonged to a chap that left his plane at our place, and he told me he always had spare gas. All I knew about the lake was that I had to go west, and my first attempt ended up in a bay. Later, I seemed to be making progress but it was starting to get dark. Then, as I was watching the shore line, I seemed to be going faster. I had to be in the river, so I went to shore. Then I could hear the rapids flowing, just ahead. Good job I stopped. ! I decided to camp there, and I got my sleeping bag and went to sleep on the rock shoreline. About 4:00 am, the entire mosquito population in Northern Ontario found me, so I slide down in the bag for another hour. When I got up, I could see the cabin, it was tucked away behind a point in a little bay. I went back and got a ten gallon drum of gas, which I knew I would have to replace as soon as possible. Then back to the Bellanca and put it in. My next move was to fly directly to Moar Lake, along the river and get more gas as I knew they had some. We were flying their guests into the tourist camp there. So I got enough gas for the trip to Selkirk and a load of empty propane tanks that needed to go south. Now I had an idea how much gas endurance I had in the "Yellow Bird".

A Volkswagen camper pulled up in the yard at the base one morning and a chap got out and said he was looking for a job. He had a commercial license and said his name was Leopold Herman, obviously very German. We told him there was a possibility, but he would have to work around the base for awhile, until we got to know him and see what he could do. It turned out that he could fly okay and even got tried out on a larger aircraft. We had a fish contract out of Ilford, Manitoba, and would be taking some commercial fishermen north to Etawney Lake and others. He was a little too brave in bad weather, especially seeing as he was unfamiliar with the area. The fishermen complained about him and we had no choice but to change his jobs. So he went to Gillam to help load aircraft. He left shortly after and went to Flin Flon, where he put an aircraft up in the bush on landing. Next, he went to Alberta, and then to Yellowknife. He was flying a twin Beech for an outfit from Edmonton, and he was doing a medivac from Cambridge Bay and went down on the tundra and spent

32 days before they found him. He was supposed to have eaten part of the dead bodies from his plane crash, only we now know his name as Martin Hartwell, but I understand that he is doing quite well now, still in the same area.

Every morning, as the calls came, and some from previous days, we made a list for the pilots of things to do and who to pick up and deliver, sometimes it was on foolscap paper, which meant it was going to be a long day. Bill Brady would do it all in the Super Cub, not stopping to socialize or have coffee, and would never overnight up north, but he would come home even in the dark. Two little lights on the river, one red and one green, would let us know Bill was back. He was a good pilot that kept things to-gether, especially the aircraft.

I was slated to go to Berens and Poplar River and inland, someplace, and at the last minute before leaving a fellow (Jacob) turned up that wanted to go to Marine Transport's pulp camp on the Pigeon River. That was okay and he got on board. He had obviously done a bit of drinking in town and had his fill. I had to stop at Black Island with some parts for the silica sand plant and when I taxied into shore and stopped, Jacob, got out the rear door to relieve himself. He missed the first step and landed on his chest across the pontoon and then fell in the water. He scrambled out and got back in the plane, after he had done his business.

Later on in the day, as I was coming home, I got a call from Marine Transport to stop at the Pigeon River and pick up a guy that was hurt. I landed and there was Jacob, standing on the dock all bent over, he was in pain. After getting to Selkirk, it was learned that he had broken three ribs when he fell out of the plane at Black Island. It took awhile for that to heal before he could go back to work.

I dabbled a bit in a pulpwood operation in both Bloodein, and

Poplar River, but it was more to get the people of the area something to do in winter. Also, they dealt with us in our little trading post in each community. Marine Transport hauled the pulpwood to Pine Falls Paper Mill during the summer months. I even sold some small pigs and chickens to Berens River to try and make farmers out of the people. Wilson Boulanger brought a small heifer calf home to Berens in his boat, that I provided, and they had it for a number of years. The people of the area were very nice, and the Priests and Grey Nuns at the R.C. Mission where particularly friendly.

I was fortunate to meet some of the old trappers of the area, and one of these was Oscar Lindokken. One day I was in Deer Lake were Oscar had a trading post and he was the only man I ever heard of that had the Hudson Bay Co. convinced that he was two tough in competition and they pulled back and said do not come to Sandy Lake and we will leave you alone in Deer Lake. They then closed their store in Deer Lake. I heard that while he and a partner were trapping in an area near the Ontario/Manitoba border that they were out checking their traps someone came into their cabin and stole the furs they had ready for sale. The rivers were just open in the spring, and they figured it was guys from Berens River. Oscar and his partner left immediately for Berens River, and paddled all day and night and in two days they got there and walked into the store, and caught the culprit in the act of selling their fur to the manager. He got nick-named "Kingwoggy" (Native Language) after that and is "Wolverine" which is a quick, clever animal. The day I was in Deer Lake, he had a pet moose in the yard and he had a fence up on the step of his house, to stop the moose from walking into the front room, or going through the screen door.

The Schutzee family, the brothers at least, went north and had a trading post in Poplar River. They also trapped and I believe taught school.

I met them one summer when they were making a tour of the area and had migrated out to the west coast to live.

There was a Withawick fellow who was trapping on Whiskey-jack Lake and he got sick and died, and as his partners could not carry him out over the portages and the ground was too frozen to bury him, they left him at the cabin. There was not too much of him left by the time they got back. His son is running a service station in Berens River and doing a fine job.

There was another chap from Rabbit Point who used to go with a horse, and his daughter to Gilchrest Lake to trap, which is north-east of Poplar River. He was checked by the game warden and other officials, maybe about having his daughter out of school, and he took exception to their intrusion and shot up the aircraft they came in on. They came back with the police and it all ended peacefully.

Then there was Joe Alix, who traded first at Little Grand and then in Berens River. He married an English nurse and he was Lebanese. The Hudson Bay would probably have liked to see him out of the area as he was tough competition. The R.C.M. Police constable that was stationed in Berens River told me that Joe would invite him over to share a bottle of rum and get him to help count his money, as he was thinking of taking a trip. Joe had his money in a satchel and he exclusively liked having $5.00 bills. He said they counted 85,000 dollars, and that was back in the late 1940's. His son took over the store, and they moved it over to the mainland, from the Island he was on, and it is still there, and flourishing with the grandson running it.

I heard a story about Buster Whiteway, a trapper and fisherman, and a voyageur, taking Hudson Bay freight up to Little Grand, and was picked up by the R.C.M. Police for a misdemeanor. He was being taken by plane to Norway House to serve time in jail, and the plane crashed near Warren's Landing, and Buster saved the life of the Policeman, who was injured. I am sure they took this into consideration in his time served.

The R.C.M.P. constable in Berens, used to like his beer and the United Church Minister was against anyone drinking, so he complained to the head office in Winnipeg about Doug. A Staff-Sergeant came out to investigate the matter. He caught me on the ice, near my plane, and I knew the fellow, from my previous years in the force. He said "You don't think the Constable here would have consumed thirty cases of beer in a month" I replied "that's an awful lot of beer, I doubt it." Case closed, and he went back to Winnipeg.

Ma Kemp at 83 was still quite lively, dancing with the local storekeeper, John Alix

Ma Kemp, had the Log Cabin Inn in Berens River, and her and her husband came to Berens River in about 1932 to build a tourist camp. He passed away a few years later and she carried on and was over 96 when she died. In the winter, the main log lodge was not open and she had a building for winter quarters. There was no water supply other than a 45 gallon drum with snow and ice in it by the wood stove to melt and be used for washing, coffee and cooking. A chap named Paul came down stairs in the morning to get coffee. He was sitting at the kitchen table drinking it and one of the young boys, her grandson, came and got up on bench and urinated in the water barrel. I guess Paul quit drinking his coffee.

One night I was spending it in Berens River and was told there was a party at Freddie and Helens across the bay, at their old house, so I decided to go and caught a ride with other people going. Lots of beer was being consumed and later on in the evening, I thought it time to leave as I was supposed to have a bed at the Hudson Bay man's house. No one was going to give me a ride at this point, and it was well after midnight, so I grabbed a canoe and paddled my way across the bay. I went to the Bay house and there were people lying all over the place, including the bed I was supposed to have. There was a barge in at the dock close by, and I knew the people that owned it pretty good, so I went down to see if I could find a bed in one of the trailers that were on board. There was lots of equipment on board the barge and a pile of hay bales. As I walked around the bales, there was a white horse standing there. I guess it was going further north with the equipment, but I tell you, it sure did give me a start. I found a bed in one of the trailers and spent the night, and went flying early in the morning.

Chapter 23

I had a trip in the "Yellow Bird", a Bellanca Skyrocket, DOF, to take a load of freight into Sachigo Lake, Ontario from Selkirk, about 350 miles. I had been there before and landed on the lake out in front of the nursing station that the crew was working on. The water in the lake was dirty, making it impossible to see any rocks. Sure enough, I hit one pretty good and damaged the bottom of the pontoon. I tied up at the dock and of course the fellows that wanted to get south, really wanted to go and I told them my problem and they said "Let's fix it". I said "Okay" but I really wish that someone would mark the spot where the rock is. A native fellow that lived there said "Everyone here knows where it is". We took off the float cover, and the water was really pouring in from the bottom. We got a whole bunch of rags, bed sheets, and anything we could find and put them in the bottom of the float, packed them down, and pumped the water out of the float. Then we put some boards on top of our temporary fix and jammed them solid with some cut to size two by fours. It seemed to slow down the leak. Then we pumped again and everyone that was going south (seven) piled in and we took off and certainly stayed away from the rock. Almost 300 miles later we arrived in Riverton and everyone was happy. Next day, in Selkirk, we had a float to repair, which was done by our competent crew.

We had plans to have a Grey Cup party at the hangar in Selkirk and borrowed a large TV and got some beer. We were watching the game and everyone got hungry. I had shot a large buck and it was in the garage next door frozen, but not skinned, and we decided to have deer steaks. So we got the chain saw out and cut steaks off a hind leg, and as the steak was cooking we peeled of the skin. The steak was good and the party grew and was a ritual every year.

Some friends of mine and me, were over industrious, and decided to make some moonshine, it was not a good idea, and we were caught and paid a fine. End of story.

There was talk of an awful lot of work this summer season, and we had a chance to lease another Norseman with a big door. It was a Mark VI and had an aluminum skin and was registered CF-UUD. Now we had a total of 12 aircraft and a crew of pilots, mechanics and helpers, and office staff of around 20 people and for sure we had better keep the ball rolling. It looked like a good season with Tourism, Hydro work, and local traffic, in all areas of the north-east that we travelled in. We had completed a fairly big job in the hangar of stripping the paint off a twin-beech on floats for Fred Chuipka of Lynn Lake and seemed to have a lot of work lined up. Our last financial statement showed a gross of over $600,000.00 with a substantial profit, and it looked like a better year coming up. I also had an offer from an accountant who was familiar with our books to take a more active interest by being a principal, and this was a deal I should have taken, as we needed someone like that, as I was away flying most of the time.

In the meantime, I had in mind purchasing another Bellanca Skyrocket in La Toque, Quebec for $10, 000.00 and this took place on the May 24th weekend. I came back from business in Winnipeg late on Friday night, and the Bank Manager, Dave told me that he would wait for me at the bank. He did and Okayed the cheque for the aircraft. I left the next morning on Air Canada for Montreal. Then I went to Grandmere, Quebec on the bus and finally to La Toque where I found out that my French was not good enough to even order breakfast, so I just pointed on the menu and got something to eat.

The owners from the airbase came to pick me up and take me to the lake where the Bellanca was tied up to the dock. Visually, the aircraft seemed alright, a non-descript grey color and this time I paid special attention to the floats for leaks. It had a 3 bladed prop and a Pratt and Whitney 550 HP engine, the same that a Norseman had. It had a fair amount of time left on the engine before overhaul and the log books were up to date as far as inspections were concerned. I noticed that it had no flaps and some of them were made that way by the manufacturer, North West Industries, of Edmonton, Alberta. A total of sixteen of these particular aircraft were made and now I was going to own two of them. There was also the Bellanca Pacemaker and the larger Air Bus, which has been restored and is now in the aviation museum. I turned it around at the dock, warmed it up and took off straight out from the dock. I circled and did a low pass and then landed and taxied back to the dock. By this time there was a bunch of guys standing on the dock and everyone talking at once, in French. One guy told me in broken English that not one of their pilots used the smaller lake for takeoff; they all taxied through the gap to the larger lake and then took off. They seemed to think that I knew how to fly the Bellanca and I guess I should because I had two thousand plus hours in DOF and now DCE. I think that Mr. Weiben would be the only one to have more time than that and he always thought that the Bellanca could carry more and fly faster than the Norseman. Soon we had the paper work finished, and the insurance in place, money changed hands, and I was gassed up and on my way west.

I passed through Kapuskasing and then on to Geraldton. I had a 45 gallon drum of gas and a pump on board to stretch my travel legs out. In Geraldton I landed and taxied into a dock and a little boy was there, and he said his name was Mike McGill. I remembered a Brian McGill from earlier times, flying a red Norseman north of Manitogan, doing something with prospectors. I think the Norseman was from Ontario, maybe Rusty Myers aircraft. I asked for his dad, as we were always looking for pilots and he had good experience, plus he had an aero mechanics license. After I gassed up I continued on my way. I think I slept overnight someplace along the way but I do not remember were, probably just pulled into shore and rolled out my sleeping bag. I got the Bellanca home and had it checked over by the maintenance guys. Within a few days I was checking Ken Hiscock out on the plane and then after some 35 hours of local trips, he was ready for a summer of float flying.

Chapter 24

Then I had a visit from the principals of a freighting outfit in the north that wanted and needed to get involved with a flying company to help them clear up a problem that was caused by an earlier than usual break-up of the roads in the north by mild weather. They wanted to buy in and had some big plans of a larger aircraft. I will call them slew-foot and liver lips, and as you may guess it turned out to be a bad deal all around. I found out that the freight in question was in Ilford, Manitoba and that it was destined for the communities of Oxford House and God's Narrows, primarily. There was a lot of housing material, and that included window casings in a large dimension. It was estimated that there was close to a million and a half pounds. Of course, this freight had to be hauled in at a reasonable rate, as I do not think the recipients would want to pay too much. I also found out that one of the principals, not present, had a drinking problem and it was partly because of him that delays occurred and the weather also took its toll. They wanted to be partners and painted a fairly rosy picture of what the future would present in business. I already had a partner that I wanted to get rid of and through this process; it seemed like the way to do it. Liver lips was the accountant and he wanted to have a look at the books. They wanted me to sign an option to purchase and it would look like this – all the assets would be valued, by me and by an estimator that they would appoint. The two prices of an item, may be a couple of thousand dollars apart, that's if you took the true value, and then that figure would be split down the middle and that is the figure that would be used. It seemed reasonable at the time. In fact, they were pulling a fast one. Example; A Norseman, Mark IV, that we had bought for $15,000.00 was priced by them at $7500.00. There was no consideration for appreciation in value of the aircraft, which there certainly was, because in time, this aircraft would be worth $100,000.00 or more, as long as it was maintained properly. This went on and on, and I had signed an option to sell, and I always thought that I had an option to back out, but that was not the case and of course, my lawyer was too busy drinking to get his thought's to-gether and I was busy flying as well, and the situation just got worse for me.. They wanted me to suggest a larger type aircraft that could be incorporated into the business that would be able to haul the freight in question and be an asset to the business, keeping in mind the poor airstrips that would be used.

One of the principals of the freighting company and I flew to St. Louis, Missouri to look at a Shorts Skyvan as the dealer was located there. It was a high wing with a boxy appearance, turbo propeller engines, and a tailgate that opened up enough to put a Volkswagen Bus inside. The cost was $600,000.00 and this appeared to be the first choice. One was available in Ireland almost immediately. So as to have an option, we went to see a Bushmaster 2000, that was being manufactured in Los Angeles. There we found an aircraft mechanic that spent time and money on rebuilding the Ford Tri-motor into what he called the Bush Master 2000. The mechanic, Savard, located a Ford Tri-motor fuselage in the rural area of Mexico, and believe it or not, there was a Mexican family living in the aircraft. He bought it from them and had it transported to L.A. and started copying the frame and wings. In all, he made four frames and then equipped one with three Pratt and Whitney, 450 HP engines, the Beaver engine, Yes, one in the nose and one on each wing. Of course, it was a tail dragger, and had pretty big main gear tires. The instruments were all installed and the outside was covered with a corrugated type of aluminum. The wing root was very thick and this gave it good lift, but not too much speed. The door on the side was fairly small and this was not good. However, did it ever take off in a short distance, 300 feet, with the three engines working, and he said you could shut down the centre engine in cruise to save fuel. It sure looked like a good bush aircraft but he did not have any others made and the company that was helping him with the finances, was being sold, that being Wittaker Tandem Gear Co.

So we went back to Selkirk and ordered a Skyvan with a $100,000.00 down payment and terms on the balance. The cheque was signed by me, as President of the company. Little did I know how things would change? We had only been gone for five days but there seemed to be a little animosity between our men (mechanics and pilots) and their crew, which were the son of the owner and the bookkeeper. The next item to look after was hiring competent pilots to fly the Skyvan and get them trained. We were lucky enough to get Eddie Johnson, a well known bush pilot with a lot of experience on different types and our mechanic, Bob, and they would be the beginning of a team to get the Skyvan mobile and in Canada ready to work. The next pilot to be hired was Brian McGill, who was the pilot from Geraldton, Ontario, father of the son, Mike that I met on the dock when I was passing through with the Bellanca on floats. I did not go to Ireland as I was too busy with the business that was already built up. The three of them went to the Short's Bros. Factory in Ireland for a three week course on flying and repairing a Shorts Skyvan, which could now carry the Canadian Registration of CF-YQY. Although the payload was not great it was a boxy aircraft and the rear door opened so you could drive a Volkswagen Van inside. This was ideal for some of the loads that we would be required to carry, such as 5 by 6 windows in the frames, and a lot of dimensional lumber. Readymade cupboards, bed box spring and mattress's and cook stoves and plywood, will be part of the fill in the spaces area with heavy items such as roofing material and cement for the foundation making the loads maximum at practically all times. All this, of course had to be tied down so as not to shift in flight.

Skyvan ready for more work

Experienced Pilots – Ed Johnson and Brian McGill

Passengers loading on Skyvan

Skyvan – CF-YQY

Part of the overall package was to have two experienced pilots come over to Canada and fly with our pilots to teach them the technical, as well as the practical aspects of flying this aircraft. The most important was loading, and flying from unimproved land strips, gravel, sand, and mud. We found out that Trans-Air from Winnipeg had also bought one of these aircraft, and the race was on to see which one got on Canadian soil first. It turned out we were ahead in this game, and maybe spoiled some of their advertizing and hoop-a-la because we made it across the pond first, via Iceland, Greenland, and then into the Northern Part of Canada. Two check pilots arrived and after a time in Selkirk the whole crew was moved into Ilford, Manitoba, to start hauling the winter freight that the transportation company had left behind due to an early spring. The airstrip at Ilford was fairly short and sand, and the one at Oxford House was newly constructed and turned to mud on wet days. God's Narrow's airstrip was probably the best one. Loads were organized at the airstrip in Ilford and the haul began.

One particular trip was noteworthy, in that the load was nine forty-five gallon drums of diesel fuel weighing about 400 lbs. each. The load was placed and tied down a little too far forward and when it was time to rotate; they were a little close to the end of the strip. They went through the tops of the poplar trees at the end of the runway and took a few branches with them. The Irish pilot who was in command on this leg exclaimed "Fooking Lovely", and when they got to Oxford House they took a few branches out from the undercarriage. This was the beginning of a full fledged haul which would last for two or three months.

Meanwhile, back in Selkirk at the base, it looked good as we were busy, but a few items of discontent appeared, especially with having to amalgamate people from two different companies and their book keeper not having any real aviation experience, but he was now issuing and signing the cheques. There was a transition taking place up north, in that, communities with a suitable place to build a land airstrip were getting them as soon as equipment could be moved in, or in some cases, use the equipment, cats with dozers, that were already at the community, i.e. Berens River. As soon as the airstrip was finished at Berens River, I was the first to land on it with a Cessna 180 on wheels. To haul people and freight with a wheel plane was a lot more economical than on pontoons, and we had mostly floatplanes. I guess we had better stick with the tourist flying and communities with a big problem in getting the airstrip in use, such as Little Grand Rapids. We had a small trading post there and were starting to build a motel-type lodge for tourists. We already had four log cabins. To be in the trading business, especially the fur trading business, made it so you were in direct competition to the almighty Hudson Bay Company who had been in business since 1674. My new partners depended on the Hudson Bay freight as that was the bulk of their winter hauling. Airplanes flew the freight to the H.B.C. stores in the summer but they could not compete with the tractor train hauling and later, truck hauling on the winter roads. I asked the head guy of the winter freighting how he came up with his rates, and he said "Just stay a couple of cents below any of the aircraft rates". Of course they were making money. We had little stores in , Poplar River, Little Grand Rapids, and were starting one at St.Therese Point, Island Lake. We already had the land acquired and logs out of the bush, and peeled to build an 'A' Frame structure, to have living quarters on top floor and store in the bottom area.

These are the logs we cut and peeled to build an "A" frame in St. Therese, Island Lake, and the pilot that took over, has a store and 3 or 4 airplanes now

I had already travelled the south area buying furs and was getting good enough at it that I was not losing any money and this was the bargaining tool that the local people had to be able to buy their groceries, etc. One thing that we had to be careful to not sell in the store was raisins, beans or yeast, as these items were the ingredients for moose milk, a powerful alcoholic concoction. I had several different fellows working in the stores and two or three were fellows who just could not adjust after the war. One was a sniper and was he ever a good shot. I saw him shoot a coyote running across the ice at quarter of a mile. I had two brothers from a large family, Wink and Jake Wheeler, in different stores, about 60 miles apart. I also had Billy Lewis and he good boxer, and won some titles for fighting in his division in the army. Boy, was he ever quick with his hands. The carpenter putting up the log structure, 'A Frame' was Siggi Austfjord, and he would have got it done too, had things gone well. All this competition to the H.B.Stores did not sit too well with my new partners, and I did not ask them to come in, although I sure did want to get rid of the 'fish monger'. Things were happening fast, and I was away flying a lot. I sure did need a member of the family, to look after the office procedures and billing, like a couple of other air charter outfits, who had their wives to run the business, when they were away. A situation arose, with family life, which will not be discussed here or any place, for that matter and I ended up 'jumping over the traces" and if you don't know that that means, talk to someone older than you, preferably a farmer. New friendships were formed, some for awhile and some were short lived, at any rate it messed up things pretty good, and I thought I was doing what was necessary. I guess a good helping of humble pie would have helped, but it was difficult to make that happen. .

In the meantime relations with the new partner were stumbling to say the least, especially with the bookkeeper, and one day the owner (partner) and liver lips walked in the office and said "I was no longer President" of Selkirk Air Services Ltd. They pulled some fancy lawyer stuff with the shares and that was it. My lawyer had not drawn a sober breath for a long time, and he was no good to me. I was basically finished with everything I had done for 10 years and putting my wages back into company to build it up; it really was my whole life. I loved to fly, I liked the idea of going up north, I thought I had a good thing going with the hangar and aircraft repair work, and the sport fishing and hunting was growing, and had the store end of things to help out in the quieter times. Dealing in wild rice, commercial fishing, trading for furs, and salvaging damaged aircraft for the insurance companies, all seemed to make a good mix and keep men working in the hanger and the aircraft flying year round.

By this time I was living in a small shack at the air base, and taking my meals downtown. My only saviour was a Cessna 180 on floats that I owned and so I went north the following spring and the good people at the Roman Catholic mission in Berens River took me in and I had basically had enough of big shots that just wanted to get bigger. What had taken place with the business just devastated me, and all I wanted to do was get away. I suppose that was sometime in 1969 or 70. The freight out of Ilford was all hauled to the different communities, and as there were no plans over the summer for new work, the Skyvan was sold.

The outfit that took over had no business to speak of and with the super-duper pilot that they put in charge, they were closed up with-in the first year and the land and hanger was sold to an individual who became more interested in the maintenance part of the aircraft business and is still operating on the land that I bought to make a seaplane base. I basically took a 8-10 year sabbatical, living up north and enjoying the people and the way of life until other opportunities came along in lumbering, pulpwood, boat freighting, and some flying…and eventually a small hotel.

It was not too long before the Manitoba Government decided to open the winter road system to everyone, which was a good idea. The rates for hauling came down and it opened the roads to independent truckers. The people who lived up north were the benefactors. I have personally seen 100 trucks on the winter road east of Bloodvein, one behind the other, to get some last minute freight into the Island Lake communities. Tractor train freighting is a thing of the past now; it all goes by trucks, tankers, van, and low beds, and opened up competition to the winter road freighting outfit that came to me for help.

I heard that one of the principals involved died of cancer, and the bookkeeper and his wife were killed in a traffic accident in the United States. Too bad this did not happen before they came sniffing around to buy a business that they knew nothing about and ruined things for me. I was too gullible, I guess, but I thought I was helping them out and it would make more flying for us. I spent a lot of time and money, (Money from a lower wage I took to build up the company) to make Selkirk Air a viable business with 12 aircraft, and a number of good employees.

The love of flying has become my first love, but I did not want to move too far away from my boys, John and Michael. So ends this part of the story.

The making of an airline pilot
(Gordon Peter Chenkie)

THE CALLING SKY

GORDON PETER CHENKIE

GORDON PETER CHENKIE

Chapter 1

It's springtime 2010, being at 34000 feet on a sunny day between Rankin Inlet, Nunavut and Winnipeg is one of my favorite flights, reason being is that flying north of sixty is where most of my destinations are, but this particular route takes me over Manitoba from the northern border at Churchill straight south to Winnipeg. On a clear day in late spring is magic to me, as the snow has melted but the lakes are still frozen giving me spectacular views of my beginning, my career, my love, flying.

Our clearance from ATC is Rankin Inlet direct Churchill direct Winnipeg to maintain FL 340. Today we are grounding 400 Knots bucking a 30 Knot headwind which is what I was hoping for as it gives me a little more time to sightsee. Just south of Gillam as I look out my window I can feel the nostalgia building and it will increase as we head south. Look! I can see as far east as Kistigan, Rorke and Stull lakes and right below me is Oxford House and 'oh my God,' there are the fish camps of Knee, Touchwood and Beaverhill lakes, to name a few. There's Gods Lake and the Narrows where I tilted numerous pints with Gilbert Burton of Taylor Airways, and there as expected, coming into view is Island Lake and the three settlements of Garden Hill, St. Therese Pt. and Waasagomach. I'm just overhead the fish camp at Stevenson Lake and looking out to my left, reminiscing about the days of Island Lake brings a tear to my eye. It was thirty six years ago that I first set foot on Island Lake, (March 1974) to be exact. I went for the month as a helper on the Norseman on skis. As

I remember those fond days of the past, the emotions where profound and poignant. At that time did I ever think I was going to be an airline pilot? No. Did I ever think that I would meet so many great people, see so much of the world, and to someday get a chance to write about it? No. All I wanted to be at first was a bush pilot like the generations before me that I so admired and still do. Now here I am thirty - six years later looking down at where it all began, and I suddenly realized, where did the time go, the so precious, irreversible time.

As Island Lake passes under my wing I look ahead and can see Poplar River, Berens River, and straight ahead are the chain of lakes called Weaver, Wrong, Harrop and of course my Mom and Dad's favorite, Eardley Lake. At one hundred and sixty- five miles from Winnipeg as I look out my window almost straight down, I can see the island that Mom, Dad, Jack Clarkson, the Skupski's', Johnny Fial, Barney and many other good friends would love do much. The cabin was called the "sugar shack" with a couple of bunk beds and a cement floor, tin walls and roof, but "Boy, if those walls could talk there would be stories of good times and plenty of laughter.

It's time now to check the weather, brief the Winnipeg Control Centre regarding our approach and landing and make a PA to our wonderful passengers for their years of support. The flight attendants bring me one last coffee and pick up our meal trays, Air traffic control clears us to seven thousand feet, as we finish the pre- decent checklist and I slowly retard the thrust levers to idle, I look to my left and see Bissett where dad ran the float base for Selkirk Air, ahead is Gimli, my favorite Grand Beach, the end of the Red River and my hometown Selkirk, I realize that not only was it such a perfect day for flying and reminiscing but something so much more important, and that is, how so very, very lucky I am.

Chapter 2

I was what you consider a lucky kid. My Mom Ella and Dad Peter grew up poor. Both came from large families whose parents generation where basically work to eat and feed your children, nothing more, nothing less. My Mom and Dad were a little better off but still being raised during the depression left them with little. They never had holidays, little if any toys, no children's camps, cottages, etc. Christmas was meager and they usually had to do some sort of labour during this most, at that time, reflective season. And as for sports, Mom and Dad had a bit in school and if there was any structured sports after school it was to be had, only after the chores where completed. Mom graduated from grade twelve but she basically had to work part time to clothe and feed herself. Dad never did graduate; he was pulled out of school after grade eight. He was much needed on the farm to help make ends meet. Soon, he was employed with many other kids his same age, at what we still all refer to as "The Mill". When we think about it today, it's unbelievable what my and your folks had to do, never mind our grandparents who I know suffered in some form, whether it was leaving families behind in another country, dealing with wars, drought, the depression; or all of the above. Dad soon left the mill and went on to be a successful businessman, first by driving the Re-Nu cleaners truck and it was on that mission that he met my lovely mother Ella.

They soon married and went on to procreate five children, myself,

Sisters Bev, Barb, Val and my brother Chris in that order. We soon moved off the farm to residential Selkirk, 149 Grain St. to be exact. Dad was in the garage business by then and Mom was your stay at home Mom, like most Moms' in those days. We where the typical "Cleaver family " and yes lucky, as I said before, even though we had most things there were still a lot of poor kids in Selkirk. We where Boomer kids as we all know now, and kids there were. We all had many friends, the streets where full of kids and Mom and Dad had the means to give us our toys, our sports gear and numerous extracurricular activities. I never went without and always got to play any sport I wanted, and I did, as Selkirk had them all. Hockey was my favorite and I think I did pretty good at it, seeing as I was quite influenced by it, not only by Hockey Night in Canada, but Dad became quite involved with the " Selkirk Fisherman", by being the General manager for 30 years. In those days it was the "team", Senior AAA hockey; it was almost pro as I remember many players then were down from the pros. In fact many names would be in the NHL today, with the expansion. The likes of Al Baty, Dickey Braun, Leo Konik, Laurie Langrill to name a few, would be there today for sure, and Marshall McCarthy, would be there a as a head coach !! The Fisherman came close in 1966 to winning the Allan Cup; they lost out to the Drumheller Miners who went on to win it. It's the closest they ever came and I do remember the excitement around town, it was euphoric. I do hope one day that Manitoba brings home the Allan Cup, and I will have a toast to Dad and the entire Fisherman Team from the past!!

Like I say Mom was a stay at home Mom and didn't start to work away from home until Chris started school. I had everything, a mother that was home when you got home from school, nice clothes, and lots of food on the table, all the toys and sports equipment I wanted, brother and sisters. In other words a fun, loving and stable home as you can get, but something wasn't right with me. I hated school and I hated it a lot, hate is a powerful word but hate school I did. I struggled with it every year except one and that was grade six. My teacher was Mrs. Dukenich and an 'angel' she was, and for some reason she had the ability to figure me out and channeled me in the right direction. I had a good year but it soon came to haunt me as the following year and until I got kicked out, was painful. I remember, report card day was always a disaster for me, I'd be ashamed and Mom and Dad would be so frustrated, especially Dad as he had to work and leave school in Grade Eight. The scene went like this, we would all be home from school before Dad, and Mom would have the table set for supper with the report cards stacked up by Dad's plate. I would then slyly sneak over to the table and put my report card on the bottom. When I think about it, that didn't really matter but that's what it did! Dad would finish his supper and just before dessert he would read his children's' report cards, of course on top would be Bev, the brain. Bev always had straight A's. He would then proceed one by one and not say too much but hmmm, good. Then came mine, there would be a long pause, Dad would choke on his tea and then say. "Jesus, the kid is doing it again." Mom would say Peter, it's not that bad, Gord got an A in phys-ed and shop!! The report cards where always the same and the teacher's comments were "Gordon is very smart and clever but he doesn't apply himself and likes to be the class clown." This went on and on until my D-day came in Grade Eleven when on my way back from lunch I stopped by the old Safeway by Walter Budy's Texaco and bought a bag of raw garlic cloves, I took them to class early and stomped on them in about ten classrooms. WELL, it was so bad they had to move all the students into the library! I'm sure Andy Cotton squealed on me because a couple of days before that Arthur Stephenson and I gave him a tighty. That's when you pull someone up by their gotch, which they have to go to the washroom, pull their pants down and pull their gotch out of their ass!! So sure enough, about two o'clock over the PA the principal said "would Gordon Chenkie please report to the principals' office." My God, was that principal MAD!! He was beet red and he just screamed at me to" clean out my locker, as I'm not only kicked out of this school but the whole division, and I also called your Dad. He wants you to stop by the garage." Well I did, and poor Dad was LIVID. Behind his desk was a big window that overlooked the shop floor. Dad was giving me the lecture of a lifetime and I had to bite my lip so hard, as the mechanics where behind him on the shop floor laughing at me, making faces and acting like clowns. I moped around the house for a few days and Dad finally said you're "starting work tomorrow at the garage."

I remember going to work then fulltime at the garage. Doing oil changes, tires, and fairly easy mechanical work, I was quite happy that I didn't have to go back to school. I was just about nineteen, had a steady girlfriend and was playing in a rock and roll band called "Black Duck". Life was good, we where partying a lot, playing on the road with the band and I was getting a paycheck from the garage. But then again something was not right with me; I started drinking more, fist fighting and generally getting more rowdy. When I look back now the flying gene was in me, just below the surface but I didn't know it. I just knew that something had to change. You see, the gene was placed in me at a very young age, seeing the float planes on the river in Selkirk were probably where it started. I remember taking Mom and Dad down to the dock one nice summer day and as they were loading up for Eardley Lake I noticed a Selkirk Airways Norseman on floats there, I walked over to it, climbed into the cockpit and curiously looked around, I remember staring at the flight instruments and dreaming what it would be like to be a bush pilot. The log book was sitting on the other seat; I opened it up and started to

The Calling Sky

read the entries. I was fascinated at the lakes the airplane had been, the pilot was Eddie Johnson, a well respected bush pilot. Mom and Dad called me over to say goodbye and introduced me to Jack Clarkson, the owner operator of Selkirk Airways. It was the first time I had met Jack and his famous and trustworthy Cessna 180. It was loaded and ready to go and I said "Goodbye, have a nice fishing trip and I'll see you back in a few days." The doors closed, the dock hand untied the floats, the engine started and Jack taxied away. Even then I noticed that the airplane was what we bush pilots' call loaded to the "nuts." I watched Jack taxi north towards the old St. John's Boy's School, the RPM increased as Jack did the run up to check the engine performance before takeoff. As he turned into wind a notch of flaps came down the water rudders came up and Jack began the long take off. I was standing beside the dock hand and he said "watch this kid, you'll see how a real bush pilot gets this 180 off the water." With the nose high in the air Jack finally pushes it over and gets on the step, a half a mile has gone by already, as the speed slowly increases the dock hand says now "watch this, kid," Jack gets the right float out of the water first to reduce some of the drag and then he pops on another notch of flap, good old IRP is airborne and slowly climbs towards the old Selkirk bridge. Jack makes a slow left turn and heads north; there goes Mom and Dad on another venture to Eardley Lake, which they love so much!! Driving back to town I remember that that experience had a profound effect on me, I still didn't know that I wanted to fly but I know now the gene had started to surface.

A few days later Mom and Dad were back and I remember how happy they where, of course Dad was bitching that Jack was late again. You know Pete; he's really three hours ahead of time. I think that was the time Jack was so late that when he was taxiing into the dock at Eardley he shut the engine off well before the dock, stepped out onto the float and said "is

211

it safe to come ashore!" But that's okay; they were back safe and sound with a load of pickerel, sun tans and smiles on their faces! Mom and Dad and their many friends sure loved Eardley Lake, and then one day it all came to an end. I don't know why, they don't talk about it; they just all of a sudden could not go there anymore. I have reason to believe that they were shoved out because it was so sudden. I f this is the case, and then I'm a firm believer that if you're mean to people on purpose then your day will come. Some people realize it on their last days and some get their due before, but your day will come and whoever you are, I don't wish you any harm but I do wish that someday you're out on a wilderness trip, a wolverine trashes your campsite when you're out, eats most of your food, shits in your sleeping bag, knocks over and shatters your whiskey bottles on the rocks and best of all, the weather turns ugly, the aircraft is a couple of days late and to top it off you get the most revenging incurable dose of crabs the Lord can bestow on you. That will serve you right, Fuck You!!!

Working at the garage (Selkirk Motor Products) was a good thing for me, unknowingly it was an avenue of many roads, I learned how to deal with customers, it helped ingrain a good work ethic into me and most importantly I got to meet all kinds of people from all walks of life, from the crying American mother and father who's car that I was gassing up, having them say " You look so much like our son, he was only nineteen and just killed in Vietnam," to the old farmer that walked in with cash in his pocket and would only talk to Peter. I got to talk to the bush pilots as I serviced their vehicles, I remember now asking more and more questions and coincidentally a few people saying "Gordie, you've got to do something with your life." The final turn came shortly thereafter I remember going to some sort of get together inside the old Selkirk arena, I was there with my usual good buddies, Dave Langrill, Bob Tyndal, Richard Campbell, Billy Atkins to name a few. We were whooping it up pretty good, just having a good old time and then all of a sudden a fight broke out behind us, tables were flying and everyone was swinging at anyone that came their way. All I remember was someone grabbing me from behind for no reason as I was just standing there watching the big scrap. I instinctively turned and punched simultaneously and clobbered some guy I never seen before, down he went, glasses broken, the fight was over. The next thing I know the cops were there and off we went to the slammer. We'll guess who the guy was that I smoked? Dad's banker, Yes, that's right, the lending manager for the Royal Bank who looked after Dad's interests at Selkirk Motor Products! This gentleman was volunteering at the gathering and was just trying to break things up. Now here I am charged with assault. Of course Dad knew most of the RCMP as we looked after all of their cars at the garage, so he found out pretty quick, and I must say Dad was really pissed with me, so much in fact that he sent a few of his buddies to come and see me at the garage and tune me up. Fortunately the charges were reduced to causing a disturbance. I had to pay a small fine, go apologize and buy the bank manager new glasses. Thank god he talked to the police as an assault conviction would have had devastating consequences on my yet unknown flying career. Not only Dad, but I was pissed with myself, I knew something had to give, I felt, as though there was a fiery rage in me, out of control and there was something out there for me. My rage soon came to an end, sometime soon after the arena incident we were all at the Selkirk Fair one afternoon, watching baseball and sitting in the beer gardens. I remember seeing this Cessna 180 on floats taking off and landing about every half hour or so, after awhile of this I said to my buddies to save my seat, I'm going to leave for a bit. I walked down over to the boat launch and recognized Bob Polinuk, he was giving float plane rides for ten dollars a person. I realized that I had never been in an airplane before so I said why not. Fortunately there was another couple that wanted to go so Bob put them in the back seats and told me to get in the front. Basically what Bob was doing was a take off towards the old bridge, a left turn, a climb to about two thousand feet. He would then head north for about five minutes and then come back in for a landing. Just enough to have a good look around and experience a float plane ride, so away we went. I remember now that soon after takeoff it started to hit me, I was getting these weird feelings that I had never experienced before, and by God I liked it! We landed, tied up to the dock and I said goodbye to Bob. From the moment I left the dock I knew without a doubt, that I wanted to be a bush pilot. No ifs, buts or maybes, a bush pilot. I remember how so good that felt, my destiny, my calling had finally surfaced. But in just a matter of minutes a new rage emerged, a rage of where and when do I begin? Look out, stay out of my way because I'm on a mission now, and I so remember saying to myself "Gordie, don't let anyone or anything no matter what stop you." That was my statement to myself. I walked back to that beer garden, and my mind was abuzz, I had a few more beers and I told my buddies that I'm going to cut out early as I wanted to go home and talk to Mom and Dad. Well you know it was one of those beautiful summer nights in Selkirk, it was just getting dark, there was a nice warm south wind blowing. I came in the house and Mom and Dad had just sat down to watch the news, after a hard week at the garage Dad liked to have a rye and chill out as the garage was closed on Sunday. This led them to look at me quite oddly, and say "why are you home so early" because usually I wouldn't be home at all or I would stagger in at some ungodly hour. "I said nonchalantly " I don't know, there isn't much going on tonight", I remember sitting on the couch hemming and hawing, trying to get the courage to tell my folks what I wanted to do with my life. Finally, I couldn't take it anymore, I said " you know Mom and Dad I went for a float plane ride today in Bob Polinuks'

180 and I finally realized that that's what I wanted to do, and that is be a bush pilot." We'll holy molly, just as I was stating my intensions Dad was taking a sip of his rye and while he was contemplating this, how would you say, shocking NEWS from another planet, his rye backfired on him and it shot across the room, a fine spray with a far enough trajectory that it splattered the TV!! I said to myself - I did it, I felt a great relief because I knew I had to get this out and start the process, and as we all know the first thing to do to tackle any mission is to take action. Mom quickly cleaned up the mess and poured Dad another drink, I let things settle down a bit and then I hit dad again, I said, " you know Dad I might need you to co- sign a loan for me so I can get my commercial pilot's license". Well, that was it, Dad blew a gasket and said, "You want to be a pilot, you ran your car low on oil last week, you're drinking and fighting and worst of all ya beat up my bank manager and now you want me to get money from him." Mom stepped in and said now "settle down Peter, I can see Gordie is really serious here and we should give it some thought." I went to bed and I'm not kidding you, the next morning which was a Sunday, I was up an at it early, so early in fact, that when I drove out to St. Andrews airport the flying clubs where still closed! I finally parked in front of Point West School of Aviation and waited until it opened; I walked in the door and never looked back.

I started taking flying lessons and ground school at Point West, my drinking and partying days came to a standstill as needed to save every nickel I had. I also needed a clear and fresh mind as this was so very new, I was in heaven, challenged, driven, focused and determined. I soloed I at seven hours, I had manuals, maps, charts, notes and various other flying paraphernalia spread out on the kitchen table. Mom was amazed at how the rest of the family was watching noisy TV, talking and laughing and I wouldn't hear a thing, I was so immersed. It's ironic when you think about it, in grade school I was in hell but in flying school I was in heaven! Mom and Dad could not help but notice how serious I was, besides working at the garage, all I did was fly and study, even my band playing days were coming to an end. There wasn't enough time. Wayne Posnick, Dennis Wall, Kenny Ledwos and Greg Mcleod where truly great musicians and I wasn't too bad a guitar player either, but I knew that it wasn't meant to be. They could see the change in me and when I look back now they slowly let me go, with class!

Mom came home one day and said she met a new lady at her PEO meeting, her name is Doreen Magill, they just moved to town and her husband Brian is the chief pilot for Ilford Riverton Airways. Mom said "Here is Brians' number, Doreen says to call if you want to talk about flying." And so I did, I went over to their home and had a nice long chat with Brian; he was very humble but straight forward and encouraging. I needed that as so many pilots tell youngsters that are interested to forget it as it is such are hard game to crack. There's an old joke that goes like this. "Please don't tell my Mom that I'm a pilot, she thinks I have a respectable job as a piano player in a whorehouse!!!" It is funny and I piss myself laughing every time I tell it, but what it really means is that most of us beginning pilots would do anything to get our foot in the door. Unbenounced to me, that visit with Brian would start us out on a good friendship as Brian hired me and gave me my first job as a bush pilot less than two years later.

Things were going good for me, I was getting more comfortable in the aircraft, I had passed my ground school with honors, and that is something I never did in grade school. But, as a lot of times in life, good things come to an end, and come to an end they did, as disaster struck and struck hard and fast. As for me and many young pilots, the dreadful thing happened, I ran out of money, and in the flying school business, no cash- no fly, plain and simple. In those days there weren't any scholarships or grants and not even credit at the flying schools. Cash, cash, cash, that's all that mattered! So guess what happened? You got it, I started drinking and partying to the dismay of my family and friends. I, they and everyone who knew me well didn't like to see that side of me again; everyone was so used to the new Gordie. This went on for the winter and I guess Mom and Dad could see that I was self destructing. Then a great thing happened, I was working in the garage as usual when one fine spring day Jack Clarkson stopped by. I could see Jack and Dad talking and I knew something was up as they kept looking over to where I was working. Finally Dad came into the garage bay and said "take the rest of the day off, you're going with Jack to St. Andrews airport, he's got to ferry a Norseman to Lac du Bonnet". So away Jack and I went, luckily the Norseman was parked at St. Andrews Airways and Jack introduced me to Ron Michaluk, who at the time was the half owner of St. Andrews Airways and who, I would eventually fly for. We had a nice chat, we said good bye to Ron and away Jack and I went. We had a good day, I met some new people along the way, got to fly in the Norseman but most importantly the fire started to rise in me again. I realized that just because I'm out of money doesn't mean that I shouldn't do something. That night while falling asleep I decided to go out to St. Andrews the next day and see if I could talk to Ron about a job, my thinking was if I wanted to be a pilot then I should start with an airline on the ground floor. You see I had my eye on St. Andrews Airways because I was out there taking lessons and at the same time watching their airplanes taking off and landing. My flight instructors Neil Stoezs, Ulrik Frey and Reed Briggs could also sense that I wanted over there; they all encouraged me to try and get on there as it would be a great little airline to start with. So the next day after work at the garage I drove out to St. Andrews Airways and as luck would have it

Ron Michaluk was there, he vaguely remembered me as we chatted and he said "do you want to go for supper at the corner café?" While we were eating I remember how I kept telling him how much I wanted to be a bush pilot and that I was hoping he would give me a job at the hanger. All of a sudden Ron looked up and said "can you start tomorrow morning? " We'll I almost choked and said I could but I work for my Dad and I would like to give him a couple of days notice," Ron said " I respect that ,so show up Monday morning at 8 o'clock." Ron even bought me supper and as I drove home I could really feel the fire raging again, but at the same time I really dreaded to tell Mom and Dad that I was leaving the garage. I should have told them that night but my good friend Bob Tyndall was getting married on Saturday and I had lots of things to do so I put it off. As it happened I got really pissed at Bob's wedding, not only because of the celebrations of your good friends wedding but because I felt as though I was letting my folks down. Unbenounced to me Mom and Dad thought different; at the kitchen table Sunday morning still hung-over as hell I broke down and told them I was leaving to work at St. Andrews Airways. Mom and Dad didn't say too much but for some reason I could sense that they we're happy for me. And the next morning I knew why, I was up at 7 o' clock, Dad was already gone to the garage and as I walked out the door Mom handed me my lunch and said "good luck son, we know you'll do well, Dad and I are very proud of you and if you can at lunch time today go to the bank and sign the papers." I said "what papers", and mom said "we co signed a loan for you for four thousand dollars!"

I'll tell ya folks; I cried all the way to the airport, I was so on fire, so proud of my parents. Here I was, a foot in the door with St. Andrews Airways, cash in the bank to not only finish my private, but to get a night rating, a float endorsement and a commercial pilot's license uninterrupted!

Chapter 3

My new life began Monday morning as I walked in the hanger at St. Andrews Airways, I noticed that the hanger was full of cargo, tools, Herman Nelson heaters', engine tents, aircraft skis and floats, and on top of it all a Beech 18 on wheels. CF - STA to be exact. Over in the far corner of the hanger were some chairs and couch or two, this was an open air coffee lunch room, there were all sorts of people drinking coffee and bs'ing there, I assumed they were a combination of mechanics, pilots and loaders as I didn't know any of them. I was sort of standing around like a spare prick in a whorehouse when Ron Michaluk finally came by and introduced me to everyone, "this is our new grunt Gord Chenkie and he's wants' to be a pilot here." Everyone was pretty accommodating I must say but there were a few snide remarks, like always when there is a new kid on the block. The one I remember the most was from Johnny Poponick when he said "go back to school". We all laughed and I still say that phrase from time to time as a joke, but deep down I knew that this was my school! Ron said "okay kid, follow me, if you want to be a pilot let's get started". I didn't know what to expect but I was really excited. I thought Ron was going to take me into the Beech 18 and start teaching me all about the aircraft and flight in general, but that thought soon vanished as I noticed a few of the guys start laughing. Well, my journey began all right, Ron grabbed an empty five gallon pail and filled it up with Varsol, he threw in a scrub brush and said "follow me", We walked over to the

Beech 18, it was in for a hundred hour inspection, the cowlings were off, the flaps extended, it was even jacked up so they could swing the gear, and most of all it was filthy, a mixture of dirt, oil, exhaust, hydraulic and fuel stains. Ron said "here you go kid; I want this airplane cleaned by the end of the day, and the cowlings too!" As the day progressed I was filthy dirty but at the same time didn't bitch at all. I noticed the rest of the guys start to be more friendly and talk more freely. Later around the coffee table the stories and BS started to fly and man, I was absorbing everything I could. Just before lunch Ralph Birch came in with the Beech 18 from Island Lake and I could tell he was so respected. I got to meet Tom Ivey the operation manager as he came to ask Ralph how much of a load he could take today. I listened to a couple of Ralphs' stories when all of a sudden someone said "hey, Gord come and give us a hand" and there I went, from aircraft cleaner to aircraft loader and gassing attendant, a promotion in one day!. When the rest of the Beech 18's came down from the north, we unloaded them, cleaned them and fueled them up for the morning. I was finally done about six and told to go home but they wanted me back at six am the next day to start loading. I was tired, hungry and dirty, but I loved it. The best part of the day came as I didn't go home; I went over to Point West and took a double flying lesson!

Life was really good I must say, I was always tired but at the same time very happy as I finished my private license and float endorsement and best off all I started my commercial pilots training. You see when you start your commercial you not only take more advanced training bit you also have to build up time, a hundred or so more hours above your training and this is where it gets expensive. Being at St. Andrews Airways was such a good move as it was not only a place to work and learn the aviation business but it was also, unknown to me at the time a place of free flying. Tom Ivey, the ops manager was a hard driving, hard working man, but if you worked like him and he took a liking to you then Tom would give you lots of leeway to pursue you're flying lessons. Well, lucky for me Tom liked me and my work ethic, he knew what I wanted and the biggest surprise came one day when I was loading up a Beech 18, Tom said "to come into his office". I thought I was on the hit list and we all know that there are dozens of pilot wantabees behind me waiting for me to falter. But that was not the case, Tom said "Gord we get a lot of calls here for charters that we can't do because they are too small, so here is this fellows name, he has a construction company and is looking to fly to Grand Rapids once a week to inspect his project, give him a call and let me know, I'll give you the required days off". Well I'll tell ya, I left Tom's office in a complete daze, I couldn't believe it! So I called the fellow up and sure enough I had five trips to Grand Rapids booked, all he did was pay for the rental and the fuel, a good deal for both him and me and it was perfectly legal. Dad also gave me a few trips, flying his mechanics mostly to Berens River. Between these trips and flying my friends to Grand Forks and over the city to observe the Christmas lights, my hours where mostly paid for. Shortly after the New Year I received my commercial pilot's license and realized that I hadn't stopped for the last ten months, no breaks, no time off, just full throttle ahead. I t was so worth it, having that piece of paper in my hand meant the world to me, my family and my friends. The new Gordie had arisen, but in fact it was just starting as the next step was to get my first job. You see, getting that first flying job is so tough because you have all the licenses but no experience, and we all know you can't buy experience, you plain and simple have to earn it! So here I was, all wet behind the ears with two hundred hours and a fresh commercial pilot's license. Every day as spring approached I would hear Tom Ivey "say so and so called looking for a job and so and so called". These guys all had way more hours and experience that me. I knew I had to do something; working at St Andrews Airways was good, the pilots, the management and owners all knew me well by now; they knew my work ethic, my personality and above all my most forceful desire to get hired. I just knew I had to do something over and above as there was just too much more experienced competition ahead of me. Then one day luck came my way again, Ralph Birch came down from Island Lake as usual on his daily trip. Ralph as I said was a very well respected pilot, he was looked upon with high regard and Ralph was also well liked as a person. He had a very easy nature to him, Ralph and I became friends almost instantly from day one, I used to love listening to his stories about his life and flying career. Ralph was always very happy, full of colorful stories and tales of days gone by, I remember loading and gassing up Ralphs' faithful Beech 18. CF-ZNC, as I walked into the hanger to have my usual chat with Ralph, I noticed that he wasn't in all that good of mood. George Brotherston, the other half owner of St. Andrews Airways asked Ralph if he wouldn't mind flying the Norseman on skis for a month this spring. The job entailed lots of physical work; it was primarily flying all the natives to their respective fish camps to make ice for the upcoming fishing season. The flying part of it wasn't too bad, that's what Ralph wasn't worried about, it was the preparation and the work involved in keeping a Norseman going in the winter, that's the hard part, not only that, Ralph had done that before many times, he was past that stage, he just wanted to fly the Beech. John Poponick heard Ralphs' reluctance to fly the Norseman and came up with the idea that I should go up to Island Lake this spring and be Ralphs' crew man on the Norseman, that way all Ralph would have to do is fly, I would do the rest. That way, I would get to not only meet the other owner, George Brotherston who lived in Island Lake but I would get to know all the lakes, the terrain and the people along the way. John noticed that I was really pumped about the idea said he would speak to George the next day when he was up in Island Lake, five minutes later I was in Tom Ivey's' office asking for the time off to go north! Luck would have it, a few days later George, Tom and Ralph all thought this was a great idea, Ralph was happy and I was going north! I was going to get to fly with Ralph Birch and learn the tricks of the trade from one of the best!

A few weeks later I was in the right seat of the Beech 18 with John Poponick heading north to Island Lake and my new adventure as Ralphs' co-pilot. We landed in Island Lake and I helped unload the Beech, I met George, big Dave Playfair and a few of the pilots. One of them in particular was Bill Kent who was very thankful that I brought up some beer and whiskey. It's a golden rule in the north that whoever comes up from the south should not land empty handed, if you know what I mean! I helped Bill and the rest of the pilots put the airplane to bed and we were soon off to the pilots shack on our skidoos, a couple of miles away from the airport. The pilot "shack" was an old twenty by forty log cabin with no electrical power, no heat and no plumbing! Just a wood stove, a kitchen and a couple of bedrooms with bunk beds in them. Bill was staying there along with me and Richard Bless who was also another pilot wantabees, as we entered my new abode I noticed that the half filled coffee cups from the morning where frozen stiff and the whole place was ice cold, I remember saying to myself "what did I get myself into". Bill said that since I was the junior, that my job was to cut wood for the wood stove as that was our only source of heat, it's dark now and I'm outside with a buck saw cutting wood for the night, Richard had the wood stove going pretty good and was melting snow for water. All of a sudden Bill came out of the pilots' shack, started up one of the skidoos with a sleigh on it and took off, me being a newbie I didn't have a clue what was going on but I was sure to find out. About a half an hour later Bill came back with the skidoo and a couple of local honeys'. We proceeded to cook steaks, drink whiskey and have a bit of fun with our new found girls. All was going well, we were having a good time and I figured that I wouldn't mind snagging one of these maidens to keep me warm tonight; Richard had already gone to bed so I thought my chances where pretty good as by now Bill had them liquored up pretty good. I no sooner put a move on one of them when Bill flew into a rage and said to me "fuck off kid, they are both for me, go get your own girls". I couldn't believe it but no matter as I just went to bed, I knew I had a big day ahead of me tomorrow! I was just falling asleep when a big racket awoke me, here the girls were fighting amongst themselves, screaming and kicking, until one of them ran out of the pilots shack half naked over to Georges', our owners house. She was pissed drunk and hysterical, Georges wife Barb got her all calmed down, she came back with her to the "shack" gave Bill supreme shit and told him to drive the girls back across to the reserve! They were fighting over who would sleep with Bill first! I got up in the morning, the "shack" was not frozen but you could see your breath, oh, I so wanted to get back into that warm arctic sleeping bag but I knew I had work to do, my first day on the job as Ralphs' helper and I had to start getting the Norseman prepared. I started the skidoo, lit a cigarette and was having a long morning piss, looking around to check the weather as most of us pilots do when we're having a leak when I noticed in a snow bank beside me; the remains of Bills goodnight piss, the words inscribed "Dirty Bill". I said to myself as I took off on the skidoo, "Welcome to Island Lake."

I must say that I had a great month of March, I learned so much. Everything about flying and keeping a Norseman on skis operational, I learned how to heat up the engine using a blow pot, how to fuel, oil, clean the wings. How to load and secure the airplane properly and above all I got to see Ralph and all his years of experience operate. Ralph taught me how to baby the engine, proper run ups, dilution procedures and best of all he showed me flying techniques such as how to check for slush below the snow. I met so many good people at Garden Hill that month of March, people that later would become good friends. I was working my ass off, but it didn't matter as I was also so into my element. I felt good, I felt challenged, I felt more driven everyday and I was learning everything that was thrown at me! The month went by pretty quick I must say, from that first night cutting wood for the wood stove to now, was a blur, but when I took a moment and looked back I realized how much more I knew than a month ago. I really became good friends with George Brotherston who would soon purchase the remaining half of St. Andrews Airways from Ron Michaluk. I got to learn where all the lakes and fish camps were and the natives that ran them. I was still such a rookie but I felt quite content, I was happy with what I had done in the last month or so, but as I was reminiscing about this most rewarding and fun experience, I soon realized that it would be time to head south again. We got the job done; Ralph was back on the Beach 18 doing his daily run from Garden Hill to St. Andrews airport. I stayed in Island Lake a few more days and helped George out at the airport and sure enough as expected George said it was time for me to head south for breakup. I don't know for sure but I'm pretty positive George could see that I was not too happy about leaving; he could sense that this is where I wanted to be, especially behind the controls of one of his airplanes! The next day Brian Magill came up to Garden Hill on the sched to ferry a Cessna 180 on skis south, Brian wanted me to go with him so I could map read on the way south. That was fine with me and it gave me a bit of a lift as I wondered if Brian was thinking of hiring me, even so, as I said goodbye to George and the rest of the gang at the airport I wondered if I would ever be back here again. As we took off, I looked out the window and could see the good old "pilots' Shack", I knew the coffee was frozen again and the place was quiet, I felt sad, I realized how much I've grown up in a few short weeks! I did the best I could, as I have said, "You can't buy experience", all I had was my measly two hundred hours of flight time, but you know what? I had my reputation. George, Tom, Brian and all the other people at the airline now knew who I was!

It just happened that the Selkirk Steelers were on their way to the Centennial Cup in Ottawa. The Centennial Cup at the time was for the Canadian junior hockey championship and they were playing the Smith Falls Bears for the cup in Nepean, Ontario which is a superb of Ottawa. I said to myself if I could get three of my buddies to come with me then I could rent an airplane and we could go see the tournament in Ottawa and I would get a few more hours plus a nice cross country flight. Well sure enough three of my buddies where raring to go, now my next step was going to be a little more difficult, as now I had to ask for more time off. I had just been gone for a month to Island Lake so I figured my chances weren't too good, but guess what? Good old Tom Ivey came through for me again and told me to go and get the hours! Man oh man; Tom was so supportive if you worked hard for him! So away we went, myself, Dave Langrill, Bob Tyndall and Kenny McCarthy, what a crew of rangatangs! Ottawa here we come, Brian Magill told me to take the southern route as the weather wasn't as unpredictable as the northern route over Lake Superior, so we went from St. Andrews to Duluth, Minnesota, Sault Ste. Marie, Ottawa. We weren't in our room in Ottawa for more than a half hour and the shit hit the fan, Mike Chubby one of the players for the Steelers came to our room for a beer, we were just being cool and having a few laughs when the there was a knock on the door. Mike hid under the bed as we opened the door and to our surprise it was the coach and all the management from the Steelers! They were really pissed with us

The Calling Sky

being at the same hotel as the team and started to give us some lip, we just kind of brushed it off when one of the managers said they can't find Mike Chubby. Right away the coach George Dorman pushed his way in looked under the bed and there was Mike hiding with a beer in his hand! Well the shit hit the fan, George and all the management went absolutely crazy, yelling and swearing at us and sure as shit they got us kicked out of the hotel! In any event we had a good time, the Steelers won the cup and we now had to make our journey back home. As we got to the airport the weather was really crappy, it was that low cumulonimbus cloud mixed with heavy rain and gusty winds, it was obvious that a cold front mixed with a low pressure system was passing through. We gasses up and went in and filed a flight plan and took off heading for the Sault. Well it wasn't long into the flight and I was getting lower and lower trying to maintain visual, it was also really rough with the turbulence knocking us around pretty good, I soon realized that it was getting unflyable so I returned to Ottawa and told the gang that we'd have to wait it out, the forecast said that in about six hours it would improve. All was well, we kind of hung around the terminal killing time when I noticed that my buddies all took off, I didn't think anything of it until they came back and said "Gord hate to tell you this but we can't wait anymore, we all bought tickets on Air Canada and we're leaving right away!" I couldn't believe it, they took off on me! So away they went, I waited for about six hours and took off for home, the weather was much better and I flew all night home buy myself. I remember leaving Duluth for St. Andrews, the sky was clear and there was a full moon out, just a beautiful night all in all. I knew that my buddies where long home now and I was thinking to myself what Brian Magill must be thinking of me knowing that my "buddies, my passengers abandoned me"! Well I was in for the surprise of a lifetime! I parked the airplane and went to the hanger straight to work, just as I started loading up one of the Beech 18's, Tom Ivey came over and said that Brian wanted to see me in his office. Tom had a funny look on his face and I said to myself, "well that's, it I'm shit caned now!" I walked into Brian's' office and we had some small chit chat about the Steelers and my trip to Ottawa, all of a sudden Brian said," well Chink, get your bags packed for next week, you're going back to Island Lake, this time as a pilot, you're HIRED!" " Now finish loading up the Beech, your hanger duties are over, we're going down to the float base as we have work to do there to get you prepared!"

Well I went home that night, dead tired. I remember I cracked a beer, sat down and told my Mom and Dad the news. Mom was in tears, Dad was silent in thoughts of pride and I was in shock. I remember savoring my beer, stunned and dazed saying to myself, "I did it, I fuckin did It!"

Chapter 4

I was going to fly the Found FBA 2c, a float plane made in Canada; it's a five passenger, a little bigger than a Cessna 180. The pilots said it's a nice airplane to fly, a little workhorse that they often call a baby Norseman. For the next few days Brian spent quite a bit of time with me, I was thankful for this extra training as I knew I needed as much help as possible, being a rookie as such. We went over everything, how to fuel and oil the airplane, how to tie the proper knots and we even made a set of new ropes for my airplane! A few days later, my bags packed, with an extra box of steaks and whiskey, I headed north to Island Lake with Ralph Birch on good old ZNC. Ralph was really happy for me and even though he didn't need one he handed me one of his sectionals and I map read all the way to Garden Hill. As we were descending for landing Ralph mentioned that the nurses where having a party at the nursing station tonight. I thought "this is cool, what a good way to start my career, A party!" After landing I helped unload the Beech, we were all done for the day, so off we went, headed for the pilots' "shack." I unloaded my stuff; put the steaks and beer in the fridge as we had power now and proceeded to have a few drinks. I remember having a beer and looking around the "shack" saying to myself "ah, it's good to be back", the radio was on with I Shot the Sheriff and Benny and the Jets as the top songs that summer. Even today when I hear those songs I'm reminded of the good old days in Island Lake! After a couple of beers we were off to the nursing station for their party, we weren't there long when one of the nurses told us all to "raise our glasses for a toast to the pilots". So here I was toasting the pilots and thinking "hey, this is pretty cool, they sure like us pilots!" Little did I know that the toast was for three Ilford Riverton pilots that had to come to the station for their VD shots! I was in stitches laughing so hard as the nurses went on to say how they got to "pull their pants down and stab those bastards in the ass!" I still tell that story especially to my daughter Brittany who is now a nurse in Yellowknife; I say "Brittany, have you pulled the pants down of a Yellowknife bush pilot yet?" She just shakes her head! We stayed a bit at the nursing station, had a good time and lots of laughs, but it was time to head home to the " shack" as we all had an early morning the next day. I remember riding in the back of the boat, smelling the fresh air, enjoying the sights, when I said to myself for the second time, "welcome to Island Lake."

The next day was a day of cleaning, we had two Found Aircraft, a Cessna 180 and a Beech 18 on floats that summer so George told me to pick my airplane and get it ready as Brian Magill was coming up tomorrow to give me my check out. So I picked out CF-SVC and I cleaned out that baby head to toe, it was shining when I was done, I put in my new ropes and equipment and even fuelled it up for the next day. I was all set but nervous as I knew that tomorrow after all this work and effort, my life was about to change forever and for the better!

When Brian got off the sched the next day we went right to work. George was sending me to St. Therese Pt. with a load of groceries, but first we went out empty and did an hour or so of touch and goes. It was a good day to start, no glassy water just a light wind out of the north. We now loaded up and I was now on my first official revenue trip as a pilot. It went pretty good I think, and Brian was happy enough to turn me loose. Back at Island Lake he shook my hand and offered his congratulations. Before he left on the sched back to St. Andrews, Brian told George to keep me between St. Therese Pt. and Waasagomach, for a couple of days before sending me out further as these were short twenty-five mile legs. I did this for a few days, just getting my feet wet, learning how to handle weight, glassy water and all sorts of different conditions. Once George seen me progress he started to send me further abroad and looking back now, I was so fortunate to have such a good boss as George, he was so patient with us young pilots. As you know being a bush pilot is very demanding, you don't have air traffic control, radar, autopilots, GPS, just your basic rudimentary winds, altimeter and meager weather information, in other words "you're on your own". I've seen many a young pilot blue and scared shitless as they have got themselves into a situation well above their skill levels, all at the hands of a ruthless operator. But George was good to us young kids; he dictated where we went, based all on our skill levels. So here I was, venturing out further and further and after a week I was starting to feel better as every day passed. Until one day, when I came back from an all day trip to Bigstone, Stevenson, and Oxford Lake, George was standing on the dock waiting for me and he had a different looking demeanor too him. He helped me tie the airplane up and offload our passengers and cargo, and he said that "your Grandpa passed away and the funeral is tomorrow". He also said " go home on the sched tomorrow and come back when you can". I was really sad but on the same token very thankful that I had a good boss in George, to let me go home and pay respects to someone I was really close too. As I said I was really close to my Baba and Gigi, my Moms' parents passed away at a very young age. I was too young to really get to know them, so having my Baba and Gigi was special to me. I'm thankful that he got to see me as a pilot and as I stood at his grave I felt very humble as I know he suffered in his day. He left his family behind in the old country to come here and start a new life,

I'm very proud of my grandparents; they all took big risks then to better their families. I know all four of them suffered in some way or another, and here I was starting a new life on my own, in a free and safe country, thanks to their vision! I'm so lucky!

After Gigi's funeral I was back to Island Lake, getting a little more confident every day. It just happened that Rodger Handel (Rodger, the dodger, we called him) took a local lady as his bride in the spring, it was evident that his flying eagerness was diminishing, Rodger just didn't want to fly that much anymore so I figured this could be a great benefit for me, and so did George! After a month and a couple of hundred hours George really started to pile the trips on me, in fact some days Rodger wouldn't come to work at all, and George didn't care as he had me. My trips where getting longer and more difficult, I was starting to fly canoes, moose meat and trappers, I was even getting trips and overnights to Norway House and Thompson and YES, a hotel bed and shower! Rodger was getting the little trips that I started on which was fine with him as he was close to home. I told George that rest was not an option, don't turn any trip down. Of course I wanted the hours and the pay as I had a debt to repay Mom and Dad, but a lot of it had to do with the fact that I wanted to do a good job and show George, Tom and Brian that they made a good choice in me. So here I was, flying from sunup to sundown day after day, week after week and before I knew it I had five hundred hours in my logbook! Before I knew it we were into August and a couple of things happened, first of all things usually slowed down a bit in August, a little break before you start hauling the trappers in the fall. This was a welcome break, as eager as I was I probably couldn't have kept that pace up for the rest of the season. George also hired two new pilots, one to replace Rodger and one for the other Found. Now I had competition but I didn't care as they were both rookies and it would be sometime before we could all fight for the same trips. In the end it didn't matter anyways as these two new pilots were good guys, Byron Spence who was native from Saskatchewan and Gerry Deasy, a wild and crazy Irishman right from Dublin! What a mixture, a Ukrainian, an Irishman and a native, and man did we ever have a good time, we worked hard and we partied hard! I didn't realize it at the time, I was so busy flying that I was just too darn tired to cook for myself. I lived on coffee, cigarettes and any food that I could steal or scrounge, when we got a supper invite it was like watching wolves devour a carcass. It wasn't a pleasant sight especially when a hot shower was offered before supper! Looking back now, I think George must have tipped off my Mom, as one day when the sched arrived, there was a huge box for me, full of all kinds of food, along with some whiskey and a couple of cartons of cigarettes. Along with that was a stern letter from my sister Barb, telling me that Mom was upset that I wasn't eating and to damn well smarten up!

Byron, Gerry and I along with big Dave (Igor) Playfair who looked after all our freight and fuel for the floatplanes became all good friends. It was late in August and I remember it was a miserable rainy day with not to much flying, Byron didn't live with us at the pilots "shack", he lived on the reserve with his wife who was a school teacher. He said, "My wife's out of town so after work let's all get together for drinks." Byron had just got back from Thompson and he brought back the "Golden Rule" a few buckets of KFC and a shit load of booze, mostly Appleton Amber rum which was the drink of choice in Island Lake, for the simple reason is that you could drink it with juice and not coke which was more expensive that the rum! So we all said rock on, big Igor said he would drive me over in his boat as he and his wife lived in a cabin not far from the "shack". We all got to Byron's' in the early evening, just soaking wet as it was just pissing rain. We were having a good time, nothing to wild or loud, just having fun. There were just us pilots along with big Igor and a few of the local ladies, after a couple of hours the door flew open at Byron's and it was the reserve cops telling us that the community hall was on fire and they needed our help to put it out. So everyone took off except me, I had one of these local lady's in my sights and I had a few drinks into her already. She looked like she was taking a shine to me so I said to myself "I'm staying here!" I found out later that Igor, Byron and the rest of them were giving the local fire boys shit especially Igor, saying you guys don't know what you're doing; you better let us take over. Well they would have nothing to do with that and when they realized that Igor and the crew were pissed, they decided to throw them all in jail! So away went Byron and Gerry to the slammer and the same for Igor. Except they had one small problem with Igor, he was three hundred and thirty pounds, drunk and mad and they just couldn't manhandle him, so what did they do? They got a fifty food extension cord, wrapped it around Igor like a mummy, tied him to the rear hitch of a pickup truck and proceeded to drag him down the muddy street to the band office! Just like in the movies except it were a pickup and not a horse. I guess the guys were saying when they got him to the band office he was like a caged animal, pissed drunk, soaking wet, full of mud and snorting like a bull! I didn't know any of this was happening and I guess one of the cops realized I was missing, so the next thing you know Byron's door flew open and in they came looking for me, and guess where I was? On the couch, my ass high in the air pissed drunk having a good time. And take a guess who that the girl was? The damn Chief's daughter! Oh man where those reserve cops mad, so away I went to jail which was not only the band office but the Chiefs' office! By the time I got there Igor's' wife Lila, who was a local native, had Igor and Byron released, so it was just Gerry and myself locked up in the Chief's office with two guards posted outside the door! As the night went on I tried to sleep but I couldn't because I had to piss like a racehorse, Gerry was passed out and I kept asking the so called guards to let me out for a squirt, but they would have none of it. Finally, I couldn't hold it anymore and I started to look around for a place to let it go but couldn't find anything that would conceal my urine, until I realized straight in front of me was the Chief's desk! And sure enough I opened the bottom drawer, it was stacked full of papers and I let her rip, I must have pissed for ten minutes! Before I passed out on the floor I knew we were in deep shit. Gerry and I both had trips at seven in the morning. Sure enough the light awoke us and we could see across the bay, to our floatplanes tied to the dock. We had trips to do, but oh no, we're in jail! The only thing that I thought might save me is that I was supposed to fly Eldon Leopkky to God's River. Eldon was with Manitoba Hydro and he was as much of a wildcat as the best of us, so if I was late it wouldn't be big issue with him. Finally the door opened about eight thirty in the morning and I figured that they would just let us go. I was sure that I could convince George not to fire us as we didn't really do anything wrong, but oh no, they didn't let us go; they escorted us straight into their conference room. There they were, the whole Chief and council all dressed up in their traditional garb and guess who was sitting beside the Chief? Yes, our owner George Brotherston! We'll my heart sank as I looked at George; he had that Scottish frown on him that I came to recognize when he was not happy. I said to myself "I'm fired now." So, we had our meeting and they let us know that they were not happy with us, coming on the reserve, raising hell and especially me for feeding their girls firewater. So the end result was that we both had to stand up and apologize to the Chief and council, we were also both banned from the reserve. We stood up and left, and as we walked down the hill to Georges' boat I heard a snickering sound, I looked over my shoulder and there was George laughing his face off! Oh man I was so relieved, George finally said "okay, no more laughing until we get to the boat, I don't want them to see us." So away we went in Georges' boat towards Stevenson Island and there was George pissing himself laughing, he thought he heard it all, until this episode. So we pulled up to the dock all composed, our customers were there waiting for us, and as we got out of the boat, George in a stern voice said "okay you two sons of bitches, get to work!"

The day went good, I was quite happy that I still had my job. But as I landed on my last trip and taxied towards the dock, I noticed George standing there, I said to myself this is weird, it's eight o'clock, and George is never here for the last trip. So as opened the door George asked me if I had enough fuel for a trip to Beaverhill Lake, I said I did but what's up? He said you're not going to believe this but the Chief wants' to go to his camp right now and he asked for you. George said "put her on the step and get over to his dock, after what happened let's do him a favor, I know it's late so get going." I said but "George, I'm kicked off the reserve" he said "don't worry the chief said you can tie up to his dock only". So away I went, I taxied over to the Chiefs dock, picked him and his load up and I was off to Beaverhill. So here I was, just caught fooling around with his daughter and now I'm taking the Chief to his camp. You know the Chief was usually a very friendly, jolly green giant sort of a guy who knew me well, but you know what? He never said a word too me all the way and I knew deep down that was his way of saying to stay away from his daughter! It's a good thing he liked me as I know he had the power to have me fired! Thank you Chief!

We were into September now, and the float flying started to get quite busy as expected. For the next six weeks we flew are asses off as the days were getting shorter and shorter. I loved flying trappers and their grubstakes out to their winter camps; they are hard working down to earth people who loved the traditional lifestyle. What you would do is fly them out in the late fall on floats, and then in early spring pick them up on skis along with their gear and of course, their fur bounty. Also in the fall where the moose hunters, now that was hard, dirty and bloody work along with the fact that you were always heavy. I must say, with the cool temperatures and a good wind, the good old Found could hall a hunter, his gear and a dressed moose all in one load! I also carried a knife under my seat for safety purposes, not from any physical threat but just in case you got caught on a rope or something, but that good old hunting knife used to cut me off some fine looking moose roasts and that my friends, used to get me allot of hot showers and supper invites!

Soon after trapping season, our flights slowly dwindled. As mid October, along with short days and freezing water rudders came about, George started to send us one by one south to the float base at St. Andrews. As my turn came, I took off towards the west, and again this time I looked down at the "pilots shack". This time I had a different feeling, I wasn't worried about if I would ever be back, I was a pilot with a job to come back to! So as I flew south, I reminisced about the summer I had. I was happy and content, I felt that George, Tom and Brian where pleased with my performance. The four thousand dollars that Mom and Dad co-signed for me, I paid it all off, in full with interest! Best of all, I pulled out my log book from my little flight bag and as I flew over Elliot Lake I said to myself, "with the two hours I have left to go, I have a grand total of seven hundred and sixty- five hours which meant that I flew five hundred and fifty hours, all on floats this summer! Not a bad start I figured, and believe it or not I was looking forward to freeze up and some time off!

The six weeks off at freeze up went by quicker than I thought, soon enough I was loaded all up with freight and my winter gear and headed back to Island Lake for the winter. The time off was good, I got to see the family and for once didn't have to worry about getting a job. Winter flying on skis is quite different than floats, keeping the airplane operational was a lot more intense. That month as Ralphs' crew man on the Norseman paid off handsomely as I knew what was required but something else had happened to me, it was insidious and I didn't even know it. I was getting to cocky and sure of myself! Sure enough in the middle of December I got caught in a whiteout on a trip back from Red Sucker Lake and instead of landing and waiting it out I decided to push it through. Well, I made it back to Garden Hill but just couldn't find the airstrip, I was flying round and round looking for something to give me some reference when all of a sudden the engine quit! It was snowing so heavy that it plugged up my intake and there I was at two hundred feet with a dead engine. I found out later that most pilots do not survive a whiteout but for me I was fortunate, I did the hardest thing you have to do with an engine failure and that is to push the nose forward. I did that along with keeping the wings level, and since I couldn't see I had no choice but to go straight ahead! It didn't take long and I didn't have time to think of the consequences when all of a sudden BANG, I hit! Luckily, it was in the middle of Waasagomach Bay, the skis where folded backwards and the gear had collapsed. Myself, and three passengers, one of them a pregnant native lady where all uninjured! It could have been a lot worse if we ended up in the bush or the rocks. I took out my sleeping bag and covered up my passengers; I turned on my master switch and called for help. Fortunately our sched was on the way to Garden Hill, they got my message and soon after when the weather lifted George and Keith Krueger in Ilford Riverton's' 185 spotted me. Keith took my passengers to Garden Hill and left George and I with the Found to survey the damage, I knew George was on one hand disappointed in me but on the other I could tell he was thankful that we were alive! Soon after Keith picked George and I up and took us back to Garden Hill. A couple of hours later I was on the sched back to St. Andrews airport, and once again as we were in the air, in the left turn, I could see the pilot " shack ," and wondered with that same sickly feeling that I first had when I left Garden Hill, "would I ever see you again?"

Since I didn't have an airplane to fly, Tom said to take some time off until George figured out what he was going to do. So I figured I would make the best of it, I went back over to Point West and took flying lessons again, this time it was for my instrument and muti engine rating. Although I was far from flying a twin engine for St. Andrews, I reasoned that this was a good time as any to get this done, and besides I had the cash. So, in a few short weeks I finished the course and had a fresh twin engine instrument rating. I felt pretty good about that. I still wasn't sure if I had a job or not so when I went over to the hanger to tell Tom and Brian that I was finished, they threw an unexpected surprise at me. Brian said, "George leased a Cessna 180 on wheel skis for the trapping season, so get your shit together and be ready in two days! Man, what a great feeling, a second chance and I said to me, "self don't fuck this up again!" So here I was, a couple of days later, with my standard fare of sched freight, steaks and whiskey, heading north to Island Lake! When I got to the pilot "shack" that night the morning coffee was frozen and those lazy pilots didn't leave any cut wood but I didn't care as I was so happy to be back. I was very much a different person, a hell of a lot wiser and not so damn cocky!

The spring season went quite well, we got all the trappers home safe and sound, nobody had any mishaps and all the airplanes were doing mostly strip to strip work as the ice had risen and was going to start to candle soon. I knew by the talk that soon, one by one we would start taking our airplanes south for breakup, and so I figured this would be a great time to have a breakup "Party". So we all got together and planned it, the wives would do the decorating and each bring a dish, we pilots, mechanics and freight handlers would chip in for the booze and George as generous as he is, said he would send it all up on the sched for free! George, also said that "any one of us coming out of the communities with an empty seat can bring back one of the nurses". I came up with this idea as a sign of thanks to all of our customers and boy, did we ever put on a bash! Len Chornoby the airport manager got us the recreation hall for free and he and his wonderful wife Barb cooked a ton of food, so we had it all ready to go when the cops showed up and said "where is your liquor permit?" Len Chornoby came to the rescue and said to the cops, "We don't need one as this is a private party and I rented the hall Gratis, but after duty you're welcome to join us." The cops said that's okay, they went home, changed and in an hour they where back drinking rum! That was great as they were one of our customers also. We had a nice party, everyone had a good time. It was a long winter, spring was in the air which enhanced everyone's mood, people were eating, drinking, dancing and socializing. As for me I was kind of behaving myself, I was mostly bartending and making sure everything was running smoothly when all of a sudden someone interesting appeared. One of the local ladies came into the party, she wasn't just any local she was a beauty, and we had been making eyes at one another for some time. Have you ever seen the movie Dances with Wolves? Well the native lady that Kevin Costner takes up with was a spitting image of this girl! So I hustled over to her, with drinks in hand and said "my party is just starting". We were having a good time and when I noticed that people were starting to leave and I realized it is almost two am, so I said to my honey "let's get out of here and head to the pilot shack." Since I was in charge of the booze I went behind the bar and scooped a bottle of rum and some mix, so here we where, drunk as skunks, pockets full of booze and on our way to the pilots "shack". We made our way down the hill to the lake, and do you think I could find my skidoo? No way, so I said to my friend "fuck it, it's nice out, let's walk." Now in the spring the snow melts and the ice lifts leaving behind a skating rink with puddles of water captured in the depressions. It's very slippery, so here we were, two drunks that can't keep their hands off each other trying to walk a mile and a half to Wass Island, which is where the pilot "shack" is located. Well, it didn't go to well, after about five minutes we must of fell ten times and now we were soaking wet! I had remembered that at the bottom of the hill were the skidoos where was Air Parks Cessna 180 on skis', so I said to my friend "let's get in the airplane" So here we were soaking wet and drunk, we mixed up the rum and climbed in and said "Hey, this is okay, it's warm and most of all dry." We were having a good time, smoking and drinking; I even heard the skidoos leaving the party. It didn't matter, we were staying put! I found out the next day from the pilots that when they left the party they noticed that the engine wasn't running but those wings were sure a ROCKIN! Anyhow we must have passed out as the last thing I remember is her head was lying on something weird; I just couldn't grasp what it was. Then the unexpected happened, the door flew open and we heard this loud yell "Holy shit, you guys scared the hell out of me, what you think this is, a fucking whore house, it smells like one. Now get the fuck out of here, I have trips to do!" Here was the Air Park pilot and I was the pilot from a competing airline, partying in his airplane! As we climbed out I noticed it was a hell of a mess, there was an empty rum bottle, sticky coke on the floor, and empty coke cans full of cigarette butts. I quickly glanced over my shoulder to see what her head was lying on? And it was a hind quarter of moose meat"!

    Soon after one by one George was sending us south for breakup, John Briggs was flying the Norseman on skis and I overheard George saying that the Norseman was due for an engine over hall. He wasn't sure if he was going to overhaul it, in fact he might park it. Having overheard this I begged George to bid on the summer fish contract out of Savage Island. I really wanted to fly the Norseman and haul fish like the many bush pilots I'd heard of. Once again I headed south and once again I was looking down at the pilots "shack" saying good bye. I knew I would be back again and besides my little incident in December, I felt quite content. The rest of the winter went well; I had just over a thousand hours in my logbook and some say that's a danger level, as most pilots think they know it all by then. I knew one thing; I was still a rookie, a lot more humble and not so damn cocky!

Chapter 5

Breakup is nice, the weather is getting warmer, and after a long dark winter we pilots look forward to summer operations. No engine tents, no sweeping off the wings, just no freezing your ass off plain and simple! As spring was rolling along I was having a great time off, the Norseman was in the hanger getting a new engine installed along with work on the set of floats George had purchased. CF-KAO was my baby for the summer, it was getting a nice overhaul to my delight, but it looked like hell! John Briggs was flying it the previous winter on skis and just happened to lose both doors on the right side of the airplane. I don't know how the right main door went missing but as for the right passenger door, it was jettisoned! John was flying a local hunter from Ste. Therese Pt. They were out doing sixty degree steep turns scouting for moose when the hunter grabbed the quick release handle to get a better view and away went the door! John said the poor fella almost fell out of the airplane! He turned white as a ghost and said "let's go home". So here was KAO with a piece of plywood on both right hand doors, George said that he would find some doors as soon as possible as flying on floats with no right hand access is not impossible but it's a handful. We never did get a right hand cargo door but George did manage to find a right hand passenger door although it was bright yellow which didn't look to good on a red and white airplane. No matter I said to myself "make do as this is something that I wanted to fly so badly." I wanted to fly fish out of Savage Island just like my predecessors a couple of generations before me. The likes of Jimmy Hoglander, Howard Hawley, Jack Clarkson to name a few, these were real bush pilots and I wanted to be just like them!

The Norseman is a great airplane, it's a man's' airplane, in other words it's not an easy airplane to fly. It doesn't have the STOL characteristics of a Single Otter or a Beaver; in fact the nickname for the Norseman is the word Crowbar. It flies like a "Crowbar," I'd often heard many pilots say "if you can master a Norseman you can fly anything!" So I was quite excited to have this chance to see if I could do what only a few have done. It's ironic but some years later I was driving to the Edmonton International airport to pick up my daughter Brittany, I was wearing a jacket that my wife at the time had made for me. She was working at a store in Yellowknife that made crests and logos, and she just happened to buy me a book on northern aviation. On the cover of this book was a picture of a Norseman on skis, which led her to make me a bomber jacket with a crest of the Norseman on the back. Now this was the time before the internet where you could check the flight times so I always went out to the airport early. Sure enough I was about a half an hour early and since I flew out of Edmonton I knew the airport quite well, so I decided that I would go for a coffee in the upstairs café and watch for Brittany's' airplane to land. All was well; I was in the lineup you know, with tray in hand sliding it towards the till when I noticed two Air Canada pilots in uniform having coffee before their flight. So as I turned inwards to pour my coffee I overheard them make a derogatory remark about me and a worse one about the Norseman. As I sat down I couldn't believe what I had just heard, here are these two pussies shooting their mouths off loud enough for me to hear. You know most of these Air Canada types believe that when they walk through the terminal building they are second to none, that's their culture! And here they are proving it! Now, as I'm sipping my coffee the blood is starting to boil and I said to myself "I'm not going to let this go, no way." I didn't care that they gave me a cheap shot, what really pissed me off was the dig against the Norseman. I wanted to go and give them an earful but I knew that these two strokers would do what I thought they would do. They would run straight to the union, make up some bullshit story and try to get my shit! So as I'm brewing like a steeped tea it struck me! I said to myself, "Hey I have my red pass with me." I never go to the airport without it. Now if you don't know, the red pass allows you access to anywhere on the airport. Our airline, Northwest Territorial Airways at the time had a code share with Air Canada; part of the package was that we used their dispatch for receiving our flight plans and weather. Now since I knew that these two klinks were on their way to the dispatch office to get their paperwork I said to myself, "I'll wait five minutes, put on my red pass and follow them there." And so I did, and on the way I was hoping that there weren't any more flight crews in the office as this would make what I was about to do much more intense. Luck was on my side! The place was empty, just those two at the computers doing their thing and here I walk in with my red pass clearly visible attached to my Norseman jacket! Now ya want to see a ghost? You should have seen the look on these two, whiter than Mister Clean and speechless! As for me, I just stood there with my mouth shut, I didn't say a word, I just stared at them. The best part was that there was no reason for me to be there, I wasn't in uniform and they had no clue that I was a jet pilot, just like them, I just stood there, they completely ignored me and I was wishing that they would say something to me, but you know what? They didn't have the Balls to do so, just as I thought! I was having such a good time watching these two fidget that I couldn't take it anymore, so I slid open the window to the dispatcher's room and asked what time our flight from Yellowknife was due in? One of the dispatchers who knew me said, "Hi ya, Gord, its due in ten minutes." As I left the room my back and the crest of the Norseman was clearly pointed their way, there was dead silence. The door closed, I headed upstairs to pick up Brittany, I felt wonderful, you humiliated me but I realized one thing. You might think that you're king shit but you're king shit with no nuts!

Breakup was almost half over; I was having lots of fun, spending lots of time with family and friends. It was getting to the point that I was becoming somewhat restless, I wanted to get going up north when tragedy struck again. My grandmother, my dear Baba, the last of the grandparents passed away. Once again, standing over her grave saying my last goodbye, I felt very humble, very fortunate, and very lucky. Here I was, starting my life with so much to look forward to, so much promise, so little to hold you back but your own self, all this for me thanks to the decisions that she and the rest of my grandparents made. Just think for a minute and really try and put yourself in their shoes. Do you think you could get on a boat and say goodbye to your loved ones, knowing very well that you will probably never see them again, your mom, your dad, your brothers and sisters, aunts and uncles, friends. I don't think so, I know, I couldn't do it and do you know why, because my grandparents did it for me. They paid the price, they sacrificed. So as I say bye to my baba, I know deep down that I will never, never ever forget what you and the rest of my grandparents did for me! So bless you baba, and may our beliefs come true and that we all see each other again, somewhere, and sometime.

Soon after babas funeral a happy occasion occurred, my good friends Dave Langrill and Val Lewis decided to walk down the aisle and tie the Knott. It was a good time; seeing good friends' were getting married is always a bit emotional especially when you're single. I was starting to think that way, taking a bride was on my mind as my career was starting to progress nicely. But that would have to wait, the Norseman was almost ready and my next journey was imminent. Brian Magill called a few days later and I was soon doing my checkout on the Norseman. I felt good as this was the same spot on the dock in Selkirk that I first looked and dreamt about what it would be like to be a bush pilot and fly this big Norseman! So with Brian's' blessing, a load of freight and the golden rule of steaks and whiskey I was headed north , back to Garden Hill and the famous pilot "Shack".

After landing in Garden Hill we off loaded our freight, talked to George and the gang for awhile and then proceeded to the pilot shack to drink whiskey and cook steaks. The start of the season is always exciting, the shack was warm, and we didn't have to cut wood or thaw snow for water. Everyone is in an upbeat mood, telling war stories and talking about our escapades during breakup. Since big Igor lived in Garden Hill full time he would enlighten us all on what happened during breakup up there and we would do the same for the southern climes. It was great to be back, we were one big family, all good people that worked hard and played hard. Business was a bit slow of course as the season was just underway, so I was getting a trip or two a day on the Norseman. This was fine for me as I wanted to get a few hours under my belt before I started the more demanding work at Savage Island. After a couple of weeks the call finally came, Nestor Shabaga the camp manager at Savage was ready for us. I on CF-KAO and our Beech 18 on floats CF-RSY piloted by the none other Ralph Birch. So I packed up my stuff and said goodbye to my friends and comrades and of course the good old pilots shack and headed twenty- five miles east to Savage Island!

I don't know where the name Savage Island came from as there is nothing savage about it. It's probably because it's inhabited mostly by the local natives and I'm sure in this day and age it wouldn't be called that. In any event here I was landing at Savage, beginning the next journey of my life. Upon taxiing to the dock I was greeted by the infamous Nestor Shabaga. Nestor was the camp manager along with his right hand man Helgi Thorvaldsen. Nestor knew me since the days as Ralphs' crew man on the Norseman and from the year before when I was flying the Found. I used to do lots of flights to Savage, bringing in all kinds of people and freight. Mostly Indian Affairs, nurses and families, and once in awhile the bosses from Freshwater Fish Marketing Corp. who at the time were the operators of Savage Island. But that was then and this is now, I'm not a guest anymore, I'm now working directly for Nestor. Nestor was a tall hard working, hard drinking Ukrainian with old school work habits and values. Nestor knew Savage inside and out as he had spent many a year there working for the Lazarenko's, who for many years operated Savage. Savage was basically a fish processing plant roughly in the middle of Island Lake. It consisted of various types of buildings, from giant coolers and freezers to bunkhouses, cabins, warehouses, fuel storage and of course the main power plant run by Jimmy Fraser who rumor has it "the only one who could keep it going because it was so ancient." Let's not forget the kitchen where Nestor sat me down to give me the one-two about how things go around here! Since I knew Nestor, I was fully aware that he has always had a love hate relationship with pilots, but I was also aware that if you did good work for Nestor he would be your best friend. Since I had five months to live here I wanted to make sure that Nestor was on my side, as it's to small of a place to be at odds with the boss. So with lunch almost done, we came down to the real issue, when do I start and finish work and the big one, how much weight will I haul? I know George talked to Nestor and told him to take it easy on me until had a few loads of fish under my belt. So we came to the agreement that when I was up to speed I would haul anywhere from twenty to twenty-five tubs of fish depending on the time of year and distance. Meaning that the colder it was and the closer the lake then the more I could haul. Now a tub of fish is a very durable plastic one foot by two and a half foot concoction with two metal handles that would fold inwards so that when you stack them on top of each other they wouldn't crush the fish below. Each tub was supposed to weigh ninety pounds including the ice that was placed on top of the fish to keep them cool. Now I knew from hearsay and fabled stories from generations gone by that the ninety pound weight of the tub was dubious, in other words every camp at every lake was different. So I told Nestor right from the start, that every lake would be different depending on how much they tried to screw me on the weight! He was a little taken back but deep down he knew that I was aware of this scam. Lunch was over and I knew Nestor was ready for his afternoon shot and siesta, so as he got up to leave he said "What time do you start work in the morning?" I said "well, what time did the other pilots start?" Nestor said "those lazy asses started at six am." And I said "well Nestor, I'll start at five am till dark!" Old Nesters' head flew around and with a smile on his face he said "you're in the first bunkhouse on the right!"

The bunkhouses at Savage were nothing but a long building with a row of beds on each side, the toilets and showers were at the end. The layout was bed, dresser, bed, and dresser and so on, with no dividers in-between, all wide open. So here I am hauling in my stuff and sitting at the end of his bed was Wade Wheeler, he looked pretty rough as he just came up from Selkirk for the summer. Wade was known as a pretty good scrapper in those days and here he was sharpening his filleting knife and staring at me, I picked a bed as far away as possible and as I was unloading my gear he said in a scrappy voice" what the hell a you doing here kid?" I said "calm down Wade, I'm not a filletter, I'm a pilot now. I won't be working with you.' So Wade was cool after that but I have to admit that the thought of that filleting knife a few beds down was a little unnerving!

The first week to ten days of flying out of Savage was pretty easy, not too heavy. I was mostly supplying the fish camps with fish nets, groceries, outboard motors and gas. Then it finally came, at the supper table Nestor said "that the first loads of fish were ready, starting tomorrow morning." Morning came and as promised I was up and at it at four fifteen, oh man was that early. I went to the kitchen, had a smoke and an instant coffee. It was dead silent, not a soul to be seen or heard, so I cranked up the Norseman and taxied out for my run up. I figured that today and every day until I leave here in the fall I'm going to wake good old Nestor up. It was my statement to him, meaning that I'll work my ass off but you can't push me around! With run up complete, I turned into wind, raised the water rudders and began my take off run. The timing was perfect! I buzzed Nesters' cabin at fifty feet, made a slight right turn and headed to the daughter of the chiefs cabin at Beaverhill Lake. After setting climb power and raising the flaps I glanced at my watch, it read five o three am! I left Beaverhill with my first load of fish, the chief was happy to see me. He knew that I would do a good job for him and you know what? His tubs were ninety pounds bang on! As I approached Savage I did a low and over to let Ralphs' wife Irene, who was cooking for the summer that I was starving. By the time I landed and walked into the kitchen she had six poached eggs on toast ready for me. With that amount of work and good food I put on fifteen pounds of muscle that summer. Yes, I'm now a Norseman pilot, I felt good and as I was wolfing down my breakfast I noticed Nestor at the counter drinking his coffee. He was giving me the evil eye and I knew he was pissed off at me for buzzing his cabin, he never said a word and either did I, we both know where we stood! My third load of fish that day was to Sharp Lake which was run by the Disbrowe clan of Red Sucker Lake. I didn't notice it but the floor on the Norseman was starting to get pretty slimy, the rule is that the natives would bring the fish tubs to the airplane and lift them up to the door. My job from then on was to load the airplane according to my liking. Being that I was a little out of shape coupled with the fact that the floor was super slippery, well, was to my dismay an accident waiting to happen, and it did. Just as I was heaving the tub up to the top row, my left foot let go and slid all the way backwards, the whole tub of slimy fish fell on top of me! So here I was soaked in fish slime from head to toe mixed with about a dozen varieties of fish slithering on the floor! Well you should have seen the Disbrowe boys, they were pissing themselves laughing so hard that even Fred the father master came up to the airplane and was soon like his three sons', rolling around the dock in stitches! I have to say it was funny and I even had to laugh at it myself. We got it all squared away in short order, loaded up and tied down when I noticed that I stank like hell. It was plus twenty-five or so and smoking hot inside the Norseman, so hot that I jumped right into the lake off the float and went for a swim. By the time I got back to Savage I was bone dry, that's how hot it is inside a Norseman in the summer!

After a couple of days I started to get into better shape and even noticed what the old timers would say "after awhile you won't smell the fish anymore." This was true; I was acclimatized to the odor. So I was trucking on, getting a little better as days went by. I really enjoyed being around when the Canso arrived in Savage, the Canso or " Pigboat" as often referred to by the pilots is a twin engine, high wing amphibious aircraft. It would come up from Gimli five days a week and bring in our fuel, groceries and whatever else the camp required. In return the Canso would leave with a load of processed fish.

I would get to talk to all the pilots and hear what's was going on in the outside world, and usually Frenchie, the flight engineer would bring me up the odd bottle of whiskey, not all the time but every once in awhile which would make it a special treat especially when the weather was out! I knew from the talk and my own observation that Nestor wasn't liked by the natives that much, Nestor ran Savage like Stalag seventeen! The job would get done no doubt, but he really drove the natives hard. Not so much for Helgi, he was more of a fisherman and more concerned about the quality and care of the product. Well one day I happened to be around when the Canso was coming in and this is when Nestor was usually out of control with the natives. For some reason that Canso arrival drove Nestor's reasoning out the window. Being an amphibian meant that there aren't any brakes, also there are no water rudders for steering on the water. The Canso is maneuvered by a combination of engines and whatever rudder you had, so you had to be very careful when sailing towards a dock. The Canso is almost thirty thousand pounds, so if you hit the dock to fast you could do a lot of damage. Nestor would be yelling at the natives, "get the houk, get the houk," for some reason he couldn't say "hook". The hook was a pole about twenty feet long with a steel hook on the end of it, it was used to grab onto the external bollards of the Canso and help pull it into the dock. Once the natives had the hooks attached you could hear Nestor screaming at them, "pull, pull, pull. Do I have to spell it for you, pull, POOL, pull?" Now today, the Canso arrived from Gimli and Nestor and Helgi where nowhere to be found. Nestor never sleeps in and I mean never, but today he did! We hadn't seen Nestor and Helgi for a day or two so we knew they were into the sauce, besides Nestor always commented how his wife would automatically send the "package." The package was usually newspapers, cigarettes, and whiskey, so for him not to be there to supervise and pick up the package must have meant that they were into the moonshine. So the Canso arrived and the natives tied it up with no problem, I was talking to the pilots, the natives were doing the turn around and were about half done, when out of the corner of my eye I seen Nestor running towards the dock with Helgi as usual about three feet in tow. Nestor looked like hell; you could tell that he was still pissed by the way he was half walking half running. By this time the natives had about ninety tubs of fish ready at the dock to load onto the Canso. There was a long slide you might say from the processing plant to the dock; it was about three feet wide on about a ten degree downward slope from the plant to the dock. This made getting the tubs to the Canso quite easy because it was not only downhill but after a few tubs the fish slime made it like a waterslide. The natives would just give the tub a toss and it would slide all the way to the Canso. Well Nestor in his stupor for some reason decided to run down the slide, he took one step onto it and his drunken feet gave way! As he tried to stay upright his feet looked like the road-runner, and finally he went down on his back and slid down the chute all the way until he hit the fish tubs! Poor old Nestor stood up again and bang, down he went again. Finally Helgi helped him off the chute and here was Nestor fully soaked in fish scales and slime! When he finally got his wits about him there were twenty natives hysterical, rolling around the dock, pissing themselves laughing! Old Nestor just stood there; he didn't know what to think. He grabbed his package from his wife, put it into a wheelbarrow and headed with Helgi three feet in tow to his cabin. We didn't see them for a couple of days and I have to admit Nestor was a little more humble and a lot easier on the natives!

Things were running pretty smoothly I must say, Ralph and I were flying our asses off to the extent that we were ahead of the game. In other words there wasn't a backlog of fish. I did notice one thing though; Tom Henry the chief cook for the summer had stopped asking us to find him some whiskey. Nestor told us in no uncertain terms "not to give Tom any booze whatsoever." Nestor had Tom all dried out and he knew that if he got a hold of any liquor he would go on a ripper. We found out that Tom was making a stash of bean juice; bean juice is a concoction of water, sugar, fruit and yeast. You theoretically mix it all together and let it ferment for a month or so, problem is if you don't wait long enough and drink it to early the consequences are sometimes painful. This would include bloating, severe vomiting, and worst of all being psychologically delusional! I guess Tom mixed up two five gallon pails of bean juice, took Nesters" canoe, paddled across the channel and hid it there on an island. Well sure enough a couple of weeks later I landed in Savage just before dark and there was no one to meet me, but Silas Monias. Silas never unloads the airplane, he usually takes care of the coolers and freezers, so I said to him "what's up Silas?" and he said "the whole camp is drunk on Toms' bean juice." I guess after supper Nestor and Helgi in their usual manner went to Nesters" cabin and started into the moonshine, meanwhile Tom snuck over to the island across the bay, picked up five gallons and canoed to Tee Pee town. Tee Pee town was just past the main camp at Savage, it was where all the native workers and their families resided for the summer. Except for the wives and children the whole camp was pissed and when I got to my bunkhouse it was like a scene from One Flew over the Coo coos Nest! Everyone was juiced, sick and delusional, one of them was walking around soaked in vomit thinking he was Buzz Aldrin! He kept on saying over and over like he was talking into a microphone "Gimli, this is one small step for Savage Island, one giant problem for Nestor Shabaga!" I went to check out the washroom and much to be expected was a war zone, there was puke everywhere, there was a runner in the toilet and upon further inspection I saw something that I never thought was possible. Vomit usually goes from a parallel to a downwards trajectory, but here in front of my eyes was flow of red puke from the toilet upwards to the roof. That's right, straight up to the roof! I said to myself "these guys are crazy," so I grabbed my shaving kit and alarm clock and slept in the guest cabin. I was in the air as usual at five am, heading up to Knee Lake which is about an hour flight from Savage. Walter Chubb and his family soon had me loaded up, I liked going to Knee Lake first thing in the morning as Walter was very dependable and when you landed at six am the load was ready at the dock, no waiting. So as I was enroute back to Savage I kind of knew what was ahead and sure enough there was Silas waiting for me at the dock. I knew right away that the camp was at a standstill! When I got to the kitchen, Nestor and Helgi were the only ones there, and Nestor, hung-over and all was fuming mad. There wasn't a worker to be found! All day Nestor was on a rampage, someone told Nestor that Tom had made two pails of bean juice. So Nestor and Helgi, like the Gestapo where searching everywhere and interrogating everyone but to no avail, they couldn't find it. After a couple of days the camp returned to normal and every one of the workers was back at it. A few days later on a Friday night Tom did the same thing. He waited until Nestor and Helgi were into the moonshine, paddled over to the island, picked up the last five gallon pail, took it to Tee Pee town and got the whole place wasted again! A few days later good old Tom was on the Canso to Gimli never to be seen again. His replacement was the well known Alice Nordal, she was hired by Fresh Water Fish and that pissed Nestor off. Alice was very outspoken and wielded a big axe handle when it came to Nestor, she didn't take any shit whatsoever from Nestor at all! Besides Nestor we all liked Alice and she liked us pilots. If you didn't give her any lip she would be your best friend and feed you accordingly, meaning that your favorite food requests would certainly be accommodated! I remember a new pilot off the Canso came in one day for lunch on the turnaround and Alice asked "who is that over there?" Someone said that's "Brian Harrison", he a mechanic on the Canso and a soon to become pilot." Alice replied, "Well I guess I'll have to fatten up that skinny little prick this summer!"

I too was also getting a little thirsty and restless; I had realized that I had been working over a month straight without a day off. Every day at four- fifteen am until dark. I needed a break so I gave Nestor some bullshit story that the Norseman needed some maintenance. I asked him to load me up for Stevenson Lake for the next morning, as Garden Hill was pretty well on track to Stevenson. I think I hit a bit of a crossroads as I was working my ass off day after day in the heat. I had visions of my buddies playing baseball and sitting in the beer gardens with their girlfriends and here I was hauling fish and sneaking down to Tee Pee town every once in awhile. I knew it was just a phase and it would pass and I routinely reminded myself of the fact that good things for my career lay ahead. So just after supper Nestor had me loaded for Stevenson Lake and I took off and headed for Garden Hill. I did this on a whim, I didn't tell anyone that I was on the way, I just wanted to get out of Savage for a night, have a few drinks with my fellow pilots and see what was going on in the world. So I landed at Garden Hill, tied the airplane up for the night and headed up to Georges' office. There was a couple of pilots and loaders there just sitting around bullshitting when I said, "when everyone's done lets head to the pilots shack for a few drinks." They all looked at me funny and said, "you know Gord, we're bone dry, there isn't a drink to be found amongst us. Nobody has been to Thompson or Norway House in ages. In fact the only thing around is that bottle of Crown Royal that's sitting on Georges" shelf, he is giving that to the Midwest helicopter pilots. They lent us a NiCad battery to start the Saunders the other day." I was a bit down as I wanted to have drink or two and as we continued to pass the stories I couldn't help but stare at that bottle of Crown on the shelf. Finally I couldn't take it anymore; with my mouth frothing I grabbed that bottle of Crown, emptied it into a plastic Pepsi bottle and proceeded to make tea in a clear glass bowl. When the colors matched I poured the tea back into the bottle of Crown, put the velvet pouch on, placed it back into the blue box and returned it precisely where George had left it! The pilots kept saying "you're crazy, you're crazy, and George is going to kill you." I said

"No matter, we're in business!" When the last 185 came in for the night big Igor drove us in his boat to the pilots shack and with a bottle of Crown in hand we were soon cooking steaks and telling war stories! I was off early in the am headed to Stevenson Lake, it was a good night. It felt good to revisit the old pilots shack and see the gang; even a couple off maidens dropped by to say hi to us badasses! The days passed on and I never thought anything about that bottle of Crown until one day. The weather was severe clear but really windy, so windy that it was gusting up to thirty-five knots. The high winds with swells and whitecaps were enough to ground the 185's, it was just too dangerous to attempt any float operations in those conditions. I'm not saying it couldn't be done but why take the risk, and George was of the same mindset, but when it comes to the Norseman, that's a different story. The Norseman can take waves and swells far bigger than most pilots can withstand, so today was just another day for me. As for today, I had five back to back loads of fish to haul out of Stevenson Lake. The track from Savage Island to Stevenson Lake would take you about ten miles south of Garden Hill, so every time I would pass by Garden Hill, the pilots who were sitting in Georges' office waiting for the wind to go down would call me up on the radio for some small chat. On one of the legs passing by, the pilots called me up and said "George is pissed with you about that bottle of Crown Royal, he's so mad that he ripped up your paycheck!" Well I found out that the Midwest chopper pilots we're back in town and staying at the Island Lake Lodge which happened to be owned by Georges' mother and father in law. Since big Igor lived next to the lodge George handed him the bottle of Crown off the shelf and asked him to drop it off after supper. So after supper with bottle in hand and a smirk on his face, big Igor who knew what was inside handed over the jug to the chopper pilots and took off. George's mother and father in law were quite boisterous in saying "this is from our son in law George for the use of your battery." Both the chopper pilots with a full tummy proceeded to pour themselves a drink of Crown on ice and savor it overlooking the quiet and glassy water bay. After their first sip they spit it out, ventured back into the kitchen and lay a tongue lashing on Georges' in laws, saying, " we know George is a Scotchman but we didn't think he squeaked that bad!" Oh they were pissed! It just happened the next morning Georges' father in law was at the airport dropping off some Americans. He went on to relay the story and without a word of lie and no investigation what so ever George said, "That fucking Chenkie!" A couple of weeks later my mail arrived in Savage, good old George sent my paycheck. Upon review there was a small deduction, the exact price of a bottle of Crown Royal!

Another few weeks passed and things at Savage were for most part running okay except for the fact that Ralphs' Beech 18 was giving him trouble. After a week or so of this it was quite evident that we were starting to fall behind. Enough behind that one morning at the breakfast table Nestor announced that Ilford Riverton Airways had just purchased a Single Otter and that it would be here today to help us out. I thought that was great because Nestor was getting awfully cranky. I could fly twenty-four hours a day and it still wouldn't be enough to catch up. I kind of forgot about the Single Otter when all of a sudden at supper time Nestor stormed into kitchen and said, "Helgi, and come with me right now. The RCMP just showed up unannounced!" Nestor was cussing and swearing about the cops not telling him like they usually do, that they are coming to Savage. I was kind of thinking like, what's your problem Nestor? The cops always come here to do business when required, no big deal. So I

The Calling Sky

figured that I would go down to the dock and help them tie up when out of the corner of my eye I witnessed what Nesters' problem was. Here is Nestor and Helgi carrying Nesters' still towards his dock. Nestor was in the process of brewing a batch as the still was steaming and all you could hear was hurry, Helgi, hurry. So with the Single Otter almost at the main dock , Nestor and Helgi proceeded to throw the still off the end of Nesters' private dock, and there it went, sizzle, sizzle, glug, glug into ten feet of water! I could see Nestor and Helgi now running towards me to greet the RCMP, and when the Otter reached the dock I almost pissed myself laughing. I couldn't believe it, it wasn't the RCMP, and it was Footsie, the pilot of Ilford Airways new Single Otter! Ilford bought the Otter from the RCMP but in typical Ilford fashion didn't paint it, they just removed the RCMP decal which was completely legal to do! Oh my God, the shit hit the fan when Nestor seen that it was Ilfords Otter. He went ballistic on Footsie, calling him all kinds of acronyms that are unprintable. As he and Helgi stormed away old Nestor said his now famous line, "Ilford Riverton pilots couldn't fly shit down a trough!" Poor Footsie got a tongue lashing from Nestor just for doing his job. I then told Footsie about Nesters' still, and we must have laughed for long time because people started to ask us what was so funny? Next thing you know there are about twenty people on the dock all laughing, visiting Footsie and all just having a good bullshit session when someone yelled, " Come over here and check this out." Here Nestor got the biggest glass bowl that he could find from the kitchen along with the Canso hook, loaded into a canoe and started to look for the still. So here are two drunks, Nestor looking through the bowl pushed into the water with Helgi on the hook and all you could hear was Nestor yelling " over here Helgi, no, this way Helgi, get the HOUK Helgi , I see it !" Surprisingly they hooked it and up came Nesters' still, risen from the dead. Nestor was so happy you would have thought it was Jesus who arose! They were walking around and laughing like two kids in a candy store. Now we all knew why Nestor was never around at supper time! He was brewing moonshine! Everyone kind of scattered off in their own direction, I went with Footsie to check out his new airplane and help him tie it up for the night. Like most pilots the first thing I did was check out the cockpit, just as I was climbing down the ladder, I noticed her coming. One of the workers was on her way to pay Footsie a visit like she did with every new pilot in town. She had just come out of the filleting station and was a sight to be seen, blood and guts all over her apron, a fish net in her hair, big long up to the knee rubber boots and best of all she was holding a ten inch filleting knife! Footsie was busy tying up the Otter and didn't see her coming when she yelled, "Pilot, what's your name?" Well, Footsie looked back over his shoulder at this ungodly sight and a knife a few inches from his face. Meanwhile I'm in stitches laughing as he nervously said, "My name is Robert Foote but everyone calls me Footsie." She then said," well Footsie my name is so and so and I fucked every pilot in Savage Island and you're next!" Well poor old Footsie was about three shades of blue and speechless, he didn't know what to do especially with the way she was waving her knife! I was in tears laughing so hard, first Nestor and the still and now a threatening piece of ass! I told Footsie that I'm off to do my last trip for the night and as he helped me push the Norseman off the dock I said, "If you want my advice, go after her sister she's better looking, and if you do the one with the knife will leave you alone!"

The heat of the summer was almost over, September was upon us and Ralph and his Beech 18 were gone. Yes, gone forever, as they found a cracked spar, so George had it ferried to Selkirk and stripped down for parts. Footsie left the zoo at Savage also, as Ilford had other commitments for its Otter. Nestor managed to find a Single Otter from The Northwest

Territories and a pilot named Merlin Carter from Hay River to help us out until the season ended. Things were going really good and all the workers were looking forward to finishing up the season and heading home for the winter. I too was looking forward to seasons end as living in a camp for months on end was a great experience ,somewhat trying at times but all in all good. Even Nestor could see the end coming; he was in a good mood one night and after supper invited us to his cabin for a drink or two. This was a rare occasion so we all figured we'd better take good old Nestor up on his offer. We were all sitting around his cabin having a few drinks and telling war stories when every ten minutes or so Nestor would get up and go to his kitchen radio and call Gimli. He would say," Gimli, Gimli, Savage Island, do you read? Pause, then again," Gimli, Gimli, Savage Island, do you read?" I know the HF signals had been out for a couple of days and this made Nestor all the more determined. After about an hour of this I couldn't stand it anymore, so when Nestor went to the kitchen again I asked one of the office workers for his office keys. I told the gang to tell Nestor that I went to the kitchen for a late snack and proceeded to sneak up to the office. Once there, I patiently waited and sure enough over the office radio was Nestor in his cabin calling Gimli. "Gimli, Gimli, Savage Island do you read?" Now after he called the second time, I waited about ten seconds knowing that he would be half way back to the living room. I put a towel over the microphone; bit my tongue really hard as I'm starting to crack up and replied, "Savage Island, Gimli here, go ahead, Nestor!" Well the gang said they were rolling on the floor in stitches as Nestor fell over backwards in retreat to the kitchen and grabbed the radio microphone and he said, "Gimli, it's Nestor, how do you read?" I said, "I can hear you pretty good Nestor, go ahead." Nestor replied, "We need milk, we need eggs, we need potatoes" and on and on and on. Finally he said, "Tell my wife to send the package." At this time

I really had to bite my cheek as I replied," Nestor, you're breaking up, say again." and sure enough Nestor repeated the whole list again verbatim! In stitches I replied, "Got it all okay Nestor, the package is here, Gimli clear." I bee lined it back to Nesters' cabin and noticed that the gang was beet red from laughter and so was I! The next morning at the kitchen table was Nestor giving me look of death; he knew he had been had! As he walked out he said, "You're the laziest pilot I have ever known, I've got ten thousand pounds of fish rotting in the bush and you're drinking coffee!" It didn't bother me as I knew this was typical Nestor!

The fishing season was almost at a halt as we were mostly cleaning up the camps and moving the fisherman and their families back to their respective homes. Later, Nestor told me to pack up tonight and head back to Garden Hill in the morning. It was the first time in months that I didn't set my alarm to four- fifteen a.m. I slept in a bit, had a nice breakfast, said goodbye to whoever was left at camp and proceeded to load my gear into the Norseman. I was just about ready to leave when Nestor came down to say goodbye, I shook his hand and wished him well and he did the same. We both could sense that although we we're at each other's throats periodically, we respected on another. As I took off westbound to Garden Hill, for the first time in months and out of respect for Nestor I didn't buzz his cabin. I remember I was a bit sad as I knew this experience would have lifelong memories for me. I looked down and said goodbye Nestor, goodbye Savage Island and I wish you all well.

Back in Garden Hill was a treat, the flying was slow and I didn't have to work near as hard as in Savage. George had me doing some cleanup work with the trappers, and to my delight my kid brother Chris came up to visit me. It was good to spend some time with Chris; he was only ten years old when I left home plus the fact that I had been gone for almost six months. Once again, when the water rudders started to freeze up,

George would start sending us south, one by one, for freeze up. My turn soon came and as usual, as I turned southbound I looked down at the pilot shack; I knew I would be back. What I didn't know, was what I was going to fly as George was going to park the Norseman for the winter. I climbed to four thousand feet, enough to see Savage Island out to the east. I had a good feeling in me, a job well done, more experience and my log book was nearing two thousand hours. I landed in Selkirk and said goodbye to good old CF-KAO, it treated me well and as I drove away I noticed for the last time the brown plywood covering the right rear door! A few weeks later Brian Magill called and said, "You're going on the Aztec." My first twin engine job and CF-CZA was my new baby!

This story ended in the fall of nineteen seventy-five and when I hear the songs "Have you ever been Mellow and Only Women Bleed" brings me surreal memories of Savage Island. That's all the girls in the kitchen played over and over again. It's now July, two thousand and ten and you have read the first five chapters of my book, "The Calling Sky". I plan to finish the rest of my book when I retire from my 737 Captain's job as I've had such a wonderful career and many more stories to share. Thank you Jack Clarkson for this opportunity to be in your book, I can hardly wait to read about you're most colorful career! Take good care and God Bless.

Here is what I am going to fly now

Manufactured by Amazon.ca
Bolton, ON